GOOD PRACTICE IN CARING FOR YOUNG CHILDREN WITH SPECIAL NEEDS

Angela Dare ● Margaret O'Donovan

Stanley Thornes (Publishers) Ltd

First published in 1997 by:
Stanley Thornes (Publishers) Ltd
Ellenborough House
Wellington Street
CHELTENHAM
GL50 1YW
England

00 01 / 10 9 8 7 6 5 4 3

A catalogue record for this book is available from the British Library.

ISBN 0–7487–2871–6

Photo credits: page 132, Sally and Richard Greenhill; cover photo, Sally Greenhill

Typeset by Columns Design Ltd, Reading
Printed and bound in Great Britain by T.J. International Ltd, Padstow, Cornwall

CONTENTS

ABOUT THE AUTHORS

Angela Dare and Margaret O'Donovan come from backgrounds of health visiting, midwifery and teaching. They worked together for many years at City and Islington College on nursery nursing and other childcare courses. Angela Dare is currently an External Verifier for CACHE courses. Margaret O'Donovan teaches at Chiltern College in Berkshire. Their previous publications are *A Practical Guide to Working with Babies*, Stanley Thornes (Publishers) Ltd, 1994 and *A Practical Guide to Child Nutrition*, Stanley Thornes (Publishers) Ltd, 1996.

DEDICATIONS

To Kieran and Kate; and to Leilah and Dominic.

ACKNOWLEDGEMENTS

The authors would like to thank their colleagues for the ongoing interest and encouragement they have shown, particularly Christine Hobart, Teresa O'Dea, Anna Mennell and Cynthia Isaac at City & Islington College and Marion Hicks, Catherine Birchall and Karen Fox at Chiltern College.

The authors also gratefully acknowledge the help received from Theresa Le Bas, Catherine Thomas, Maureen Cotterell and Francesca, and Ben and Beth O'Brien.

They are most appreciative to staff, parents and children for permission to use photographs taken in Bromley Hall School, Poplar, London E14; and of The London Borough of Greenwich Portage Scheme.

The Scope bookmark on page 40 is reproduced by kind permission of Scope (0171 636 5020).

The photograph on page 54 is reproduced by kind permission of WRK Developments.

The photographs on pages 224, 225 and 226 are reproduced by kind permission of the Cystic Fibrosis Trust (photographer: Camilla Jessel).

The extracts on pages 70, 71, 73 and 76: Crown copyright is reproduced with the permission of the Controller of Her Majesty's Stationery Office.

INTRODUCTION

This book looks at the broad issues concerning the care of young children up to eight years old with special needs. Although it is written primarily for use by nursery nurses and other carers in a variety of settings, we feel much of the content will also be relevant and interesting for parents.

The book provides the underpinning knowledge for NVQ Level 3 endorsement E (Special Needs). Keep any material you collect, following completion of the integrated activities, for inclusion in your portfolio. Your assessor will need it for evaluation of your understanding.

Our intention has not been to cover the delivery of the curriculum, although teachers in nursery, infant and primary schools may find some of the information helpful.

The book is divided into two parts. In part one we have addressed the background to disability, the complexity of the current legislation and other related matters in a user-friendly form.

Part two gives factual information and practical care advice on some of the more common conditions of young children. Inevitably not all conditions are included, but many of the care practices discussed will be transferable to children with differing needs.

You may wish to use the book in various ways, perhaps as a reference for information regarding specific legislation or for updating your knowledge on management issues for children with certain conditions. Whichever method you choose we hope you will find the information both easy to understand and useful.

With regard to terminology: in the early chapters, concerned with setting the scene for the subject area, we refer to 'disability' and 'special need'. For the remainder of the text the term 'special need' is used. Although we use the word 'parents' we recognise and value that some children will be looked after by other prime carers. We use 'he' or 'she' in alternate chapters or sections of chapters except where this would be inappropriate.

At the back of the book you will find a table of child developmental norms; a compact glossary; a list of useful addresses; and a further reading list.

We have tried to develop and present a comprehensive book that brings together diverse information about the subject of special needs. We hope childcare workers will find the book a helpful source of reference.

PART ONE
Introduction

Increasingly, children with special needs are attending a variety of inclusive and integrated childcare and education settings. As a childcare worker you require particular knowledge to enable these children to take part in everyday living on equal terms with all children.

The earlier a child's special need is recognised and assessed, the sooner effective ongoing provision of specialist help and family-centred support can be provided.

Chapter 1 gives an important insight into how people with disabilities were treated in the past. It addresses the needs of families who have a child with special needs and identifies the professionals from health, education and social services who are likely to be involved in caring for and supporting the child and her family.

Chapter 2 focuses on disability awareness. Over the past twenty years or so disability organisations have campaigned for a greater awareness of disability, a more informed society and an accessible environment which affords disabled people the same opportunities and rights as non-disabled people. The chapter emphasises the uniqueness and individuality of each child and suggests how you can promote self-esteem and a positive self-image in children with special needs. The provision and ethos of an inclusive daycare setting is also discussed.

Chapters 3 and 4 set out current legislation and statutory provision for children with special needs. They explain how local health, education and social services departments must take into account what the law says when providing care, management and education for children. The Education Act 1981 was instrumental in moving the focus away from a child's particular condition, concentrating instead on the child's ability and specific educational need. Its requirements were extended and carried through into the Education Act 1993 (Part 111) and the Code of Practice 1994. The Children Act 1989 is the major piece of legislation for safeguarding and protecting the welfare of all children. Because legislation is subject to revision and amendment it is essential that you keep up to date with future changes.

The concepts of empowerment and advocacy – listening to children, giving them choices and acting on their behalf – are included in chapter 3.

The nursery education voucher scheme for all four-year-old children is explained in chapter 4. Future changes to the scheme, which became available nationwide in April 1997, are likely.

Finally, chapter 5 addresses the role of parents as partners with the professionals and their right to be consulted and involved in all aspects of their child's care, management and education programmes. Such a partnership acknowledges parents' skills and expertise and the fact that they know their child best. The chapter also describes your role as a key worker in a daycare setting.

Voluntary organisations play an important part in supporting families and many of them provide care, education and support services for children with special needs and their parents. Some voluntary provision is detailed in this chapter.

1 BACKGROUND TO DISABILITY AND SPECIAL NEEDS

This chapter covers:
- Disability
- Special needs
- Definitions of impairment and disability
- Types of special need
- Possible causes of special needs
- Towards prevention and early identification of special needs
- Meeting the needs of parents and family
- The multidisciplinary team

This chapter provides an insight into some of the issues surrounding disability and special needs. Understanding past and recent attitudes towards disabled people will help you to develop an awareness of their concerns, dissatisfactions and desire for rapid change.

The term 'special needs' is explained, the types of special needs identified and some possible causes given.

The parents and siblings of children with special needs have their own particular needs which must be acknowledged and supported by all those involved in helping the family – professionals, friends and wider family members as well as parent support groups.

The chapter identifies the professionals in the multidisciplinary team who care for children with special needs and their families. In whatever setting you work you will be part of this team – caring for the children, liaising with parents, attending meetings and helping to formulate activity and learning programmes for individual children.

Disability

Everyone has their own perception of disability which varies according to personal knowledge and experience. Perhaps you know a child or adult who is disabled and understand something of his or her needs. Perhaps you are also aware of the different attitudes of society towards people with disabilites and the barriers they frequently encounter in their everyday living – social barriers of discrimination (being treated differently and unequally), prejudice and isolation, as well as physical barriers of access. Or, perhaps your only understanding of disability is seeing disabled people out and about from time to time, watching an occasional documentary programme about disability or reading fleeting references to disabled people in books or articles. Many disabled people are 'invisible' because they have no easy access to an environment planned and constructed by able-bodied people.

KEY POINT

Children and adults with disabilities are entitled to the same rights and opportunities as other members of society.

GOOD PRACTICE

Professionals involved in caring for children with disabilities must listen sensitively to what the children and their parents are saying about their situation.

Activity

Imagine you are a wheelchair-user going out and about in your local neighbourhood.

1 How easy or difficult is it for you to get around the streets and shops?
2 Are there any particularly accessible facilities such as public transport, leisure and entertainment services? If so, identify what makes them user-friendly.
3 What specific improvements would be necessary to make your neighbourhood physically accessible to wheelchair-users?

The physical environment must be accessible to all children

Throughout the ages disabled people have been pushed to the margins of society and different cultures and religions still have differing attitudes towards those considered 'abnormal'. A disabled relative was frequently considered a 'shame' on the family and was sometimes cast aside to make do as best he or she could while others were left to die or were even killed – especially in societies where everyday life was such a struggle for survival that those who were unable to contribute fully to their society were rejected. Even Aristotle called the deaf 'senseless and incapable of reason'.

The 'insane' were often thought to be possessed by the devil and were put to death. In ancient Rome deformed children were drowned in the Tiber. Women who gave birth to disabled children were frequently assumed to be witches and both mother and baby would be killed. Disabilities in babies were sometimes deemed to be 'God's punishment' for the sins of the parents, while in other cultures people with disabilities had mystical powers attributed to them.

Most disabled people, though, have been tolerated in varying degrees. In rural societies such as in Britain, disabled people made a valuable contribution to their family and community by undertaking the less demanding work around the farms and helping in the traditional cottage industries of weaving and basket and chair making. However, in the nineteenth century, when large sections of the population moved to the bigger towns and cities as a consequence of the Industrial Revolution, there was little work for those who were disabled. Many were abandoned by their families. The more liberal members of society and church organisations founded institutions where abandoned disabled people could find shelter and basic care. Gradually, more and more families used these institutions as a way of unburdening themselves either of the financial or 'shameful' burden of disabled relatives.

With the advance in medical treatment doctors sought to 'cure' disabled people and return them to society. Most of those who could not be cured remained in the institutions to live out their lives there, often completely abandoned by their families.

In Britain today, which in world terms is rich, disabled people's expectations are for equality, integration and equal opportunity. Large long-stay institutions have disappeared. As far as possible disabled children and adults are supported within their own families or in small community homes. Such residential homes are often frowned upon by some members of the local community who would prefer them to be elsewhere. These same people are often outspoken about the cost of medical care, both in hospital and the community and the general financial cost to the tax payer of ongoing support and resources. People may have these reactions because they lack knowledge of disabilities or, perhaps, believe perpetuated myths about disabled people.

KEY POINT

Society frequently sees the birth of a baby with a disability as a tragedy, so subscribing to the medical model of disability (see page 31, chapter 2). Friends may offer condolences rather than congratulations because they do not know what to say.

PROGRESS CHECK

1 What social and physical barriers do people with disabilities encounter in their everyday lives?
2 Why are disabled people often 'invisible'?
3 Why is it important to understand past attitudes towards disability?

Over the last twenty years attitudes and assumptions have been slowly changing. Through education and moves towards integration and inclusiveness there is better awareness of the issues surrounding disability.

EDUCATION

- Campaigns by disability organisations have provided greater 'disability awareness', equal rights and opportunities for disabled people.
- Disability awareness training helps people to examine their own attitudes towards disabled people and to implement good practice and courtesy towards them in their workplace and wider environment. Professionals caring for people with disabilities need to learn about disability directly from disabled people. For blind people, for example, the biggest problem is often the lack of skills in sighted people needed when assisting a blind person.
- Legislation for equal rights and opportunuties is provided in the Children Act 1989, the Education Act (Part 111) 1993 and the Code of Practice 1994 (see Chapter 3).
- Attempts are being made by the media to positively portray people with disabilities (although images on the television tend to remain rather negative).
- National and international sporting events for disabled people such as the paralympics and marathon races, although exclusive activities, raise the profile and visibility of disability.

INTEGRATION

- The integration of people with disabilities into the community and all areas of public life is taking place.
- Integrated day nurseries, nursery schools and classes and schools provide facilities for disabled children.
- There is better access to public transport, libraries, social activities, local amenities (such as sports facilities) and holiday venues.

All these changes have led to a more informed society and have benefited children and adults with disabilities by promoting confidence and removing social isolation.

KEY POINT

In spite of legislation and greater efforts to educate people about disability there is still much to be done towards achieving a fully integrated society.

PROGRESS CHECK

1 What do you understand by disability awareness training?
2 How does a more informed society benefit disabled people?

Special needs

Whether caring for children in a nursery, nursery class/school, infant or primary school or home setting you are constantly identifying, responding to and satisfying children's ordinary, everyday needs.

Satisfying children's ordinary, everyday needs

The term 'special needs' is used by childcare and educational professionals in relation to children whose development is atypical – not following the recognised pattern seen in most children. All children are on a continuum of development – they start out at the beginning of the same track and move along in a continuous process of development. But, as you will know from observing children in your workplace, not all children of similar ages are at the same stage of development. Children with special needs are simply at different points in the developmental continuum.

KEY POINTS

■ Children with special needs have the same requirements for love, security and protection as the other children you care for. They will have individual personalities, likes and dislikes, some will be strong willed and others easygoing.

- Take time to get to know children with special needs and give them plenty of attention and encouragement. Ensure you offer them the opportunity to make and maintain friendships and help them to become independent.

Activity

Carry out a detailed written record observation on each of three children of the same age in your work setting. The aim of your observation must be the same for all three children. Your evaluations should be clear and objective. Compare the developmental stages and abilities of each child. Are all the children at the same stage and level of development or are there obvious differences?

LABELLING CHILDREN

Labels such as 'handicapped' and 'subnormal' (see page 39, chapter 2) which focus on a particular disability and fail to understand the essential differences between children are no longer used. 'A child may be unable to walk, yet may be confident and determined, able to use elbow crutches to move around the room. Labelling this child "physically handicapped" focuses on his disability only, and tells nothing of how he is coping with that difficulty' (*Children with Special Needs*, Woolfson, 1991).

KEY POINTS

- There is no group of children called 'the disabled' or 'the handicapped' but there are individual children who happen to have different conditions. Current preferred terms are 'children with disabilities', 'disabled children' and 'children with special needs'.
- Using the term 'special needs' recognises the uniqueness of each child and recognises each child's particular strengths, abilities and level of development. It focuses positively on the 'need' rather than the disability, enabling appropriate levels of care and resources to be provided to support the child in leading an ordinary life. Unfortunately, the term is seen by some as just another label implying separateness and segregation.

PROGRESS CHECK

1 What do you understand by a 'continuum of development'?
2 What is wrong with using labels such as 'handicapped' and 'subnormal'?

Definitions of impairment and disability

While definitions may help to identify and explain a degree of need more readily and assist in planning future services, there are no universal, precise definitions. Any definition is subject to the views, attitudes and influences of those formulating it and there is continuing debate about acceptable definitions and terminology. What really matters is the individual child, how the child's needs are met and the attitudes of society towards the child. The definitions in the table on page 00 originate from the World Health Organisation (WHO), the Union of Physically Impaired Against Segregation (UPIAS) and The Office of Population Censuses and Surveys (OPCS). You may find them useful.

STATISTICS

There are approximately 10 million disabled people in Great Britain, many of whom would not consider themselves part of this statistic, particularly older people who have developed conditions or impairments in later life. Within this figure there are 360,000 children with impairments.

Nationally, 20 per cent of all children may have some form of special educational needs at some time during their school career and 2 per cent of all children will receive a statement of special educational needs (see page 72). In 1995 the number of children with a statement of special educational needs was 217,000.

Types of special need

There are many types of special need. As a childcare worker you will need to find out about the degree of difficulty a child is experiencing. To do this requires a thorough knowledge of child development. The developmental charts on page 366, 368 and 370 will help you. In addition, through talking to the child, her parents and the professionals caring for her, you will be able to understand a child's particular needs. Not all children with special needs have a special educational need but when necessary special educational provision is determined through a process of assessment (detailed in chapter 3).

KEY POINTS

- Remember, the word 'types' refers to the special need not to the child.
- Many children may, at some time, have short-term special needs, for example, following bereavement or other emotional trauma, or a period of illness or hospitalisation. Unless their needs are adequately met at the time they may develop emotional, social or learning difficulties.

You may care for children with any of the special needs identified in the table on page 11. The key points on page 11 are explained in more detail in part two.

DEFINITIONS

Impairment	Disability

BASED ON A DEFINITION FROM INTERNATIONAL CLASSIFICATION OF IMPAIRMENTS, DISABILITIES AND HANDICAPS (WORLD HEALTH ORGANISATION 1980)

1 Any loss or abnormality of psychological, physiological or anatomical structure or function.	1 Any restriction, or lack (resulting from impairment) of ability to perform an activity in the manner or within the range considered normal for a human being. Examples of difficulties/inabilities due to impairment:
	■ inability to walk
	■ mobility and postural difficulties
	■ poor vision and hearing, blindness or deafness
	■ inability to make and maintain effective relationships or maintain codes of behaviour.

BASED ON THE DEFINITION FROM THE UNION OF PHYSICALLY IMPAIRED AGAINST SEGREGATION

2 Lacking all or part of a limb, or having a defective limb, organ or mechanism of the body. These two definitions imply some part of the body is missing or not working properly. Examples:	2 The exclusion of people with physical impairments from community life and social activities due to the attitudes and situations imposed by society – personal and social disadvantage. Examples of personal and social disadvantage:
■ loss of whole/part of a limb	■ a child using a wheelchair is unable to manage steps into a building – society disables the child if no ramp is provided
■ juvenile arthritis	
■ cerebral palsy	
■ eye or ear defects	■ a person with visual impairment is disadvantaged if information is not readily available in large print or Braille.
■ brittle bones disorder	
■ emotional/psycho-social disorders.	

DEFINITION FROM *THE PREVALENCE OF DISABILITY AMONG ADULTS*, 1988, THE OFFICE OF POPULATION CENSUSES AND SURVEYS

	3 A restriction or lack of ability to perform normal activities which has resulted from the impairment of a structure or function of the body or mind.

TYPES OF SPECIAL NEED

	Physical conditions	Speech, language and sensory impairment	Learning difficulties	Emotional and behavioural difficulties
Cause	Damage to the body and its physical functions, including injuries: ■ to the brain and spinal cord ■ to the body systems ■ affecting the control of movement.	May be physical or emotional, leading to difficulties with the development and functioning of one or more of the senses.	Various: a child has a learning difficulty if he/she has greater difficulty in learning than most children of his/her age (see also chapter 3). Learning difficulties can be: mild, moderate, severe or profound.	■ emotional events and experiences ■ learning difficulties ■ physical conditions or sensory impairments ■ illness
Examples	■ cerebral palsy ■ spina bifida ■ cystic fibrosis ■ sickle cell condition ■ arthritis ■ limb deficiencies ■ muscular dystrophy.	Speech and language difficulty including: ■ stammering ■ poor pronunciation ■ difficulty in understanding the meaning or structure of language. Vision and hearing impairment.	■ Down's syndrome ■ fragile X syndrome ■ autism ■ speech/language and sensory impairment	Children can become: ■ unhappy ■ disruptive ■ angry ■ aggressive ■ withdrawn ■ anti-social ■ uncooperative
Key points	■ The effects of every condition will vary from child to child. ■ Children with physical conditions frequently require physiotherapy to help with posture, balance and mobility. Many children will have specialist equipment such as wheelchairs, walking frames, braces, crutches, callipers or artificial limbs to help them to get around. They may use particular feeding aids and require help in feeding, dressing and toileting routines. Lifting, handling and positioning techniques are important to avoid injury to the child or carer. Special needs such as medication and hospital care will vary from child to child.	■ The degree of learning difficulty will vary according to the level of impairment. ■ Early identification of speech and language difficulties is important for a child's emotional and social development and for later school performance. ■ Support for children with sensory impairments includes adapting materials and providing opportunities and stimulation to promote independence and confidence. Special equipment such as spectacles, artificial eyes, hearing aids and amplification systems will be used.	■ A specific learning difficulty is a difficulty in a clearly identified area and includes dyslexia and dyspraxia. ■ Careful observation of children with learning difficulties is necessary in assessing needs. Activities and learning programmes must match their actual level not the level expected for their age.	■ Emotional and behavioural difficulties may also arise from factors within a school environment. ■ A high adult to child ratio, one-to-one care and small group activities are beneficial for children with emotional and behavioural difficulties. Alternatively, individual learning programmes and behaviour management may be appropriate. The education welfare officer or social services department is likely to be involved with the child and family.

Which child has a special need?

PROGRESS CHECK

1 Name the four types of special need.
2 What do you understand by the term 'learning difficulties'?
3 Name two conditions which are classed as 'specific learning difficulties'.
4 Why might a young child have emotional and behavioural difficulties?

Possible causes of special needs

Special needs may be caused by:
■ hereditary factors

- prenatal, birth and postnatal developments
- childcare and management factors.

Sometimes it is not possible to identify a clear cause.

Recognising special needs

Special needs may be recognised:

- prenatally
- at birth
- through child health promotion and surveillance programmes
- by follow-up to a parent's observation and concern
- by professional observation of children in care and education settings
- following an accident or serious illness.

The table on page 14 sets out possible causes of special needs.

Towards prevention and early identification of special needs

Preconception care reduces many of the risks to the unborn child and helps to make the womb a healthy environment in which the baby can safely grow. Prenatal care aims to prevent, as far as possible, any problems with a pregnancy. Special tests such as amniocentesis, chorionic villus sampling, ultrasound scanning and particular blood tests may identify certain conditions but cannot alter them.

KEY POINTS

- Parents have a right to all available information about special needs. While some special needs may be identified before birth, the importance of every child as a unique individual with his or her own potential must be recognised and valued.
- Parents may need information about an inherited condition and the risk of passing it on to children or grandchildren. Genetic counselling can advise a couple on the probability or degree of risk and the choices they need to think about. It is a sensitive area of medicine which must support a couple in the decision they make.

Activity
Find out about the special tests of pregnancy. At what stage of a pregnancy would these tests be offered? How are the tests carried out? What specific conditions might these tests identify?

GOOD PRACTICE

- Throughout infancy and childhood, child health promotion and surveillance programmes should be offered. Observation of children by family doctors,

SOME POSSIBLE CAUSES OF SPECIAL NEEDS

Hereditary factors

Genetic inheritance — Cystic fibrosis, sickle cell and thalassaemia conditions, phenylketonuria, Tay-Sachs disease and others (some of these are discussed in chapter 7).

Chromosomal inheritance — Down's syndrome, fragile X syndrome (see chapter 9).

Sex-linked inheritance — Haemophilia, Duchenne muscular dystrophy (see chapter 7).

KEY POINTS:

■ Inherited disorders are passed on from parents to their children and are *always present at birth* even if not immediately identifiable.

■ *One or more* special needs may be present but *one* may predominate.

Prenatal factors — Substances: drugs, tobacco, alcohol.
Maternal infections including: rubella, toxoplasmosis, cytomegalovirus listeriosis, HIV, some sexually transmitted diseases (STDs).
Threatened miscarriage.

At birth — Anoxia (lack of oxygen), prematurity, postmaturity, low birth weight, difficult delivery.

Post-natal factors — Infections including: bacterial meningitis, measles, mumps, diphtheria, poliomyelitis.
Accidents/injuries: particularly those damaging the brain and spinal cord.
Childhood cancers: leukaemia, sarcomas, retinoblastoma, Wilm's tumour.
Child abuse of any kind.
Allergic reactions including: asthma and eczema (see chapter 6).

Child care and management factors — Frequent changes in prime carers during early years.
Emotional deprivation.
Family stress.
Difficulties with parenting.

Unknown factors — Sometimes it is not possible to identify a clear cause for a special need.

KEY POINTS:

■ Conditions present at birth are said to be *congenital*.

■ *Congenital* conditions are not necessarily *hereditary*, for example congenital heart disease, congenital dislocation of the hip.

■ Special needs may not become obvious until a baby grows and develops, hence the importance of health promotion and developmental assessment programmes.

health visitors, nursery and school staff and parents can identify, at an early age, those who may have special needs. Appropriate help can often limit or reverse the difficulties or delay.

■ Immunisation is an effective form of preventive care for infants and young children. It is offered routinely from the age of two months. Occasionally, there are contra-indications to immunisation.

The list, 'Towards prevention and early identification of special needs' sets out measures which may prevent, or identify, special needs at an early stage.

TOWARDS PREVENTION AND EARLY IDENTIFICATION OF SPECIAL NEEDS

■ Genetic counselling
■ Preconception care: medical care and positive health advice given to a couple before starting a pregnancy. It includes self-care by continuing or changing to a healthy lifestyle.
■ High standards of prenatal, perinatal and neonatal care.
■ Immunisation programmes.
■ Comprehensive child health services for child health promotion, screening and developmental assessment programmes; and efficient referral systems for specialist care and investigations.
■ Loving and secure emotional environments in which children can thrive and be happy.
■ Healthy and safe environments which lessens the risk of childhood illnesses, infections and accidents.

PROGRESS CHECK

1 What do you understand by a) hereditary b) congenital?
2 Name three prenatal factors which may have adverse effects on the unborn baby.
3 What particular infections may result in a baby or young child having special needs?
4 What is preconception care?
5 Other than through preconception care, how else might special needs be prevented or identified at an early stage?

Meeting the needs of parents and family

PARENTS

No parents expect their child to have developmental delay, require additional help, perhaps need intrusive medical procedures or even to die in early life. The whole sudden experience of having a baby with special needs can be deeply upsetting and isolating.

Recognising a special need

Sometimes the diagnosis is very obvious and clear at, or just after, birth. For some children and their families it may be many months or even years before a diagnosis can be made. When a special need is recognised in a child the parents inevitably need time to understand, adapt and accept. They need time to adjust and learn about their child as an individual with her own personality and potential. Often, the only information parents have about certain conditions is affected by the prejudice of society. Their own experience may be very limited.

KEY POINT

A child's special need may affect only a minor part of the child's life, or it may be a major and challenging factor.

Parents' reactions

Many parents will go through the different emotional stages associated with bereavement – grieving for their apparently 'lost' child – before they are able to accept, adjust and take pleasure in her. Such reactions are seen across all cultures and social classes. Typically parents experience the following.

- Shock, grief, numbness and confusion, inability to come to terms or fully comprehend and take in what has happened.
- Denial of any long-term disabling condition, feeling their child 'will grow out of it' or 'catch up later'. Of an older child they may say she's 'just lazy' or 'shy'.
- Feelings of guilt and apportioning blame, particularly if the child has an inherited condition or the mother smoked or drank heavily during pregnancy. Anger and blame may be directed at the doctor for not recognising or preventing the special need prenatally or at birth. Parents may blame themselves or each other if their child is disabled following an accident or serious illness.
- Gradual orientation, acceptance and adjustment. Parents become able to relate to their child as an individual with her own personality and potential.

KEY POINT

There is no time limit to this process of acceptance and adjustment, it may take up to several years. Parents work through the stages in their own time.

Adjustment

In spite of the sadness and stress they feel, most parents learn to love their child and are aware of the greater degree of dependency and responsibility there is always going to be. Their protective instincts are usually heightened, sometimes to the point of overprotection. Adjusting to the implication that their child will not get better and striving to provide the care, opportunity and stimulation required by the child (often despite the attitudes of society) can be a challenging process.

KEY POINT

Some parents find it difficult to cope and may never reach this stage of adjustment. They may be reluctant to share their anxieties either with family or a professional carer. Some children with special needs are fostered or adopted.

Questions parents ask

Initially, many questions are asked – 'Why did it happen?', 'What is it?', 'Why us?' Parents want quick answers to questions such as 'Will she die?', 'Will she learn to walk and talk?', 'Will she be able to go to ordinary school?' or 'What quality of life will she have?' There may be no ready answers. Sometimes, the cause is never determined, possibly making the situation harder for the parents to accept, although knowing the cause does not automatically make it easier.

PROGRESS CHECK

1 Describe the typical emotional stages parents go through when their baby is born with a special need.
2 Why might parents feel guilty or seek to blame themselves?
3 How long might it take parents to reach the stage of acceptance and adjustment?

Areas of difficulty

Mother—baby bonding

For medical reasons mother and baby may be separated from each other, or a mother may be reluctant to hold, cuddle and feed her baby, fearful of yet more powerful emotions should her baby die. Parents may find their baby's physical appearance upsetting. The baby may be rejected.

KEY POINT

A mother may have mixed feelings of love and dislike particularly if there are feeding difficulties or she receives no response from her child to caring overtures.

GOOD PRACTICE

While family and friends may be attentive and caring it is important that sensitive professional counselling and support is available. Parents need to be listened to and helped to recognise and express their feelings.

Relationships

Family routines tend to revolve around a child with special needs. Twenty-four-hour care is often necessary, with parents taking 'turns'. As their child gets bigger and heavier, routines of carrying, lifting and bathing may become more difficult and parents feel exhausted. The child may be sleeping in the parent's room or a parent may sleep with the child in her room.

Financial pressures can occur from loss of earnings due to caring responsibilities, extra laundry, heating and lighting costs. Transport to and from appointments and assessments plus possible adaptations to the home (there may be grants towards these) all quickly add up. Stress and anxiety can lead to irritability and arguments. Strained relationships, separation and divorce are not uncommon. For some families, though, relationships grow stronger as they find the determination and energy to face the difficulties and strive to find the support and provision they know is best for their child.

Isolation

Many parents feel isolated from family, friends and their local community because their child is 'different' and does not fit into the normal pattern. They may feel they are the only people to have a child with a special need. Their isolation may be partly self-enforced as a way of coping or to avoid the hurt and embarrassment of unsocial behaviour – many people today still have little awareness of special needs. Equally, there is less time for socialising. Day-to-day activities which most mothers and young children do together are limited, especially while the child is not walking.

Parents' needs

When the needs of parents are recognised and supported there is less stress and anxiety within the family, often reducing the length of time towards acceptance and adjustment.

KEY POINT

Support and advice from the different agencies (statutory and voluntary) must be offered sensitively and with understanding and direction.

In particular, parents need the following.
- Information about their child's condition and the help available. They have a right to know about their child's difficulties and where to go for help – not knowing is confusing and stressful.
- Support for their own emotional needs. As a child reaches the age at which she would have achieved particular milestones such as sitting up, walking and talking, the sense of loss and sadness frequently re-emerges. Unsupported needs have damaging and destructive effects on the whole family.
- Practical help in the home will be required either from relatives, friends or the social services department.
- Parents need contact and friendship with other parents whose own experiences provide valuable insights into many aspects of special needs. Special needs support groups or self-help groups provide the opportunity to share feelings and concerns, perhaps saying things which could not be comfortably shared with the professionals. Information about play and school facilities, financial benefits, baby- and child-sitting and so on will be available within these groups. Parents whose children are older can say what did and did not help them. (More details of befriending schemes are included on page 157.)
- Parents must have time to be with other members of their family and meet their needs.

KEY POINTS

- Parents need assurance that their emotions are normal reactions. Pretending they do not exist does not make them go away.
- Help and counselling are available. A 'special needs' health visitor can be a vital point of professional contact. A health visitor is outside the family circle, someone in whom parents may find it easier to trust and confide.

GOOD PRACTICE

Link workers from black and ethnic minorities should be available from both statutory and voluntary agencies to enable families to obtain the support, information and resources they need. Similarly, parents for whom English is not their home or community language or who have communication difficulties, need interpreters who are skilled in special needs issues, as well as information presented on tapes, in large print and in Braille.

KEY POINTS

- Over-saturation with information and conflicting advice is a common experience. Parents need to pull back from time to time and listen to their own feelings and instincts.
- Parents from ethnic minorities may experience lack of effective communication from the professionals. They may be unclear about the specific roles of the professionals and the terminology they use.

PROGRESS CHECK

1 Why is it important to support parents' emotional needs? How can this be done?
2 How can the needs of parents from ethnic minorities be identified and supported?

Activity

Imagine you are employed as a nanny caring for a baby, now ten days old, with special needs. The baby's mother is distressed and reluctant to hold, cuddle and care for her baby although she will offer her the bottle.

Think of ways in which you could help and support the mother to get close to and relate to her baby.

THE CHILD

Most children with special needs are loved and accepted within their family but some experience loss of love and approval from the important people in their life. The negative attitudes of many in society lead to discrimination and isolation. For a child with restricted mobility there is greater dependence on parents, perhaps resulting in over-protection and greater control in the child's life.

The child's needs
All children with special needs have a right to be part of a family, a community and society. They also have a right to:
- love, security, respect and stability of care
- be valued for who they are
- appropriate specialist care and therapy
- play opportunities, stimulation and social interaction
- integration into daycare and education settings with key worker support and flexible provision.

GOOD PRACTICE

Professional carers must help parents to find a healthy balance between caring and protecting and allowing their child to develop the confidence necessary for independence and quality of life.

KEY POINT

Too great a preoccupation with their special need or using it to gain attention is damaging to a child's social and emotional development.

Further references
Throughout the book there is emphasis on the uniqueness and value of every child. Chapter 2 details ways in which you can help a child develop self-esteem and confidence. Most chapters detail specific support and provision such as health care, play and education opportunities. Chapters 4 and 5 detail the role of a key worker in caring for children with special needs.

THE SIBLINGS

The effects on brothers and sisters vary according to their ages, birth order and the number of children in the family.
    Siblings may experience the following.
- Over-protection or, possibly, neglect.
- Resentment at the amount of attention given to their brother or sister, including continual discussion about the child between parents and other adults.
- Jealousy.
- A shift in the family balance which means they have to take on a domestic role.

Siblings may feel anxious and concerned

- Worry and anxiety that they will 'catch' their brother or sister's condition.
- Fear and concern at witnessing their parent's distress or rejection of the child.
- Teasing and social isolation.
- Emotional swings, from being loving and protective to disturbed behaviour such as regression, attention-seeking, moodiness, anxiety, low self-esteem, embarrassment or guilt.

KEY POINTS

- Not all siblings will experience such emotional or social disadvantage. Much depends on individual personality and the bond between them and their brother or sister with special needs. Many remain happy and well adjusted.
- You may care for siblings in a nursery, school or home setting. Observation of their play and behaviour (perhaps in the home corner) or of their drawings, painting and general demeanour, may indicate they are experiencing difficulties. They may exhibit regressive behaviour, resort to temper tantrums or become withdrawn and clinging.

The siblings' needs
- Individual attention and reassurance they are loved and valued.
- One-to-one key worker provision for a child in a nursery or education setting.

Siblings need individual quality time with parents

- Opportunity for older children to express their feelings and be listened to uncritically by parents, carers or professionals such as the family doctor, health visitor, nursery nurse or child psychiatrist.
- Time on their own with parents.
- Correct information appropriate to their level of understanding. There may be a misunderstanding or lack of knowledge about the special need which is causing unnecessary worry.
- Encouragement to care for their brother and sister in small everyday ways just as an older child normally would for a younger member of the family. This includes cuddling, talking and playing with her and fetching nappies and clothes during bathing and changing routines.

GRANDPARENTS AND OTHER CLOSE FAMILY MEMBERS

Grandparents, other close family members and involved adults may initially feel confused and lacking in confidence. They can be encouraged to treat the child just as they would any other child in the family. They will quickly learn the care and management routines, often becoming great sources of strength and support both practically and emotionally.

CASE STUDY

Sammy was three and a half years old and had attended the nursery since he was eighteen months old. He had always been a happy, sociable and

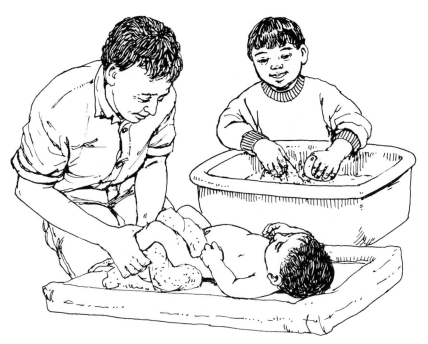

Sibling participation in a caring routine

helpful little boy. An only child, he was particularly looking forward to the birth of his baby brother or sister and kept telling the nursery staff how he was going to bring 'his' baby to the nursery every day so that he could look after 'it'.

Susan was born six months later with cerebral palsy and a visual impairment. She was cared for in the special baby unit for two months before coming home.

Her parents cared for her with love and commitment but were, naturally, very worried, especially as she had marked developmental delay. They were also very tired. Inevitably, they had less time for Sammy who still wanted to take Susan to the nursery and could not understand why she was not smiling and chuckling when he talked to her or gave her a tickle.

At the nursery a childcare worker noticed Sammy had started to suck his thumb again (he had given that up a long time ago) and had become rather clingy. He also had had several 'accidents', although he had been clean and dry since he was two and a half.

Several times Sammy threw the bricks he was playing with across the floor and spoilt a friend's painting.

1 Would you have been concerned about Sammy? Give reasons for your answer.
2 In what ways could the nursery staff have supported Sammy and his family?

'Hello grandad'. Grandparent support for the sibling

The multidisciplinary team

Team work is essential in assessing and supporting a child's abilities and needs as it would be unusual for one individual or profession to have all the necessary skills and expertise. Professionals from different disciplines come together as a team to support the immediate and changing needs of individual children with special needs. Children's best interests are served if there is close cooperation and a flexible cross-discipline approach between all the team members. Parents are always considered valuable members of the team and should be invited to participate in meetings concerning their child.

KEY POINTS

- Nursery nurses are members of the multidisciplinary team. They have a unique child health, education and social care training enabling them to recognise early signs of difficulty in children. Opportunities exist for nursery nurses to work in a variety of settings such as daycare, education (including special schools), the home and hospital. In some areas nursery nurses assist health visitors in their work with families with young children.
- Under eights officers are employed by local authorities either by social service or education departments. All officers have experience and skills in working with young children and their families. Their functions may include registration and inspection of day nurseries, pre-schools, playgroups and

childminders, advising on good practice and current legislation and providing training.

The following lists will help you to identify the professionals and the skills they provide.

WHO'S WHO

Health service professionals
Paediatrician
Consultant/specialist
Child psychiatrist
Child psychologist
Child psychotherapist
Family doctor
Health visitor
Community paediatric nurse
School medical officer
School nurse
Speech therapist
Physiotherapist
Occupational therapist
Dietician
Play therapist

Education service professionals
Education psychologist
Education welfare officer/education social worker
Special needs support teacher
Special needs adviser
Special needs assistant

Social service professionals
Social worker
Nursery officer
Residential social worker/childcare officer

Health, education and social service professionals

PROFESSIONALS AND THEIR SPECIALIST SKILLS

Health service professionals

Paediatrician (hospital or community based)
Paediatricians are doctors specialising in the diagnosis of illness, disorders and special needs in children and the provision of medical care. They work in hospitals or as members of the community child health service and may become involved with children with disabilities or special needs in the maternity unit, paediatric ward, out-patient department or a child development centre.

Consultant/Specialist
Consultants/specialists care for children in hospital who have short- or long-term serious medical or surgical needs. They have in-depth expertise and skill in specific conditions. An important aspect of their work is liaising with the family doctor and the school medical officer. They also contribute to assessments or reassessments of any child for whom they are caring.

Child psychiatrist

Child psychiatrists have a medical degree and specialise in child mental illness. They work in hospital child psychiatry units and community child guidance clinics providing individual, family or group therapy for children with emotional or behavioural difficulties. In particular, child psychiatrists work as consultants giving insight and understanding to the origin of a child's problems so enabling members of the team working directly with the child to offer effective help.

Child psychologist

Child psychologists are non-medical professionals working in child development centres and child guidance clinics. They observe and assess children's social, emotional and behavioural development and needs. Understanding the dynamics, relationships and circumstances of the family is an important part of their work. Particularly, they offer advice on how to manage difficult or unusual behaviour.

Child psychotherapist

Child psychotherapists work in child guidance clinics and are concerned with child development and the way relationships develop within the family. They help children and families to work through their problems.

Family doctor

The family doctor (or general practitioner) is the key professional in the primary health care team and an important person in the lives of all families, especially those with young children. He or she is often the first point of call for worried parents. A family doctor may work from a health centre or surgery and will care for the general health needs of a child with special needs including attending to every day ailments and carrying out child health surveillance and immunisation programmes. Children can be referred by their doctor for specialist care and therapy. Access to accurate and updated information about service provision enables the family doctor to discuss options of care and management for the child and support for the family – for example, Portage and respite care.

Health visitor

Health visitors have a background in nursing, obstetric training and the health and development of infants and young children. They are members of the primary health care team working in the community with people of all ages. They have particular responsibilities towards all children under five years, visiting them and their families at home. A health visitor may be the first to identify a possible special need in a child and is frequently the Named Person (see pages 62 and 72, chapter 3) for a child under five years with a special need.

Many health authorities employ specialist health visitors to work with families who have a child with a special need. They offer help, counselling, support and advice and provide a link between the hospital and community services. They know how to access the right statutory and voluntary services and provide information about local support groups, playgroups and toy libraries. At all times they work and liaise with a family's regular health visitor.

A regular or specialist health visitor will visit the family as often as necessary to offer early support and build up an in-depth relationship with the child and the family.

Community paediatric nurse

Community paediatric nurses are specialist children's nurses working in the community from a hospital or health centre base. They help and support children in their own homes who require nursing care and who, without this service, would need to remain in hospital. Through an assessment process they are able to identify the nursing and equipment needs of babies and children with profound and complex special needs. They liaise and coordinate care with the hospital and primary health care team. The paediatric community nursing service is not available in every health authority or National Health Service Trust.

School medical officer and school nurse

School medical officers are concerned with the health needs of school children and advise the local education authority on the medical aspect of children's development. They provide medical supervision for children with special needs in the school and may be part of a multidisciplinary team assessing pre-school children with special needs. They do not directly treat any medical condition but refer a child to the family doctor or appropriate specialist.

School nurses discuss health issues with children and their parents offering health-promotion advice and referring children when necessary to the school medical officer. They test vision and hearing and check height and weight of pupils. They may pick up difficulties in these areas. Many work in special schools where they supervise the routine medical care of children with special needs.

Speech therapist

Speech therapists are concerned with all aspects of communication. They assess children's hearing, speech and language and check mouth and tongue movements. They prepare individual programmes of activities and exercises for children to help them acquire language and use speech. Children with a cleft lip and/or palate, cerebral palsy, a hearing impairment or a stammer are particularly helped by speech therapy. Children with speech and communication difficulties often have secondary behavioural and social problems. Speech therapists work either in the community, hospital clinics or schools.

Physiotherapist

Physiotherapists assess children's motor skills and help those with movement, positioning or balancing difficulties. Their aim is to provide exercises and activities to improve these skills. They demonstrate exercises to help breathing and coughing in children with cystic fibrosis which parents or carers can carry out at home or in school. Physiotherapists work in hospitals, health centres and schools.

Occupational therapist

Occupational therapists are concerned with the practical and functional skills needed for everyday living. They particularly assess children's fine and gross motor skills in relation to their ability to feed, wash and dress themselves appropriate to their age. They give advice regarding toys and suitable home equipment which will help a child to play constructively, move around, sit and position themselves independently. Occupational therapists work either in hospitals or in the community.

Dietician

Dieticians give advice on a range of special diets. Children with diabetes, cystic fibrosis and coeliac condition have dietary requirements which enable them to remain healthy. The dietician will support the child and family in managing the special diet and offer ongoing advice as the child grows or a dietary need alters. Dieticians may work in hospitals and in the community.

Play therapist

Play therapists work with individual children or groups of children in paediatric wards, or sometimes in day nurseries, to alleviate stress and anxiety through play. They provide a range of play experiences for children to help them 'play out' emotions such as fear, discrimination or aggression. Play therapists may hold a Diploma in Nursery Nursing or other childcare award and may also have the Hospital Play Specialist Board Certificate.

PROGRESS CHECK

1 Which health professionals work in a child guidance clinic?
2 Describe how the family doctor might be involved in caring for children with special needs.
3 How can specialist health visitors help children with special needs and their families?
4 Which health service professional would assess the nursing needs of a child with special needs being cared for at home?
5 How does a physiotherapist help a child with cystic fibrosis?

Education service professionals

Educational psychologist

Educational psychologists advise teachers and parents about children who may be experiencing learning or behavioural difficulties and prepare educational assessments for children requiring a statement of special educational needs (see pages 72 and 74, chapter 3).

Education welfare officer/education social worker

Education welfare officers provide a link between children and their families, the school and local education authority. In particular, they are concerned with the welfare of children whose school attendance is irregular. They may negotiate alternative education provision for excluded pupils and can be a main contributor of social information in any assessment procedure.

Special needs support teacher

Special needs support teachers, sometimes called learning support teachers, are teachers with additional training and experience. They may be appointed to work in a particular school teaching individual children or they may be peripatetic – moving from place to place – teaching children in different schools and visiting pre-school children with special needs in their own homes. In particular, they work with children with vision, hearing, speech and language impairments.

Special needs adviser

Special needs advisers are peripatetic teachers with specific expertise, who travel to the schools of a particular local education authority giving specialist advice and support both to children with special educational needs and to the schools.

Special needs assistant

Special needs assistants (also known as learning support assistants or special schools assistants) are non-teaching members of staff who provide extra help and support for children with special needs and are seen as members of the school team. They may be qualified nursery nurses or childcare workers or may hold the Certificate in Learning Support. Some may be trained teachers who do not want the responsibility of a full teaching role, others may have no formal qualifications but have worked with children in a variety of ways. They provide learning support for individual children or groups of children, some of whom may be 'statemented'. Specific training will be needed when working with children who require medical routines such as physiotherapy.

PROGRESS CHECK

1 Describe the work of an educational psychologist.
2 A special needs support teacher may be 'peripatetic'? What do you understand by the word peripatetic?

Social service professionals

Social worker

Social workers are employed mainly by local authorities but may also work for voluntary organisations. They are based in hospitals or a local area office. They hold a social work qualification and undertake different kinds of social welfare responsibilities for children with special needs and their familiies, including advising on accessing resources, benefits and services to which children and parents are entitled and acting as an advocate to enable them to obtain these services. They are able to counsel parents or carers and help them to understand the special needs of their child. Social workers are involved in assessment for daycare, respite care and family aide provision. They have statutory child protection duties towards children with special needs and are responsible for the quality of care for those looked after in residential care homes.

A psychiatric social worker has special expertise in working with school children with emotional, behavioural and learning difficulties and is often a member of the child guidance clinic team.

Nursery officer/supervisor/manager
Nursery officers (also known as nursery supervisors or managers) may be qualified nursery nurses or hold an NVQ Level 3 or CACHE advanced diploma qualification. They may work in day nurseries, combined nursery centres or family centres run by local authorities or voluntary organisations or they may work in private nurseries. They will be in charge of the nursery setting.

Residential social worker/childcare officer
Residential social workers or childcare officers provide day-to-day care and support for children, including those with special needs, living in long- or short-term residential care homes. They may also be key workers for individual children in these homes maintaining an overall interest in their welfare.

PROGRESS CHECK

How might social workers be involved in supporting children with special needs and their families?

Activity
1 Find out further information about any three of the professionals listed above. Write down your findings.
2 In what circumstances might a nursery nurse caring for children with special needs liaise with (a) a health visitor, (b) a physiotherapist, (c) a speech therapist, (d) a social worker?

KEY TERMS

You need to know what these words and phrases mean. Go back through the chapter and make sure that you understand:

disability
disability awareness
education service professionals
health service professionals
impairment

multidisciplinary team
social service professionals
stages of bereavement
types of special need

2 PERCEPTIONS OF DISABILITY

This chapter covers:
- The medical model of disability
- The social model of disability
- Disability awareness
- Positive images of disability and special needs
- Language used
- Attitudes and behaviour
- Discrimination and stereotyping
- The child's self-image
- Access and inclusiveness
- Inclusive daycare provision

This chapter briefly identifies the medical and social models of disability. These models provide a framework to explain, in simple terms, the ideas and issues surrounding disability. As knowledge increases so the models and perceptions of disability change. The medical and social models of disability, which view disability from different perspectives, are frequently referred to in text books, journals and articles.

The chapter focuses on the basic human rights of children with special needs to live ordinary lives and be treated with respect, dignity and equality. It also aims to help you understand the importance of using appropriate language, challenging discrimination and stereotyping and helping children with special needs to develop a positive self-image.

Because more and more daycare and education settings are integrated and inclusive you are increasingly likely to care for children with special needs on a daily basis. The last part of the chapter concentrates on how to provide a daycare setting which recognises and values **all** children and promotes equality of opportunity.

The medical model of disability

The medical model, sometimes known as the 'personal tragedy' model, views disability as a sickness and labels disabled people as 'ill', and as 'medical cases' who need treatment. It fails to take into account disabled people's own views and feelings, leaving them powerless and dependent on others. The focus is on the disability, rather than on the needs of the person, with emphasis on medical explanation, treatment or a cure (usually provided by able-bodied professionals). Where there is no 'cure' disabled people are often cared for in a community home.

The phrase 'suffering from' (cerebral palsy, Down's syndrome and so on) is commonly heard. Some disabled people talk about 'belonging' to the medical pro-fession – the medical model contributes to disabled people being thought of as patients, reluctant to give up the 'sick role' so encouraging dependency on profes-sionals, family and friends and leading to over-protection and social isolation. Parents may sometimes feel guilty and at fault for their child's impairment. They try to compensate by seeking different medical opinions, cures and alternative therapies and take on the role of 'nurse' to their child.

Within the medical model society responds to disability by determining where disabled children should be cared for, go to school and, later, where they should live and what type of work would be suitable for them. This attitude reinforces reliance on others, giving disabled children no control over their lives and denying them opportunities for choice.

The Disability Movement (a growing group of disabled people and their sup-porters) rejects the medical model of disability because it discriminates, patronises and fails to accord disabled people the opportunities and rights available to others.

However, within the medical model, there are the positive values of pain relief, medication and provision of specialist resources such as surgery and a range of therapies. Without medical treatments and therapies many children with disabili-ties would die. For example, regular physiotherapy, medication and dietary management are essential if children with cystic fibrosis are to remain well. Babies born with spina bifida may require life-saving surgery with ongoing nursing care and physiotherapy.

The social model of disability

The social model of disability came about through The Disability Movement, and other organisations, campaigning for equal rights and opportunities for disabled people. It rejects the medical model of disability. Within the social model it is soci-ety that disables people by creating barriers of rejection, discrimination, prejudice and physical access so preventing them from making choices and decisions which affect their lives. The real 'cure' for disability is restructuring society and planning the environment to take account of their needs.

The social model does not deny the need for medical care but it also acknowl-edges those with disabilities as people first who should be enabled to participate fully in society and take charge of their own lives. Within the social model of think-ing, society and the environment should be inclusive, integrated and accessible, supporting personal rights, choice and freedom.

We (disabled people) reject the inhumanity of the 'medical model' of thinking, involved in labelling and identifying people by their impairing conditions. Calling someone a 'Down's child' or a 'spina bif' makes the child no more then their condition . . . the social model of disability identifies prejudice and discrimination in institutions, policies, structures and the whole environment of our society as the principle for our exclusion . . . we must reject the legacy of the past that has excluded us and see children as they really are – not 'categories' but as citizens and with contributions to make, if we let them (Micheline Mason, 1994).

PROGRESS CHECK

How would you describe and present to your peer group the perceptions of disability contained in the medical and social models?

Disability awareness

Disability awareness is about understanding different disabilities and responding to what disabled children and adults consider to be important in their lives. Important principles of disability awareness include the following.

■ Professionals, parents, carers and all members of society listening and talking to disabled people, so learning directly from them.
■ Recognising and challenging all forms of discrimination such as inappropriate language and behaviour, negative attitudes and stereotyping.
■ Displaying and using positive images of children with disabilities in books, playthings and in the media.
■ Understanding the need for social integration and an accessible, inclusive environment.

Social interaction and integration

KEY POINT

Disability awareness training is available through courses and learning packs organised by disabled people themselves. The resources can be adapted to meet the needs of particular groups. Those working with disabled young children in care and education settings should consider using this facility to understand and learn more about their special needs.

'Please will someone come and play with me?'

Equal opportunities policies in establishments such as day nurseries, nursery schools and schools must make reference to children with disabilities and special needs indicating how their needs will be met and setting out agreed procedures for dealing with incidents of disability discrimination or harassment.

Activity
Look at a variety of catalogues advertising children's clothes, toys and nursery furniture. Are children with disabilities visible in these books?

FEAR AND EMBARRASSMENT

Many people have deep-seated fears about disability or are embarrassed by it, particularly if they have no experience or understanding of it. Perhaps they feel unsure how to approach or speak to someone who is disabled, often assuming a child or adult with a physical condition is also deaf (especially if they are in a wheelchair). They may be disturbed by the physical appearance of people with Down's syndrome and feel threatened by people with mental disabilities. To overcome fear and embarrassment they may stare at, ignore, ridicule or speak disparagingly of disabled people possibly not fully realising how offensive their behaviour and remarks are.

PROGRESS CHECK

1 What do you understand by the phrase 'disability awareness'?
2 What facility could you use to learn more about disability awareness?

EQUAL OPPORTUNITIES

All children are equal and must be accepted and valued for who they are. For some children sign language will be their first language, for others mobility will be by wheelchair. Being unable to walk or communicate verbally are differences, not failures. Children with disabilities and special needs are children first and foremost and while they may require special learning programmes or different forms of therapy, they also need plenty of opportunities to play, make choices and interact with their carers, friends and peers. Like all children they will have particular interests and talents, for example in music, reading and drawing which must be encouraged and supported.

Some children will have a particular interest and talent

- Always look beyond the disability and make sure children's 'special needs' do not overshadow their 'ordinary needs'. Be positive and think about what each child **can** do, not what the child **cannot** do.
- No child should be left out of any activity because of his disability or special need. Help the other children to understand **all** children have a right to be included in the activities of the setting.
- Non-disabled and disabled children (including those who use wheelchairs) can learn about each other through 'pairing' in activities such as music and dance, ball games and so on. After a while the children will initiate pairing themselves.

KEY POINT

Children with disabilities and special needs also have 'ordinary' needs which must not be overlooked.

DEVELOPING CARE SKILLS

Initially, you may feel uncomfortable and unsure about how to care for children with disabilities and special needs, how to pick up a child with a physical condition without distressing him or how to feed a child with cerebral palsy who has difficulty in chewing and swallowing. You will be helped by those who have the expertise and

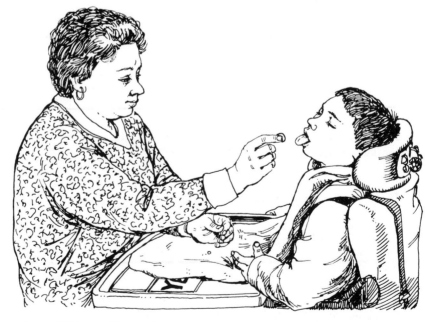

Some children with special needs require considerable help when eating

skills, for example, the nursery staff, teachers or specialist carers. A good relationship with parents is essential – they are the principal experts and will tell you how and what their child can manage in areas such as mobility and independence skills and how best to communicate directly with him.

GOOD PRACTICE

When caring for children who do not find verbal communication and self-expression easy, be patient and wait until the child indicates by a sound, eye movement, nod or other small gesture that a need has been expressed or a choice made. It may take time and many guesses before you get it right.

PARENT WORKSHOPS

Workshops, organised by the nursery or school, can offer guidance, support and encouragement to parents. The sessions need careful planning. Specialist speakers, or parents with a particular expertise in the area of special needs, can be invited to give talks and lead discussions on topics chosen by those attending the workshops. Examples might be:

- adapting play materials and activities
- accessing support services
- the process of statementing
- how to prepare for a special educational needs Appeal Tribunal.

Such workshops enable parents to support each other, become more confident in their ability to help their child and find their way through what, at times, may seem a mass of red tape.

GOOD PRACTICE

Establishing a relationship of respect and trust with parents is essential for the well-being of children with disabilities and special needs.

KEY POINT

Setting up workshops for parents enables them to become informed, develop confidence and gain new skills to help their children.

Positive images of disability and special needs

Positive images of children and adults with disabilites and special needs from different cultures should be represented in care and education settings through books, pictures, posters, displays and puzzles. Toys, including wheelchairs, crutches, splints, glasses and hearing aids are valuable in helping children gain accurate and visible information about disability. Dolls and puppets can reflect both boys and girls with different kinds of disabilities.

KEY POINT

Dolls, in particular, help children to understand how someone can be different in one respect but similar in other ways, for example, a doll with a disability still needs to be bathed, fed and cuddled.

A collection of items for the 'home corner'

Activity

Check the books, pictures and posters in your work setting. Do they reflect positive images of different groups and individuals including children and adults with disabilities?

SPECIAL EQUIPMENT

Equipment such as wheelchairs, walking frames, wedges, artificial limbs and a variety of hearing aids may be puzzling to some children. Talk to them about the different equipment, how it is used and how to care for it. They may ask to try it out. Make sure you always have permission from the child or his parent for this, that the equipment (which may be expensive) is not damaged and is returned to the owner when finished with.

Language used

Language carries many powerful messages. It *reflects* and **shapes** attitudes. The use of inappropriate words and terms when talking about disability is insulting and not only devalues disabled children but labels and categorises them, so reinforcing negative attitudes and influencing the way society perceives disability.

Incorrect and offensive terminology oppresses, offends and patronises. It contributes to poor self-image and lack of self-esteem among disabled children.

INAPPROPRIATE LANGUAGE

Examples of inappropriate language include:
- abnormal, deaf and dumb, dummy
- daft, lunatic, mental, mongol
- spastic, cripple, hop-a-long
- the disabled, the handicapped
- the Down's boy in reception class, the deaf baby in the nursery, the cerebral palsied child.

Such language is hurtful to a child's dignity. It also focuses primarily on the disability rather than the child.

'It hurts when I'm called names. I just go away and cry'

Through education and the work of disability organisations, society is now much more aware of what is acceptable and preferred language. Non-disabled people should always be guided by disabled people in the language they use.

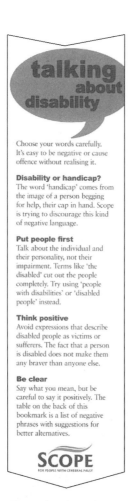 

The Scope bookmark sets out appropriate words and terms

CHILDREN'S AWARENESS OF DISABILITY AND SPECIAL NEEDS

Children are naturally curious. They usually become aware of disability some time around three years of age and will ask many questions about a child they perceive as being different. Children need accurate and developmentally appropriate information about their own and others' disabilities. They may wonder if a condition is catching or if it hurts. Ignoring their questions or failure to resolve any fears and anxieties they may have can reinforce myths and lead to later bias and discrimination. Children will copy the language used by their adult carers and older children. Be very careful about your own language and terminology.

GOOD PRACTICE

- Always use appropriate language yourself and teach children correct words and terms if they are known.

- Do not criticise children for being curious and asking questions. Answer them as honestly as you can.

PROGRESS CHECK

1 How does inappropriate use of words and terms affect children with disabilities?
2 Why must you be careful about the language you use?
3 Why is it important not to ignore children's questions about disability?

Attitudes and behaviour

The following unacceptable and offensive attitudes and behaviour can have a negative influence and detrimental effect on the way children and their families react to and cope with disability.

- Brusqueness of professionals during conversations or assessments.
- Talking to the carer instead of to the child.
- Assuming the child is deaf or unable to understand and communicate.
- Concentrating on a child's disability rather than his ability.

*'I'm happy when you talk to **me**'*

- Staring at the child.
- Behaving in a patronising way towards the child.
- Seeing and talking about children with disabilities as objects of curiosity and pity, deserving sympathy, for example 'Poor little thing', 'What a pity he can't walk on his own'.
- Pushing, teasing, name calling and bullying the child.

Activity

'The central stigma in a disabled person's life is the absence of acceptance – a failure to record them respect and regard' (Goffman 1968).

'They only ever see the chair, not the person sitting in it' (The Spastics Society, now Scope, advertising poster in 1985). The words were written underneath a picture of a child in a wheelchair.

Read these two quotations carefully. What messages do they convey to you? Discuss them with your class group and tutor.

Discrimination and stereotyping

DISCRIMINATION

Instances of discrimination or prejudice on the grounds of disability or special needs must be challenged in the same way as any racial, religious or gender discrimination. Children can be upset or frightened by disability and may reject a disabled child. Give them the opportunity to talk about how they feel in an open and honest way. A child who has been discriminated against, perhaps by being teased or bullied or excluded from an activity or game, needs comfort, support and help to talk about how he is feeling. The other children will need reminding of the rules of the setting and through stories, role play and small-group work you can emphasise and reinforce what is hurtful and what is acceptable behaviour.

STEREOTYPING

Stereotyping – having pre-conceived ideas or making assumptions about – children with disabilities usually occurs because of ignorance. Labels and categories emphasise the differences between 'them' and 'us' and suggest the disabled are weak and dependent. For example, children with disabilities may be seen as:
- tragic victims, to be pitied and a burden
- helpless, needing to be cared for by 'normal' people.

Physical appearance is important in our society. Books, theatrical productions and films often deliberately portray their characters as disabled to provide greater atmosphere and dramatic effect or to emphasise wickedness (Long John Silver in *Treasure Island* and Captain Hook in *Peter Pan* – blind in one eye and with a wooden leg or only one hand).

Instances of discrimination against a child with special needs must always be challenged

In some countries children are deliberately maimed and disfigured before being put out to beg in the hope of evoking pity, guilt and a greater financial contribution from passers-by.

GOOD PRACTICE

Support and care for all children's needs without bias or discrimination and challenge any attitude or behaviour, from wherever it comes, that stereotypes, hurts or unfairly treats children with disabilities.

Activity

Write a story suitable for children aged three to five years. Without making any assumptions or being in any way patronising include a child or children with special needs in the story.

PROGRESS CHECK

1 In what ways might children with disabilities be discriminated against?
2 What do you understand by the word 'stereotyping'?

The child's self-image

All children need to feel good about themselves with a clear sense of who they are in order to develop into well adjusted and independent members of society. Terms such as 'self-image', 'self-esteem' and 'positive identity' are all used in referring to how a child perceives himself.

KEY POINT

Children develop their self-image and identity from the attitudes of others towards them and the way their family, friends and carers interact with them.

A POOR SELF-IMAGE

Children compare themselves with others. A disabled child may have a poor self-image and lack confidence because of the differences (especially physical differences) he sees between himself and his friends or because of inappropriate comments made about his lack of progress in a particular developmental area. He may also hear adults make comments such as 'I don't know how you manage to look after him'. Over-enthusiastic attempts to make a child walk or talk at all costs and too much emphasis on treatment and cure will have a negative effect on a child's attitude towards himself.

PROMOTING A CHILD'S SELF-IMAGE

There are many ways in which you can help a child with a disability or special need to develop a positive self-image.
- See the child before the disability or special need, value the child for himself.
- Always use the child's name.
- Encourage the child himself, and others, to use positive language. Challenge any inappropriate language or behaviour from other children or adults.
- Help the child to be aware of the needs of others, to develop social behaviour skills and operate within the rules of his peer group.
- Develop good listening skills and be sensitive to non-verbal communications.
- Be positive, do not underestimate ability.
- Offer choices and allow him to make decisions e.g. 'Which jumper would you like to wear?', 'Would you like jam or honey in your sandwich?' 'You choose the colours you would like to use for your painting'.
- Avoid rigid expectations and set goals and targets he is likely to attain. Frustration and boredom lower esteem.
- Encourage success and independence by breaking down activities and skills into slow, small steps in correct sequence.
- Care for the child's intimate personal needs with sensitivity.
- Always praise achievement however small.
- Make sure the child plays with other children, is included in team games and is never isolated.

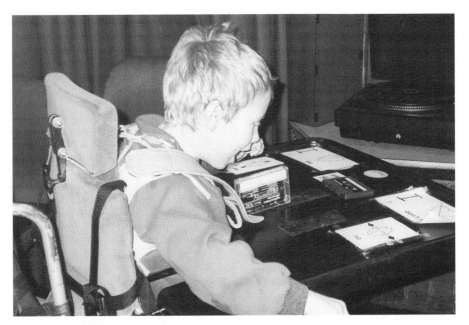

Offer activities which are pleasurable as well as stimulating

■ Support parents and listen to any concerns they may have. Take into account their ideas and wishes in any care or learning programme.

KEY POINT

Disabled children need disabled adult role models who feel good about themselves if they, too, are to grow up with a positive self-image.

PROGRESS CHECK

1 Why might a child with special needs have a poor self-image?
2 How can you prevent a child with special needs from becoming frustrated and bored?
3 How can you help a child with special needs to take part in activities?

Access and inclusiveness

Accessible, inclusive and integrated are words that are frequently used in the context of disability. Access means a way into or freedom to obtain or use something. It means that planners, architects, employers and others must think in terms of 'inclusive' design and create an environment which can be used by **all** people. For society and the environment to be truly inclusive disabled children must have equal access to:

Storytime at playgroup – adult role model

- the physical environment – indoors and outdoors
- the learning environment – all levels of education according to their needs and abilities
- appropriate health and social care provision
- training and employment opportunities when they are older
- information about services available to them including financial benefits, as and when they can understand them
- sports, leisure and holiday facilities.

Inclusive daycare provision

Children, including those with special needs, need play opportunities and the experience of mixing with other children. With the emphasis on inclusive settings, in which all children, with and without special needs, are cared for together, more and more nurseries, combined nursery centres, pre-schools and playgroups are re-thinking their policies and procedures with the aim of providing an inclusive and integrated environment which recognises the value and equality of all children. Daycare provision may be recommended in a pre-school child's assessment or statement of special educational needs. An inclusive setting must be the choice of the family, it may not be appropriate for all children.

Children with special needs must have equal access to inclusive sports and recreational facilities

STAFF DEVELOPMENT INITIATIVES

Some establishments may feel unsure about admitting children with disabilities and special needs. Disability awareness training is available to provide information and advice and voluntary organisations may offer specialist help in handling and lifting techniques as well as administering medication. Learning Makaton and how to administer British sign language will enable staff to communicate with children with hearing impairment and particular learning difficulties.

KEY POINTS

- Children with special needs benefit from the bustle and atmosphere of a mixed group. The Pre-school Learning Alliance (previously the Pre-school Playgroups Association) promotes awareness among its supervisors and helpers of the need for integrated care and encourages inclusive settings.
- Whether specialist or inclusive, a daycare setting should have a clear policy statement for admitting children with special needs.

Activity
Write a policy on including and caring for children with special needs in your work setting.

KEY POINT

A higher staffing level will be needed in an inclusive setting to care for children requiring a great deal of help with mobility, eating, drinking and toileting routines.

PARENTAL CONCERNS

Parents of children already attending the setting may worry that their children will not receive adequate attention. They need reassuring about the value of integration for all children and the opportunities for their children to learn about those who are different and need particular help. By developing a caring ethos for all children the staff will be able to allay any fears and anxieties that parents or other children may have.

KEY POINT

In an inclusive daycare setting children who do not have special needs have the opportunity to learn about, respect and respond to children who are different.

GOOD PRACTICE

- In an inclusive daycare setting the environment, curriculum and resource provision should reflect the ethos that all children are cared for and valued.
- Remember to care for children's ordinary needs as well as their special needs

An inclusive daycare setting welcomes children with and without special needs

AN INCLUSIVE SETTING

The environment should be caring, understanding and supportive in which a child with special needs and his family feel comfortable and valued. Appropriate physical access must be provided. All the staff should know the strategies for challenging any discrimination, inappropriate language or behaviour towards children with special needs and support any child who has been isolated, bullied or teased.

GOOD PRACTICE

The environment must be safe. Always follow these safety principles.

- Familiarise yourself with the Health and Safety policy of your workplace. In particular, know the procedures for fire practice, dealing with accidents, prevention of infection and handing children over at 'home time'.
- Make sure the adult:child ratio meets local authority requirements.
- Maintain appropriate supervison of children both indoors and outdoors.
- Be a role model for safe practice – the children will copy you.
- Check equipment, furniture and toys regularly. Make sure gates and fences are secure and in good repair.
- Avoid clutter in playrooms and corridors – this is especially important for children with visual impairment or mobility difficulties.

Equipment

Equipment and facilities should be 'integrated' – a mixture of standard and special. Safety must be a major consideration. Sturdy versions of standard equipment and playthings together with existing facilities and resources can often be imaginatively adapted to suit special needs. Local and national government funding is usually scarce but voluntary organisations may provide help and parents with creative DIY skills can often make special pieces of equipment. Children's specific needs should be discussed with their parents.

KEY POINT

- Some children require special equipment to enable them to take part safely in everyday play activities. Planning advice and suggestions about equipment and furniture can be provided by specialist teachers, educational psychologists, physiotherapists and occupational therapists as well as voluntary organisations.

Partnership with parents

Cooperation and partnership with parents helps effective communication and sharing of information. A daily or weekly diary or record card, filled in by both staff and parents can detail a child's progress or area for concern and provide helpful suggestions for activities at home. Most daycare settings are happy for parents to enquire about their child at any time. Flexible visiting times can be arranged.

Play opportunities

Young children are naturally curious, wanting to explore and investigate their environment and discover how things work. They do this through play. Children with special needs may not always show this natural curiosity but that does *not* mean they are uninterested in playing or cannot play. It *does* mean they need more encouragement and help to become involved, thus developing interest and skills in play activities.

Play materials, toys and equipment

Play materials, toys and equipment should be:
- well made, sturdy and safe
- attractive, colourful and enjoyable
- stimulating and versatile
- appealing to children with and without special needs.

Special books and catalogues are useful sources of help in choosing suitable items. The health visitor, occupational therapist and child development centre will be able to offer advice about special toys. Parents, too, may know about particularly appropriate toys and activities.

Play opportunities

The following list offers helpful suggestions on children's play.
- Match activities and toys to the actual level of development not the level you would expect for age.
- Prompt a child to pick up a toy and encourage him to actively explore it.
- Offer toys which guarantee 'success' when played with. For example, there is no right or wrong way to play with a ball or a pile of bricks, whereas posting shapes into a box is dependent on getting the correct shape into the correct hole. Children become frustrated and lose interest when they cannot succeed.
- Place a toy in the hands of babies and children with visual impairment and cerebral palsy. Move their fingers over it so that they can understand its shape and what it does.
- Provide activities which are graded in sequence of difficulty. This promotes confidence and a sense of achievement as each small step is mastered.
- Creative play materials and jigsaws made of light but strong foam plastic benefit children with poor hand control.
- Push-and-pull toys, tricycles, climbing frames, rope ladders and swings promote muscle tone, coordination and balance.
- Allow children to progress at their own pace and consolidate achievement at one level before suggesting something more difficult.

■ Always be positive in outlook, encourage and praise. Never show disappointment or anxiety at any perceived lack of progress.

■ Make sure *all* children take part in the activities of the setting. Do not exclude any child.
■ Remember to offer toys, games and activities which promote all-round developmental skills – physical, sensory, cognitive, social and emotional. Change the activity if it becomes too difficult or boring.

Specific facilities
Certain adaptations to the environment and equipment will be dictated by individual special needs.

For children with mobility difficulties
■ Plenty of empty, uncluttered and well planned space allows wheelchairs to wheel around and children to crawl, ride and slide around in safety.
■ Ramps, lifts in multi-storey settings, grab-rails, wide entrances and automatic doors provide easy access.
■ Large toilet, washing and changing facilities are essential. A separate toilet for disabled children is unnecessary as large toilets can accommodate wheelchairs and walking frames. Privacy and respect must be maintained particularly when disabled children are using nappies, pads or catheters.
■ Long-handled taps are easier to manage.
■ Suitable seating is needed: adjustable chairs with attachable trays for eating, drawing and playing; specially designed tables with space cut out for a child in a

A special table and seat

Going ...   *going ...*   *gone!*

wheelchair to enable him to engage with his peers in group play or at meal-times; corner seats for sitting at floor level.
- Soft play areas, beanbags or soft mattresses facilitate crawling, rolling and jumping. Ball pools stimulate the whole body and help muscle tone and posture.
- Sloping foam or canvas wedges support a child lying prone, enabling floor play with free arms.

Carer and child interaction. Floor play is possible when lying prone on a wedge

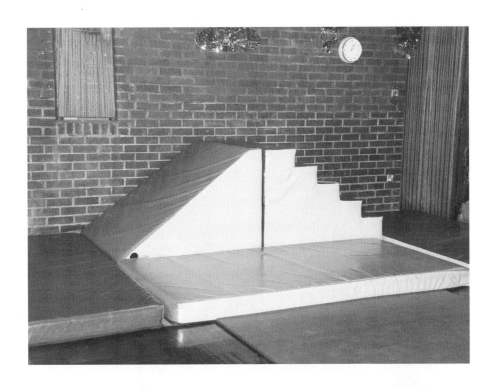

Soft play areas and equipment

- Sand and water trays with detachable legs allow children to lie on sloped wedges round the trays and enjoy the tactile stimulation of the sand and water.
- Prams and other pushing toys weighted with sandbags assist balance and walking.
- Children may have their own particular equipment:
  - a prone board which gives the sensation of standing and enables play at a table
  - a mobile standing frame (for a child who cannot stand unaided) or a wheelchair
  - a tricycle with pedal straps to support the feet and a seat belt
  - head sticks for painting and drawing.

Adjustable bikes for children with special needs

For children with visual impairment
- Lay out equipment in a familiar pattern each day.
- Provide plenty of light.
- Ensure there is no clutter.
- Brightly coloured arrows should lead to areas such as the toilet and outdoors with bright Day-Glo strips on the edges of steps, including steps to the climbing frame.
- Different textured surfaces to indicate specific outdoor areas such as the climbing frame area and the sand pit area.
- Raised or beaded edges to activity tables prevent objects falling off.
- 'Feelie' bags and boards help to develop muscle tone and flexible hands – necessary when using a Braille machine.

- Provide large print names, signs and symbols; magnifiers; and signs in Braille.
- Provide large print books, talking books and tapes.
- Clear Vision (print and Braille) books can be read by a sighted or visually impaired person to children to begin to familiarise them with Braille in the same way that sighted children become familiar with print.

For children with hearing impairment
- A system for recognising the fire alarm is required.
- Provide access to language and communication through a signing system and speech therapy programmes.
- Ensure there are lots of signs, pictures and symbols.

KEY POINTS

- Children with learning diffculties and emotional/behavioural difficulties will also benefit from many of the facilities set out above. In addition they may follow structured activity and learning programmes and take part in small group activities with the help of a key worker.
- A sensory area providing a range of visual, auditory and tactile experiences provides pleasure and learning oppportunities for *all* the children in the setting.
- An enlarged home corner enables children with mobility, vision and hearing difficulties to engage in imaginative play.

You will will find further provision for children with mobility difficulties in chapters 5 and 7, vision and hearing impairment in chapters 8 and 9, and learning difficulties and emotional and behavioural difficulties in chapters 8 and 9.

Activity
Plan a sensory area for the benefit of all the children in a daycare setting.

MUSIC ACTIVITIES

Making music is an activity which can be enjoyed by all children. It is an especially beneficial therapy for children with severe learning and communication difficulties. They are often isolated with little control over their lives. Choosing and taking turns with different instruments and being offered the opportunity to 'lead' the group enables them to take the initiative, so building confidence. Through music children can express emotions such as pleasure, anger or frustration in a safe, accepting environment. They also interact with each other and the carer or therapist, at the same time learning about sharing and taking turns.

Ben has always enjoyed making music. For a time he attended a music therapy project where this photograph was taken

Activity

Think about the care or education setting where you work. Is it an integrated and inclusive setting? Is it accessible to children with mobility difficulties or hearing or visual impairment? What modifications might be needed or possible to make it an inclusive setting? Draw a plan of an ideal indoor and/or outdoor inclusive setting.

CASE STUDY

Adam was seven years old and had just started a new school. He had visual impairment and wore glasses with thick lenses. Through PTA fund raising the school had an outdoor grassed area where the children could enjoy ball games, group activities and races. Adam loved being outside playing with his classmates. However, several children in Adam's class had recently ganged up on him excluding him from joining in their games. They called him 'four eyes' and laughed at him when he missed catching or kicking a ball. On one occasion they broke his glasses.

1 How would you have cared for and supported Adam's needs?
2 Give possible reasons for the children's behaviour.

3 Give a detailed account of how you might have challenged the other children's inappropriate language and behaviour and ways in which you could have helped them to understand the rules of the setting.

KEY TERMS

You need to know what these words and phrases mean. Go back through the chapter and make sure that you understand:

access

Clear Vision books

disability awareness

disability equality training

inappropriate language

inclusive daycare provision

inclusiveness

models of disability

preferred language

---

3 *REPORTS AND LEGISLATION*

This chapter sets out essential facts on current legislation relevant to children with special needs and special educational needs. Anyone providing services for children with special needs – health, education or social service departments, as well as voluntary organisations – must act within the legal framework. Legislation can change at any time and all health, education and social care practitioners (including nursery nurses) must keep up with current legislation.

Reports may make recommendations but these have no basis in law unless they are accepted by the government and enshrined in Acts of Parliament or Regulations which are laws (legislation) and must be put into practice.

Empowerment and advocacy, important concepts which need to be understood by all who care for children with special needs, are discussed at the end of the chapter.

KEY POINTS
- There are no 'Good practice' headings in the legislation text. Complying with the law is, in itself, good practice.
- Reports are not legally binding. Legislation is the law of the land.
- The words 'handicap' and 'handicapped' were used at the time of the Court Report and the Warnock Report and feature in the text below.

The Court Report 1976 – 'Fit for the future'

BACKGROUND TO THE REPORT

Under the chairmanship of Professor Donald Court a committee examined child health services for children in England and Wales and made recommendations for future developments. In particular, they looked at community health services, primary health care and the hospital service.

Child health services were considered to be an important element in the country's future and the committee worked on producing a structure for an integrated child- and family-centred health service which would most effectively meet the needs of all children.

SUMMARY OF THE REPORT

- The report recognised the many improvements in the health of children in England and Wales during the twentieth century. In particular, immunisation programmes, better nutrition and living conditions were identified as being major factors in these improvements.
- The committee expressed concern about apparent differences of health provision for children among the social groups with more money being spent in wealthier regions.
- Health surveillance and an integrated approach were thought to be essential in the early detection of handicap.
- A strong school health service was seen as an integral part of a good child health service.

RECOMMENDATIONS OF THE REPORT

- An integrated child- and family-centred service (particularly for children with a handicap) would provide a continuum of readily available skilled help and care for a child's total needs – physical, emotional, social, psychological and educational. Services would follow a child's development from early pre-school years through school and adolescence. Parents needed a 'single door' leading to assessment, explanation and treatment – these services should not be fragmented into 'pre-school' and 'school'.
- A basic programme of health surveillance and referral procedures for all children should be provided.
- Better coordination of health, education and social services for children in the community, hospitals and schools should be available.
- Local child development centres should be developed with a multidisciplinary professional team to provide care and management programmes for children with handicaps.
- Appointment of general practitioner paediatricians (GPPs) and child health visitors (CHVs), to concentrate solely on health care for children and their families, should be made. The health visitor, with the tradition of special responsibility for children and their families, would be a familiar figure to whom families could turn for advice or help.

KEY POINTS

- The Court Report model of a child- and family-centred health service was not adopted and implemented at the time. However, it prompted attempts at better coordination of hospital and community services.

■ Today, many more family doctors are involved in child health promotion and surveillance programmes. The health visitor's role as the key point of professional contact for parents, is more important than ever. Child development centres provide multidisciplinary assessment of children's special needs.

Health for all Children, 1996, edited by David M. B. Hall, published by the Oxford University Press, recommends particular programmes for child health promotion.

The Warnock Report 1978 – 'Special educational needs – the education of handicapped children and young people'

BACKGROUND TO THE REPORT

Mary Warnock chaired a committee of enquiry into 'the education of handicapped children and young people'. It was the first enquiry to review educational provision for all handicapped children in the United Kingdom since 1889. The considerations were based on the philosophy that all children are entitled to an education whatever their disabilities and stressed the importance of focusing on a child's *educational need* rather than on his or her disability.

SUMMARY OF THE REPORT

■ Warnock endorsed the recommendations of the Court Report that a basic programme of health surveillance should be provided for all children to help in the early identification of disabilities or significant difficulties.

■ The report recognised the 'special responsibility' of health visitors for children under five and their families, and their important role in detecting disabilities.

■ Of professionals other than those in the health service the report says:

> . . . *they may be instrumental in the discovery of handicapping conditions in children attending nurseries, nursery schools, nursery classes and those playgroups with which they have effective contact. The staff of day nurseries and playgroups have excellent opportunities to discover such conditions among children in their care.*

■ While concluding that up to one child in five (20 per cent) is likely to require special educational provision at some time in their school career the committee believed that 'no child should be sent to a special school who can satisfactorily be educated in an ordinary one'.

■ A child's educational needs and special provision should be identified through a process of assessment.

■ The practice of categorising and labelling children according to their handicap

Nursery workers in a daycare setting observing and interacting with children. Opportunities exist to identify children who require extra help

should be abolished. It creates a distinction between the handicapped and the non-handicapped.

■ The report recognised the important role of early education for handicapped children under five years.

■ At all times there should be a partnership of trust and understanding between the parents and those offering a professional service to the family.

■ Parent workshops could be a valuable form of support provided they met the specific needs of parents of different backgrounds.

RECOMMENDATIONS OF THE REPORT

KEY POINTS

■ While continuing to use the terms 'sensory disabilities' and 'physical disabilities', labels such as 'remedial', 'maladjusted', 'educationally sub-normal' or 'mentally handicapped' would be replaced by 'children with learning difficulties'.

■ Learning difficulties could be described as 'mild', 'moderate' or 'severe'. Children with particular difficulties, such as specific reading or writing difficulties, might be described as having 'specific learning difficulties'.

The following are further recommendations of the report.

- The adoption of the term **special educational need.** This would take into account a child's abilities as well as disabilities.
- A five-stage assessment process, with an annual review of progress, to identify a child's specific educational needs. At all stages parents would be fully involved and informed.
- Access to the school curriculum through a) specialist help adapted to the particular needs of each child b) provision of ramps or handrails to the classroom c) equipment such as hearing aids or techniques for teaching through Braille, should be provided. A special curriculum would be provided for children with severe learning difficulties. Some children would benefit from being taught in small groups or a special class.
- Whenever possible, children with special educational needs should be integrated into ordinary schools. Three forms of integration were envisaged.

Locational integration

Special classes, for children with special educational needs, located in an ordinary school *or* a special school and an ordinary school sharing the same school site. In either situation there would probably be little contact between pupils in the special classes/school and those in the rest of the school.

Social integration

Children with special educational needs would attend a special class or unit located on the site of an ordinary school but there would be planned opportunities for integrated out-of-classroom activities such as assembly, playtimes and meal times.

Functional integration

The fullest level of integration would be children with special educational needs in the same classes as other pupils, mixing freely with them at all times and receiving appropriate additional help and resources. This type of integration would make the greatest demands on an ordinary school because the teaching programme would have to be planned for the benefit of all children whether or not they have special educational needs.

RECOMMENDATIONS FOR THE UNDER FIVES

- A Named Person would provide the family with a point of contact for advice and support. An obvious choice for a very young child would be the family health visitor. For an older child it might be a social worker or a teacher. He or she would be someone who understood the family's cultural and ethnic background, making sure their special needs and anxieties were followed up and supported. The Named Person would provide a link between the parents, the family doctor and specialist health sevices, teachers (including home visiting teachers), social services, support groups and voluntary organisations.

- Provision of nursery education in nursery schools/classes for children with special needs.
- A range of provision, such as day nurseries, play groups and opportunity groups to provide crucial early learning opportunities for young children with special needs.
- A peripatetic teaching service for children with hearing and visual impairment, physical disabilities and learning difficulties of any kind. Teachers would visit children either at home or in a day nursery setting.

In all, over two hundred recommendations were made in the Warnock Report many of which were included in the Education Act 1981.

KEY POINT

Terms such as 'special educational needs', 'children with learning difficulties' and 'specific learning difficulties' were promoted in the Warnock Report.

PROGRESS CHECK

1 In what ways did the Warnock Report envisage children with special educational needs gaining access to the school curriculum?
2 Briefly describe the three levels of integration suggested in the Warnock Report.
3 What is meant by out-of-classroom activities?
4 What specific provision did Warnock recommend for children under five with special needs?

Activity
Find out how you could gain access to your Member of Parliament to discuss issues surrounding inclusive education.

The Education Act 1981 and The Education Act 1993

THE EDUCATION ACT 1981

The Education Act 1981 plus the education (Special Educational Needs) Regulations 1983 were a direct result of the Warnock Report. The Act was concerned only with children with special educational needs and brought about major changes for their education.

KEY POINT

In particular the Act recognised the essential role of parents as partners with the school in the education of their children.

PRINCIPLES OF THE EDUCATION ACT 1981

- Labelling a child acccording to handicap was abolished and the concept of *special educational needs*, focusing on a child's learning needs, was introduced
- Statutory duties were placed on local education authorities and school governors to meet learning needs through *special educational provision*.
- Procedures were introduced for *continuous classroom assessment, statutory assessment* and preparation of *a statement of special educational needs*.
- Where possible, children with special educational needs would be educated in ordinary schools.
- The role of parents in education was seen as crucial to children's progress. Parental wishes on integration into ordinary school had to be taken into account.

Parent and sibling involvement in education

- Parents were given a right of appeal against local education authority decisions about their child.

Activity

1 Find out who your local councillor is and discuss with him/her your local authority's policy on inclusive education.
2 If possible, observe a council session on relevant education matters.

THE EDUCATION ACT 1993

The Education Act 1993 (Part 111) builds on the 1981 Act and is now the current legislation for children with special educational needs in England and Wales. The Education (Scotland) Act 1980 (as amended) and Article 8 (3) of the Education (Northern Ireland) Order 1996 includes provision for children with special educational needs.

DEFINITIONS FROM THE EDUCATION ACT 1993

- 'A child has **special educational needs** if he or she has a **learning difficulty** which calls for **special educational provision** to be made for him or her.'
- 'A child has a **learning difficulty** if he/she:
  - (a) has a **significantly greater difficulty in learning** than the majority of children of the same age
  - (b) has a disability which either **prevents or hinders** the child from making use of educational facilities of a kind provided for children of the same age in schools within the area of the local education authority
  - (c) is **under five** and falls within the definition at (a) or (b) above or would do if special educational provision was not made for the child.'

    The Act further states: 'A child must not be regarded as having a learning difficulty solely because the language or form of language of the home is different from the language in which he or she will be taught'.
- '**Special educational provision** means:
  - (a) for a child **over two**, educational provision which is additional to, or otherwise different from, the educational provision made generally for children of the child's age in maintained schools, other than special schools, in the area
  - (b) for a child **under two**, educational provision of any kind.'

KEY POINTS

- A child has a **special educational need** if he or she has **greater difficulty** in learning than most other children of the same age and requires **special educational provision**.
- A child does not have a learning difficulty just because his or her home or community language is different from the language in which he or she will be taught.

PROGRESS CHECK

1 Why was the Education Act 1981 so important?
2 What are the main principles of the Act?
3 Which Education Act sets out the current legislation for children with special needs in England and Wales?
4 What do you understand by the term 'special educational need'?

The Code of Practice 1994

The Code of Practice issued in 1994 offers guidance on the standards required to implement the provisions of the 1993 Act. This means that all local education authorities, as well as governing bodies of all maintained schools, must consider what the Code says when identifying and assessing a child with special educational needs and planning how best to meet those needs. The Code of Practice also extends parents' rights of appeal to a special educational needs tribunal if they are unhappy about local education authority provision set out in their child's statement of special educational needs. The Code of Practice is supported by the Education (Special Educational Needs) Regulations 1994.

THE PRINCIPLES AND PROCEDURES SET OUT IN THE CODE OF PRACTICE

Schools are required to:
- create a positive partnership with parents
- listen to what children have to say when considering their special educational needs
- draw up a special educational needs policy and appoint a special educational needs coordinator
- maintain a register of children with special educational needs
- identify and assess a child's special educational needs through a five-stage model of assessment
- consider parents' wishes about the school they wish their child to attend
- work in close cooperation with local health and social services departments.

PROGRESS CHECK

1 What is the importance of the Code of Practice?
2 In what ways must schools have regard to the Code of Practice?

IMPLEMENTING THE CODE OF PRACTICE

Partnership between school and parents
An active partnership between parents, the school and the local education authority is considered crucial to children's education and progress. Schools must act on any parental concerns and involve them in all stages of assessment, review and decision making. Information about voluntary organisations which offer advice and support concerning education should be available through the school.

Listening to children
The Code states that children have important and relevant information to offer about their education. They have a right to be heard and should be encouraged to take part in decision making about provision for their special educational needs.

SPECIAL EDUCATIONAL NEEDS POLICY

1.

AIMS

Our school aims for the best standards of education for each individual pupil, with full and equal opportunities for physical, intellectual, social, moral and spiritual growth, responding to every child's changing needs and equipping children with the skills to meet the demands of a changing society.

With this in mind, and having regard to the guidance in the Department for Education and Employment Code of Practice, our school aim is that children, staff, parents, governors and outside agencies will work in partnership to ensure:

– the early identification of children with Special Educational Needs and appropriate intervention and provision

– that all children with identified Special Educational Needs have access to a broad and balanced curriculum, including the National Curriculum.

Having regard to our school's Equal Opportunities Policy we will ensure that:

– decisions relating to Special Educational Needs are based solely on the ability and needs of the individual child

– children with Special Educational Needs are encouraged and assisted to reach their full potential

– language support for children of ethnic minority backgrounds is provided in the classroom whenever necessary

Part of a school's SEN policy

2.

PARTNERSHIP WITH PARENTS

Our school values the importance of a close working partnership with parents.

In addition to the formal consultations with parents planned to take place throughout the year, teachers may make contact with parents to highlight any particular success or concern and to discuss or review progress. Contact may be made in person at the end of the school day, or by letter or by telephone. When a teacher contacts a parent, he or she will note this in the child's records.

Equally, teachers welcome the opportunity to meet parents, by appointment, who wish to discuss their child's progress. If a concern (which has not previously been identified by either the child's teacher or parent) is expressed by a parent, it is recorded, investigated and the results discussed with the parent within ten days. All concerns should be directed, in the first instance, to the class teacher who will consult, where necessary, with the Special Educational Needs Co-ordinator. Where parents notify the school of their child's special educational needs on first registering their child with the school, records will be requested from the child's previous school. If records are not available the concerns of parents will be recorded and acted upon as above (or at the appropriate Stage of Assessment).

Parents of children who are on the Special Educational Needs Register are invited to the school at least every term to review their child's progress and to share their views. They will have the opportunity to view and discuss their child's records of Special Educational Needs. They will also be offered suggested activities or support strategies in order that they may share in the practical support of their child at home.

The Special Educational Needs Co-ordinator has regular meetings with our Special Educational Needs Governor at which parental opinions related to the general strategies employed by the school are discussed.

Part of a school's SEN policy (cont.)

Special educational needs (SEN) policy

All state maintained schools must publish a SEN policy stating their arrangements for assessing children with SEN plus the support and services available for them within the school and from the local education authority. Policies should stress the rights of parents to be involved and informed at all times. All parents have a right to read the SEN policy and where necessary, the information should be in Braille, on tapes or in the family's home or community language. See part of a typical SEN policy on pages 67 and 68.

Special educational needs coordinator (SENCO)

A member of the teaching staff is appointed SEN coordinator responsible for the day-to-day administration of the policy. He or she maintains the school's SEN register, coordinates the provision for children with SEN and liaises with their parents and other members of staff.

Five-stage assessment model (including statutory assessment and statement of special educational needs)

The Code of Practice recommends a five-stage model, or step-by-step, approach towards early identification of children with special educational needs. However, there is flexibility within the Code for the number of stages as long as schools take proper action on behalf of a child.

The school is responsible for stages one to three. The school and the local education authority share responsibility for stages four and five. Each stage must have clearly stated aims and a record of the action taken to meet the child's needs is maintained. Only a small number of children need help beyond stage three. At all stages the child and his or her parents are fully involved.

Stage 1

A teacher, parent or health or social services professional may express concern. The child's teacher gathers relevant information, including details from parents about their child's health, development and/or behaviour and makes an initial assessment. The child's name is placed on the SEN register. A record of special help to be offered, such as periods of special attention or specific teaching within the normal classroom curriculum, is made. A review date is set and progress monitored. The review may decide the child:

- no longer needs special help or
- should continue at Stage 1 or
- should move to Stage 2.

Stage 2

The SENCO becomes more involved. Following discussion with the child's class teachers and parents an individual educational plan (IEP) is drawn up. It might include extra help from a teacher and set specific achievement targets. The subsequent review may decide that the child:

- continues at Stage 2 or
- reverts to Stage 1 or

Assessment Stage I: the period of special attention

- no longer requires special help or
- moves to Stage 3.

Parents are invited to contribute to Stage 2 reviews and always advised of the outcome. They must be consulted if the school is considering moving the child to Stage 3. A review date is set.

Tommy is now eight. He started at his infant school in the term before he was five. At first he seemed to be coping but by the end of the year he had made very little progress and was well behind the others in the class in his reading, writing and number work. His teacher was worried and spoke to his parents. During his second year, Tommy got extra help in class from his teacher and a classroom helper. His teacher set some targets for Tommy to reach by the end of the term, but he did not make as much progress as was hoped and he did not reach all his targets. Following a review in which his parents took part, he was moved on to Stage 2. During his next year at school the teacher set some new targets within an individual education plan, with the help of the school's Special Educational Needs Co-ordinator. After some assessments had been carried out, Tommy reached most of the targets but his progress was still slow. Tommy moved on to junior school as a slow-learning child who would continue to need some special help from his teacher and the Special Educational Needs Co-ordinator. His progress will need to be reviewed regularly so that the school can decide whether any more help might be needed, perhaps at Stage 3.

From the DfEE publication Special educational needs – a guide for parents

Stage 3

Where a child's progress causes concern, outside specialist help is sought, perhaps from an educational psychologist, a specialist teacher for hearing or visually impaired children or an SEN adviser. A further IEP is developed, possibly introducing specific activities, materials or equipment. The Stage 3 review is attended by the SENCO, teachers and specialist. They may decide that the child:

■ continues at Stage 3, perhaps with a new IEP and new targets or
■ reverts to Stage 1 or Stage 2, or
■ is referred to the local education authority for statutory assessment.

Parents should be encouraged to attend the Stage 3 review and always be told the outcome.

Robert was slow learning to speak and his speech was difficult to understand. After he had had several ear infections, it was found that he had 'glue ear' which caused occasional hearing loss. Grommets were fitted when he was three and his hearing improved. He had some speech therapy before he started school until his speech became reasonably clear. His teacher found that Robert's attention wandered at school and had to keep him close to her table to be sure that she had his concentration and that he followed her instructions. His language development worried his teacher as well as his mother. He made no real progress at reading and writing even with extra help from his teacher and the school's Special Educational Needs Co-ordinator. At six and a half he was referred to the educational psychologist who, with the teacher from the LEA's Hearing Impaired Service, drew up some language work for his teacher to carry out. This was an important part of Robert's individual education programme at Stage 3. He is now making good progress and it seems that at the next review he may be moved from Stage 3 to Stage 2.

From the DfEE publication Special educational needs – a guide for parents

---

Most children's special educational needs will be identified by this type of continuous assessment and review procedures and met by their school's resources such as an IEP, extra help from a teacher or special needs assistant or some other specialist. For those whose needs are more significant or long term (approximately 2 per cent of all school children) the local education authority is obliged to arrange a statutory assessment and, if necessary, draw up a statement of special educational needs.

Stage 4: statutory assessment

A statutory assessment is a detailed examination of a child's special educational needs carried out by the local education authority in cooperation with the school and parents. It can be requested by a child's school, or professionals such as a doctor, therapist or social worker. Parents can also make a request if they are concerned about their child's work.

A **named officer** from the local education authority advises and helps the parents over all arrangements relating to a statutory assessment.

Parents may wish to have independent help and advice at the beginning of the assessment procedure. A **Named Person** (see page 62) helps them to express their views and provides information and support. He or she may be from a voluntary organisation, a parent support group or a professional from the health or social services department.

KEY POINTS

- The local education authority considers all the information and advice from the school, a doctor or paediatrician, educational psychologist, other professionals and parents before deciding whether the child's needs can be adequately met through the school's resources or whether a statement of special educational needs is necessary.
- If a statement is not being made a 'note in lieu' is usually sent to the parents explaining the decision and recommending appropriate provision for their child.

Stage 5: a statement of special educational needs

A statement is a legal document which sets out a child's special educational needs and details the provision the local education authority considers necessary. It forms the basis for a child's future educational plans. Special provision is funded by the school although the local education authority is required to make additional resources available.

KEY POINT

Whenever possible, arrangements are made for education to continue in an ordinary school. However, a child's needs may be more adequately met by the facilities, specialist teaching, expertise and adapted buildings of a special school.

At all times the parents are fully involved, their views are sought and they are advised of procedures. A draft, or proposed, statement is sent to them. If they accept the contents it becomes final. However, they have a right of appeal against all or any part of a statement (see page 74). A copy of the completed statement is given to the parents.

KEY POINTS

- Parents are involved at all times with their child's progress including the process of assessment and statementing.
- Stages 1 to 3 of the five-stage model are school based. Assessment at Stage 4 and drawing up a statement is the joint responsibility of schools and local education authorities

Activity

Create a flow chart of the processes of assessment and statementing to present to a group of parents.

KEY POINT

A statement must be reviewed every year. It may last for the whole or part of a child's school career. It ceases at sixteen years if a child leaves school at that age. A local authority may maintain the statement if a child remains at school until nineteen years old.

Provision of resources identified in a statement can be expensive and may be at a time when school and local education authority budgets are tightly controlled. It is often felt that statementing is resource-led rather than needs-led and many parents express concern that their children are not receiving the level of support indicated in the statement.

> **John** went to a nursery school and then to a primary school. Although he did well in some areas of his work, his parents were worried that he was getting behind with his reading. Both schools arranged extra help for him but by the age of eight he was still having difficulties. His school discussed his problems with a visiting specialist teacher. This teacher did some tests with John and gave his teacher some advice about work that she could do with him. His parents were still worried, and his school agreed to refer him to the LEA, who decided to carry out a statutory assessment. After hearing the views of his parents and taking the advice of specialists, they decided that his problems were not so severe as to need a statement, but that he did have special educational needs. The LEA issued a note in lieu and sent his parents and, with his parents' agreement, his school, all the advice they had received during the statutory assessment. Now John is registered by his school as having special educational needs at Stage 3. He gets special teaching twice a week, in a small group, when he does work that has been carefully planned just for him.

From the DfEE publication Special educational needs – a guide for parents

KEY POINTS

- Not all children who are formally assessed go on to receive a statement of special educational needs.
- Parents have a right to express a preference for a particular school including the school their child already attends.
- Parents have a right to appeal against part or all of a statement.

Statement of special educational needs

A statement is set out in six parts.

■ Part 1: the child's and family's name, address, religion and home or community language.

■ Part 2: the child's special educational needs. This part is usually in the form of a report setting out developmental attainments to date and identifying areas where special help is needed.

■ Part 3: the proposed special educational provision. The recommendation might be for an extra or specialist teacher to deliver a planned numeracy and literacy curriculum. Speech and language therapy may also be advised.

■ Part 4: the name of school the authority considers appropriate for the child. Parents have a right to state a preference for a particular school including the one their child already attends. The local education authority will take into account the needs of the other children at the school plus available resources before agreeing to the request.

A 'preferred' school

■ Part 5: the non-educational needs of the child. This may include help to develop self-care skills, occupational therapy or physiotherapy, or transport to school.

■ Part 6: details of how provision for Part 5 will be carried out. A special needs assistant may be appointed to help with self-care skills. A special bus or taxi might provide transport to and from school.

Non-educational provision identified in a statement

PROGRESS CHECK

1 Outline the three school-based stages of the five-stage model of assessment.
2 Who is responsible for the procedures of a) statutory assessment b) drawing up a statement of special educational needs?
3 What non-educational needs might a child have?
4 Why might a special school be more appropriate for a child with SEN?

Activity
Prepare a leaflet for parents at the infant school where you work explaining a statement and the procedure of statementing. Include a section on the rights of parents in the statementing process.

ASSESSMENTS AND STATEMENTS FOR THE UNDER FIVES

Children under the age of five years old can be assessed and statemented by the local education authority in much the same way as children of compulsory school age. However, most local authorities are reluctant to do so unless specifically asked by parents, in order to avoid 'labelling' at an age when all areas of development are so important.

A statement for a child under five years is based on medical and developmental assessments undertaken at a child development centre. Special educational provision might be attendance at nursery class or school (in an ordinary or special school) or at a day nursery or playgroup. A home-based learning programme such as Portage (see page 152, chapter 5), or a peripatetic teacher for a child with hearing or visual impairment may be recommended. Statements for children under five are reviewed informally every six months and formally every year.

Carol was premature and very underweight at birth. She was found to have cerebral palsy. It was soon clear that she was quite seriously handicapped. She had a three month review at the Child Development Centre when it was decided to inform the LEA and, with the parents' agreement, to arrange a visit from the home teaching service. The home visitor came weekly and set small tasks for Carol which her parents carried out with her. During the first year the home visitor sought the advice of both the physiotherapist and speech therapist who were already working with Carol. Their advice was invaluable and was included in the home teaching programme. At the age of two, Carol was assessed by the LEA. All the professionals who had been working with her were asked to give their advice. Because of their work with Carol, her parents were also able to help with the assessment procedure. Carol was given a statement of special educational needs which named a local special school. The home teaching stopped just before Carol's third birthday when she started school, where the programme continued. The same physiotherapist and speech therapist now see Carol at school. Her parents are still involved and are carrying on the work at home.

From the DfEE publication Special educational needs – a guide for parents

KEY POINTS

- Any concerns the staff in a daycare or education setting may have about a child's developmental progress should be shared as early as possible with the local education authority.
- Assessments and statements for children under two can be undertaken only with parents' consent or at their request.
- A statement for a child under two years is very rare.
- For families whose first language is not English, local education authorities should offer translations of documents in the home language or provide translaters.

Activity

A child with a statement of special educational needs is to be admitted to the infant school where you work. What does this mean for the child? What duties does this impose on the teaching staff?

Steven aged twenty months with a Portage home visitor

SPECIAL EDUCATIONAL NEEDS TRIBUNAL

The special educational needs tribunal considers appeals by parents against local authority decisions about their child's SEN. It is an independent tribunal, unconnected to any local education authority. A decision is made after considering all written and verbal evidence including whether the local education authority has acted within the guidance set out in the Code of Practice. The Government cannot influence its decisions.

Reasons for appeal
- If the local education authority decides against making a statutory assessment or does not issue a statement of special educational needs after making a statutory assessment.
- Against the description of a child's special educational needs and/or the special educational provision the local education authority has identified.
- Against the school named in the statement or the refusal of the local education authority to change the school named in the statement.
- If the local education authority refuses a request for a further assessment or ceases to maintain a statement.

KEY POINT

Appeals *cannot* be made about the way the local education authority carried out the assessment, the length of time it took or the way the school is meeting a child's educational needs.

Information for parents

Parents need to make their appeal within two months of the decision they are appealing against. While they would be encouraged to attend the hearing they are not obliged to do so. A representative, such as the family's Named Person or an advocate may attend on their behalf. Children may attend the tribunal or present a written statement if they have a particular view they wish to express about their education. The appeal application can be withdrawn any time before the hearing. The appeals procedure usually takes between four to five months from the time the appeal is received to the tribunal's decision. Parents and the local education authority are required to accept the decision of the tribunal.

KEY POINT

Parents can get advice about the special educational needs tribunal and help in preparation of their appeal from: the local education authority; the SENCO of their child's school; voluntary organisations such as the Citizen's Advice Bureau or a society representing their child's particular special need, for example Scope, The Down's Syndrome Association or The National Autistic Society; and the Named Person or an independent advocate.

Ben – a true story

Ben is a five-year-old boy with Down's syndrome, who lives with his parents and two-year-old sister Beth. Outgoing and sociable, Ben readily makes friends with other children and adults and with members of his wider family who are all very important people in his life – loving, caring for and supporting Ben, his parents and his sister. Ben is a treasured son, brother, grandson and nephew.

Ben was a happy baby and toddler and made slow, steady progress. He had repeated upper respiratory tract infections which have lessened over the years although he still has frequent catarrh. His development was regularly assessed and Ben received all his immunisations.

Between the ages of eight months and two and a half years (when he began to attend day nursery) Ben received weekly help from a Portage home visitor which proved extremely beneficial for him. He was usually able to perform the weekly set task before the next session. His family were involved and enthusiastic participants in the programme. Physiotherapy, speech and occupational therapy services were all provided. Ben always enjoyed his therapy and exercise sessions although they could be tiring for him.

Ben walked at two years. When he was four years old he attended gym sessions for children with special needs which increased his physical ability and confidence. He learnt to walk along a form, climb wall ladders, commando-crawl under, over

'Whoops! Mummy didn't tell me about the landing'

and through hoops and tunnels and, with help, hang by his hands. Now, at five years, he can run around and climb up and down steps and stairs.

Although he would rather just play with the water, Ben makes a good effort at washing his hands and face and cleaning his teeth. Dressing and undressing can be tricky. He can take off his shoes, socks, trousers and sometimes a top item, like a tee-shirt, with help. He can put on and pull up his trousers but needs help to get them over his bottom, he also needs help to get his socks over his toes and heels. Undoing a zip poses no problem but he is unable to manage buttons, press studs or buckles.

Ben demonstrates symbolic play and hand–eye coordination

Ben is an enthusiastic but slow eater. He is able to use a spoon and fork (and sometimes a knife) independently but there are times when he prefers someone to feed him – particularly when he sees Beth being fed. He eats a range of food and has been able to chew properly since the age of three. Ben has learnt to push his plate away when he has had enough as he is unable to say 'I've had enough' or 'I'm not hungry'. He drinks from a training beaker.

Ben is in control. He signs for others in the setting to be quiet. They can 'wake-up' when he signals by loud banging on the tambourine

Ben has a well developed pincer grasp although his hands are weaker than those of a child without special needs. He manages simple three-piece jigsaw puzzles, threads beads and can turn large objects such as taps. He plays enthusiastically and is able to engage in simple sequencing activities. His play, at a little over four years, was assessed at the developmental level of two and a half years.

Ben's comprehension is improving. He understands positional language such as in, on, under, up and down, and he readily fetches things and responds to little commands. He has a spoken vocabulary of about twenty words and is beginning to pick up simple phrases he hears Beth using such as 'Go away' and 'Get away!' Ben uses up to a hundred and fifty Makaton signs. Beth copies her brother's signing – a positive example of sibling interaction.

Because Ben has no way of expressing himself verbally he does become frustrated. He may throw things or refuse to get dressed. When being read a story he may push the book away. At times he will rush around in a state of high spirits.

Ben received a statement of special educational needs when he was four-years-and-four-months old. His parents were unhappy at the recommendation that Ben should attend a special school. They felt strongly it would be more beneficial for Ben's overall development if he attended his ordinary, neighbourhood school.

Family interaction. Even Beth joins in signing

They appealed to the special educational needs tribunal and their appeal was upheld.

Ben is now settled and integrated into the school of his parent's choice. Two special needs assistants provide a total of thirty-five hours help per week. Ben also has one session of speech therapy per month. Full-time education is tiring but apart from a few tears, particularly at the beginning of term, Ben is happy. He is making all round progress and can now join up the dots of his name. Since attending school he has learnt to sit on and use a child's toilet.

The Education Reform Act 1988

The Education Reform Act 1988 introduced the following concepts.

- A national curriculum which all children, including those with special educational needs, are expected and entitled to follow. This inclusive approach has meant a move away from separate special classes for children with special educational needs to a policy of in-class support teaching.
- The rights of all parents to send their children to the school of their choice provided it has room for them.
- A school's right to opt out of local education authority control, if a majority of parents voted in its favour, under the new concept of Local Management of Schools.

KEY POINT

Children with special educational needs must have access to the National Curriculum.

The Children Act 1989

The Children Act is the legal framework for the *care and protection* of children in England and Wales. It established a new approach in England and Wales to services for children and their families. The Act recognises the importance of families and that, wherever possible, children are brought up within their own families.

Families are important

In particular, disabled children are now included in children's legislation as a new legal category and local authority social services departments are required to register children with disabilities and provide care services for them.

The Act encourages better coordination of services between local health, education and social services departments.

DEFINITIONS FROM THE CHILDREN ACT

The Children Act (Part 111 Section 17) defines children as *being in need* if the following apply.

- He or she is unlikely to achieve or maintain, or to have the opportunity of achieving or maintaining a reasonable standard of health or development without provision for him or her of services by a local authority under this Part (of the Act).
- His or her health or development is likely to be significantly impaired, or further impaired without the provision for him or her of such services.
- *He or she is disabled.*

The Children Act states that: '*A child is disabled if he is blind, deaf or dumb or suffers from mental disorder of any kind or is substantially and permanently handicapped by illness, injury or congenital deformity or such other disability as may be prescribed.*'

KEY POINT

Children in need means children, including those with disabilities, who require specific help and services to ensure 'a reasonable standard of health and development'.

PRINCIPLES IN THE CHILDREN ACT

The following principles are enshrined in the Children Act.
- The welfare of the child (whether disabled or not) is paramount and should be safeguarded and promoted at all times by those providing services.
- Children with disabilities are children first with the same rights as all children to services.
- Parents and families are important in children's lives. Local authorities should support them in carrying out their responsibilities.
- Parents should be valued as partners with local authorities and other agencies such as health and education services.
- Children have a right to be consulted and listened to when decisions about them are being made. Their views and the views of their parents must always be taken into account.
- Health, education and social services for children with disabilities should be coordinated.

REGISTRATION

Local authority social services departments are required to keep a register of children with disabilities – where possible, a joint register between local health, education and social services departments. Such a register makes it easier to plan and coordinate services for a child and her family. Inclusion on the register is voluntary and parents have a right to see what is written. Provision of services is not dependent on registration.

A register of children with disabilities is totally separate from, and has no connection with, a child protection register.

PROGRESS CHECK

1 What is the *main* objective of the Children Act 1989?
2 What do you understand by the phrase 'children in need'?
3 What are the principles of the Children Act?

The National Health Service (NHS) and Community Care Act 1990

The National Health Service and Community Care Act 1990 followed from the 1989 White Paper 'Working for Patients'. With the Act came 'purchasers' and 'providers' of services and the creation of NHS Trusts providing NHS care commissioned by District Health Authorities. Many family doctors are now fundholders responsible for purchasing certain hospital and community health care for their patients.

Under the NHS and Community Care Act 1990, local authorities have a duty to make assessments of need for community care services. For children with special needs community care means providing health and social care services, as well as support, to enable them to live as independently as possible in their own family homes or 'homely settings'. A 'seamless care' plan should demonstrate a holistic approach to assessment and provision.

The Disability Discrimination Act 1995

The Disability Discrimination Act introduced new measures aimed at ending the discrimination which many people with disabilities face. Further measures will take effect in 1997. The Act provides new rights for disabled employees and job applicants and makes it an offence to discriminate against people solely on the grounds of disability. However, disability rights campaigners are not satisfied that the measures go far enough.

The Act defines disability as a 'physical or mental impairment which has a substantial and long-term adverse effect on a person's ability to carry out normal day-to-day activities'. People who *have* a disability and those who *have had* a disability, but no longer have one are covered by the Act.

The Disability Discrimination Act supports the policies and requirements of the the Education Act 1993 to provide all children with special educational needs an education and school place appropriate to their needs

PROGRESS CHECK

1 What does the NHS and Community Care Act 1990 say about children with special needs?
2 How does the Disability Discrimination Act 1995 support the Education Act 1993?

Children's rights, empowerment and advocacy

CHILDREN'S RIGHTS

Children are dependent on their parents for basic needs such as food, warmth, shelter, clothing, protection and love but they are also subject to adult preferences, rights and power. Adults may not always understand or meet children's needs.

Children now have rights enshrined in laws. Technically, the days when children were 'seen and not heard' are over. Action has been taken to ensure children, and their families, know what their rights are and how to put this entitlement into practice. Children must be empowered to secure their rights and make their voice heard. Young children can be represented by an advocate to speak and interpret on their behalf.

KEY POINT

Remember, the fact that children have been granted legal rights does not automatically mean those rights will be respected.

The Convention on the Rights of the Child

In 1959 The United Nations, formerly the League of Nations, made a Declaration of the Rights of the Child. During the International Year of the Child in 1979, Poland proposed a Convention on the Rights of the Child. It was an important step in recognising the child as a person worthy of respect and with rights. The Convention was completed and adopted by the United Nations General Assembly in 1989 and ratified (formally approved) by the United Kingdom government in December 1991. Countries which have ratified the Convention are known as States Parties and are legally bound by its provisions.

Activity
Find out the current number of States Parties to the Convention on the Rights of the Child.

KEY POINT

The Convention on the Rights of the Child is the first universal, legally binding code of child rights in history.

The Convention on the Rights of the Child declares that children have the following rights.
- Life.
- An adequate standard of living – food, shelter, medical care.
- Education, play, leisure and cultural activities. Access to information and freedom of thought.
- Protection against all forms of abuse, neglect and exploitation, including child labour and sexual exploitation.
- A say in matters affecting their lives and opportunities to take part in the activities of their society in preparation for responsible adulthood.
- Article 23 of the Convention (summarised) states that *a disabled child has the right to special care, education and training to help him or her enjoy a full and decent life in dignity and achieve the greatest degree of self-reliance and social integration possible.*

KEY POINT

The Convention on the Rights of the Child recognises the rights of parents or carers and in no way promotes conflict between them and their children.

The World Summit for Children in 1990 created a Committee for the Rights of the Child to monitor the way in which States Parties implement the provisions of the Convention.

Rights of children with special needs

Children with special needs in the UK have, through Acts of Parliament, a right to education, health care and a range of services which promote and safeguard their welfare. Local education authorities, local health authorities (through their hospital and community health provision) and social services departments have duties to provide appropriate care and support programmes through continuous assessment and review procedures. Multidisciplinary teams (see page 24, chapter 1) work and plan with the parents and child, to provide a 'package of care and support' to meet individual and changing needs.

KEY POINT

Any care and support plan must be flexible. The overall aim is, as far as possible, to maintain and support children with special needs within their own families. Children being looked after by foster carers or living in residential homes have a right to be placed near their family homes – often placements are many miles away making parental visits time consuming and expensive.

Listening to children

The Children Act 1989 and the Code of Practice 1994 require that children are listened to, consulted and involved in decision making which will affect their lives. Young children with special needs must be listened to, whatever their age, and their wishes and choices respected and encouraged. It is sometimes hard for people, including professionals, to understand that children have rights independently of the adults around them, especially their parents. Newell (1988), commenting on the Cleveland crisis on child abuse in which the professionals were clearly not listening to what the children were saying, but rather they were acting in the children's best interests, wrote 'let no one forget after Cleveland that "best interests" are no substitute for "rights".' Lord Justice Butler-Sloss in the Cleveland Report said 'the child is a person, and not an object of concern'.

'Now, will somebody please listen to me!'

KEY POINT

The family's Named Person is able to act as a coordinator in securing the appropriate information, help and support.

PROGRESS CHECK

1 What is the importance of the Convention on the Rights of the Child?
2 What does Article 23 of the Convention say about the rights of disabled children?
3 To which particular services do children with special needs have a right in this country?

4 What comments were made by Newell and Lord Justice Butler-Sloss with regard to the Cleveland child abuse crisis?

EMPOWERMENT

The word empower means to enable, to give power or authority. Young children with special needs must be enabled to make their wishes known to their adult carers and to make choices, however small, in matters affecting their everyday lives. The motto of The National Children's Bureau is 'The powerful voice of the child'. All children, including those with special needs, have the right to be heard and given a sense of control over their lives. Frequently, children 'fall in' with whatever plans their parents have for them without being asked whether or not they have any choice or preference. Listening to children, taking into account their views, allowing them to exercise choice and involving them in planning and decision-making procedures come within the remit of The Children Act 1989.

Offering choices

How often are non-disabled children given the chance to make a choice or say 'yes' or 'no' during the course of a day? Typically, you ask them 'What would you like for your lunch?', 'Would you like an orange or an apple?' 'Which story would you like?', 'Where shall we go for our walk today?'

The Children Act 1989 says:

Learning to make well-informed choices and making some mistakes should be part of every child's experience. Children and young people should be given the chance to exercise choice and their views should be taken seriously if they are unhappy about the arrangements made for them.

GOOD PRACTICE

Make sure you offer choices to children with special needs and encourage them to make decisions in care, education and home settings.

On a small scale you can offer children similar choices to those above such as which clothes they would like to wear, what activity they would like to do next or whether they would like a rest. Choice of a music tape, appropriate television programmes or a special treat can also be offered. Older children can be actively involved in decisions about education and be given certain responsibility within the school environment. They can be asked their views on management of their health care and medical needs.

Scott makes a choice

KEY POINTS

■ A balance must be struck between giving children a voice and offering them choices and decisions about which they cannot make an appropriate judgement on their own.
■ Giving children the opportunity to choose and make decisions in small ways increases self-image and promotes the confidence and independence to make later major decisions affecting all areas of their lives.

Activity

If you are caring for children with special needs think how many times you offered them choices today. How were the children with complex special needs able to respond to your offers?

Child protection

Children need protection from all types of child abuse. Children with special needs are particularly vulnerable to the possibility of abuse and must be empowered to recognise appropriate and inappropriate touching, as well as behaviours such as verbal abuse and discrimination. They must be given the words and language to use in defending themselves.

Your role and responsibility as a childcare worker in protecting children with special needs and identifying possible abuse is the same (if not more so) as protecting other children (see page 363, chapter 9).

Understanding and interpreting children's needs

Not all children with special needs will be able to make their voices heard through the spoken word, even so their vocal communications, actions and behaviour can reveal their wishes and feelings. You will need to be patient and learn to interpret their clues and gestures, such as nodding or shaking their head, pointing, facial expressions as well as recognising the messages they give through their play and creative activities. Children with severe learning difficulties or communication skills can be helped to make their needs and preferences known through sign language, an interpreter, large print, Braille and information technology.

Children communicate in a variety of ways

KEY POINT

Through observing children you can pick up any stress, anxiety, aggression or pleasure which may indicate a particular need or a wish to express a view.

Empowering parents

The Children Act 1989, the Education Act 1993 and the Code of Practice 1994 have empowered parents of children with special needs to enter into a parnership of support and cooperation with the professionals. This concept recognises that parents know their children best and professional services cannot be wholly effective without their support. However, families cannot be empowered unless they are informed. Professionals must be sure that families receive appropriate information about the range of services available. Information should be freely accessible through outlets such as public libraries, local child health and development centres, daycare and education settings, hospitals and surgeries.

Information must always reflect the needs of families from a variety of ethnic and cultural groups.

Activity

Check in various outlets, such as those mentioned above, in your own locality for leaflets or information sheets on services available to children with special needs and their families. Do you have information available in your work setting? Is the information available for families of different ethnic groups and those with sensory impairment?

PROGRESS CHECK

1 What do you understand by the word 'empowerment'?
2 Why is it important to offer young children with special needs the opportunity to make choices and decisions?
3 In what non-verbal ways might children with special needs make their wishes and choices known to you?

ADVOCACY

The movement for child advocacy started in America in the 1960s. It is now enshrined in the Children Act 1989. Children with special needs are those least likely to be able to speak up for themselves and their rights. Those who are unable to make themselves heard or who are denied appropriate services and support need an adult to act as advocate, interpreting and articulating for them. An advocate will *listen, interpret, liaise* and *negotiate* to secure their rights. Parents can be enabled to speak on their child's behalf (or another advocate can speak their words for them). Where a child's needs appear to be overruled or ignored an advocate can help the parents to gain information and support. This may be a professional such as the family health visitor or social worker (perhaps in their capacity as Named Person), an ethnic link worker, or someone from a voluntary organisation. Some local authorities employ children's rights officers as independent advocates for older children with special needs to make sure they are 'heard' when plans for their future are being discussed.

Where advocacy is helpful
Advocacy is helpful if:
- parents have insufficient knowlege of English to make themselves understood
- parents lack knowledge about services and resources available to their child and family
- professionals will not listen to the child or the parents.

Advocacy and schoolchildren

Children with special needs attending school have a right to be involved in their own school-based and local authority assessments and decision-making processes. The Code of Practice 1994 states:

> *Special educational provision will be most effective when those responsible take into account the ascertainable wishes of the child concerned, considered in the light of his or her age and understanding.*

KEY POINT

- Advocacy may be important if parents are unsure about the statutory assessment procedures or how to appeal against a statement of special educational needs.
- Children looked after by the local authority may require access to an independent advocate.
- Where children's rights have been obstructed or violated, the child, or an advocate (parent, carer, social worker, the police, social service department or other person or organisation) can seek help for the child through the courts.

Advocacy and parents

Advocacy training programmes for parents enable them to become confident and assertive advocates for their children. They gain information about the rights of children with special needs and learn how to access the resources available for them.

Self-advocacy is a form of self-help in that it empowers parents to speak out effectively for their own needs.

Activity

Think of instances which might constitute obstruction or violation of a child's rights.

PROGRESS CHECK

1 What do you understand by the word 'advocacy'?
2 Who might act as an advocate on behalf of a child with special needs?
3 Why might the parents of a child with special needs require an advocate?

CASE STUDY

A family had recently moved from Bangladesh to join their extended family in Britain. Both parents had limited English. Their five-year-old child, Depesh, was to join his cousins in the local infant school.

On admission to school Depesh was found to have marked developmental delay and arrangements were made for him to be formally assessed and receive a statement of special educational needs.

Depesh's parents had no knowledge of the education system, the support available or their rights. There was unanimous agreement at a case conference that Depesh's needs would be best represented by an advocate and an ethnic link worker. The assessment and statementing procedure was commenced.

1 In what other situations might an advocate be better suited than a parent to represent a child's needs?
2 How could Depesh's parents gain access to the information needed to make a suitable choice of school for their son?

KEY TERMS

You need to know what these words and phrases mean. Go back through the chapter and make sure that you understand:

advocacy	empowerment
Children Act 1989	learning difficulty
children's rights	NHS and Community Care Act 1990
Code of Practice 1994	reports and legislation
Court Report 1976	special educational needs
Education Act 1981	special educational provision
Education Act 1993	Warnock Report 1978

4 STATUTORY SERVICES AND SUPPORT FOR CHILDREN AND THEIR FAMILIES

> **This chapter covers:**
> - Health service systems and support
> - Social services systems and support
> - Education authority systems and support
> - Social security benefits

This chapter sets out the statutory care and support available for children with special needs and their families. Laws, or statutes, are passed by Parliament and either impose a *duty* (must do) or give a *discretionary power* (may do) to central or local government departments or agencies to provide a service or carry out certain obligations. The three main statutory service providers for children with special needs are:

- the health service
- social services
- education authorities.

Across these three types of service there is a wide range of support and care for a child and his family, which is described in this chapter. Professionals from the different disciplines interlink to offer the necessary provision – for example, a child with cerebral palsy may receive physiotherapy from the health service, day nursery provision from local authority social services and, later, special educational provision from the local education authority (see page 108). Research shows that families appreciate services being available all in one place. Too often they are spread over a wide area causing confusion as to where to find help.

KEY POINT

The key to successful assessment, review procedures and provision of services is an effective working partnership between all those providing a service. This is particularly important for children who have wide ranging and complex needs.

Health service systems and support

The National Health Service (NHS) in the United Kingdom was introduced in 1948. It is a comprehensive service providing health care, within available resources, for all members of the community. The National Health Service and Community Care Act 1990 brought health care into the 'market place' with purchasers and providers of services. The purchasers are health authorities and General Practitioner fundholders who purchase (buy) health care on behalf of the

HEALTH SERVICE PROVISION

Hospitals — in-patient care
— out-patient care

Consultant/specialist advice
and care
- neonatologists
- paediatricians
- neurologists
- ophthalmologists
- ear, nose and throat
  specialists
  (and others)

Hospital/hospice respite care

Child psychiatric clinics

Community child health services

*Primary
health
care
team*

Family doctors ——— referrals
prescriptions
care of unwell child
child health promotion
immunisation

Health visitors / Special needs
health visitors

Community midwives

Community paediatric nurses
nursing care
equipment loans

Child health clinics
Child development centres
Child guidance clinics

School health service
Dentists

Toy libraries
(also social services provision)

KEY POINT

Physiotherapists, speech therapists, occupational therapists and dieticians may be hospital or community based.

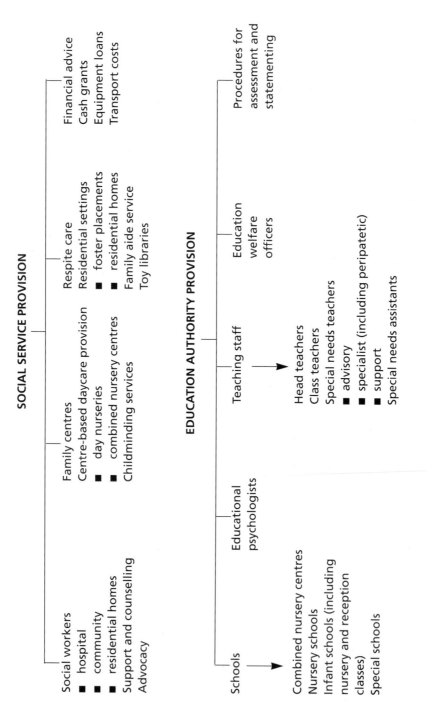

SOCIAL SERVICE PROVISION

- Social workers
  - hospital
  - community
  - residential homes
- Support and counselling
- Advocacy

- Family centres
- Centre-based daycare provision
  - day nurseries
  - combined nursery centres
- Childminding services

- Respite care
- Residential settings
  - foster placements
  - residential homes
- Family aide service
- Toy libraries

- Financial advice
- Cash grants
- Equipment loans
- Transport costs

EDUCATION AUTHORITY PROVISION

- Schools
  - Combined nursery centres
  - Nursery schools
  - Infant schools (including nursery and reception classes)
  - Special schools

- Educational psychologists

- Teaching staff
  - Head teachers
  - Class teachers
  - Special needs teachers
    - advisory
    - specialist (including peripatetic)
    - support
  - Special needs assistants

- Education welfare officers

- Procedures for assessment and statementing

KEY POINT

Provision of nursery education is at the discretion of local authorities.

communities they care for. Providers are all General Practitioners (fundholders and non-fundholders) and NHS Trusts who have contracts with the purchasers to provide health care services.

The Department of Health (DoH) has overall responsibility for the National Health Service.

Some health service professionals are identified and described in Chapter 1 (see page 25).

Usually, the first professionals a child and his family see are from the medical profession. For many children identified with special needs through the health service the most likely causes will be a physical condition, sensory impairment or developmental delay. Sometimes needs can be assessed in a child health clinic or surgery but usually children are seen in a child development centre which provides multidisciplinary assessment.

KEY POINT

Children with special needs may require hospital care. Some will receive health care at home from the family doctor and community paediatric nursing team. Ongoing physiotherapy, occupational or speech therapy can be provided in hospital, the local child health clinic, in the nursery or school or at home.

HEALTH SERVICE SUPPORT AND PROVISION

Health service support and provision includes the following.

Health service professionals
See page 95.

Specialist/consultant care
Many children need specialist assessment, treatment and care including surgery, investigations and a range of therapies. Parents are often overawed by a hospital environment and are particularly vulnerable when waiting for new information, such as the results of tests or investigations, or are bringing new concerns to the doctor's attention.

KEY POINT

Any visit to hospital can be a stressful and difficult time. A sensitive approach by the doctors and other staff can allay fears and anxieties.

Primary health care
Routine health care for children with special needs is always available in the community from the primary health care team. The family doctor cares for day-to-day health problems and concerns. Home nursing care and loans of medical equipment such as suction apparatus, injection pumps, feeding tubes, oxygen and mobility aids are provided by the community paediatric nursing service. The health

visitor sees the family at home, offering advice, support and information often in the role of Named Person.

A special needs health visitor may also visit the family.

Home nursing care equipment and mobility aids

Assessment of needs at the child development centre

Assessment of a child's needs usually takes place in a child development centre which may be in a community or hospital setting. It provides facilities for health and developmental assessment, ongoing therapy and care for children with special needs. The centre is a 'single door' (recommended in the Court Report) through which children and their families have access to the necessary services. Referral is usually through the family doctor.

Typically, the core members of a centre's multidisciplinary team would be: paediatrician, psychologist, social worker, health visitor, play specialist, teacher, speech therapist, physiotherapist and occupational therapist, community paediatric nurse and nursery nurse. The parents are always valued members of the team – they have the day-to-day knowledge of their child's progress and needs. Developmental assessment may take place in a playgroup setting at the centre over a period of a few weeks. For parents, it can either be a time of worry and anxiety or a relief that, at last, something is being done for their child.

Play activities are provided with the nursery nurse and teacher observing behaviour and play skills. Other members of the team assess the child in their own field of expertise. Ongoing support and therapy is frequently required with further assessment every six months or so.

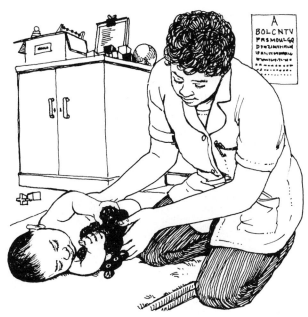

Physiotherapist assessing muscle tone in a child development centre

Child development centres serving ethnic communities should have access to a community link worker to interpret and advise as necessary.

The child development centre

The child development centre offers the following benefits.

■ An accessible setting for children and their families with familiar layout and staff.
■ Opportunities to meet other families with children with similar special needs. Families can share experiences and knowledge and learn about family support groups and other voluntary organisations.
■ A link worker to advise, interpret and support families of different cultures.
■ Daycare or playgroup facilities.
■ Transport arrangements for children who live far away or who have mobility difficulties.

Activity

Find out about a child development centre near you. Gather information on:
1 the services provided at the centre
2 the method of referral and details of a typical assessment programme
3 the role of the nursery nurse at the centre (if one is employed).

Child psychiatry service and child guidance clinic

Children with emotional, behavioural and school difficulties can be seen, with their families, in a child guidance clinic or unit based in a child development centre, child health clinic or hospital. Professional staff include a child psychiatrist, psychologist, psychotherapist and psychiatric social worker and, usually, a psychotherapist and family therapist. Because of the link between disturbed behaviour and home/social circumstances the service is orientated towards family as well as child therapy. Typically, a child would be referred to a child guidance clinic because of emotional problems such as fear, anxiety, sadness or unhappiness or because of aggressive, anti-social and defiant behaviour.

Parent and child attend a therapy session

KEY POINT

The aim of all child psychiatric intervention is to help children live a more normal life both individually and within the family so that they can grow up settled and secure.

Activity
Think of reasons why a young child might display a) anxiety and b) aggressive behaviour over a short- or long-term period.

Child health promotion programmes

Child health promotion includes positive efforts to promote good health and prevent illness, and to encourage immunisation and child health surveillance (growth and developmental assessment and screening programmes). Assessments and screening may take place in a child development centre, child health clinic, hospital or surgery, or in ordinary or special schools as part of the school health service.

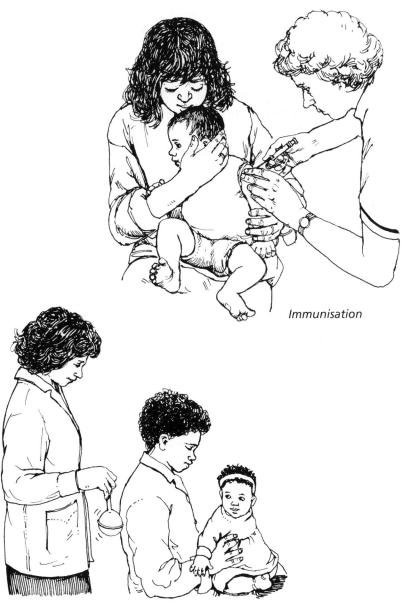

Immunisation

A hearing test: the baby locates the sound stimulus

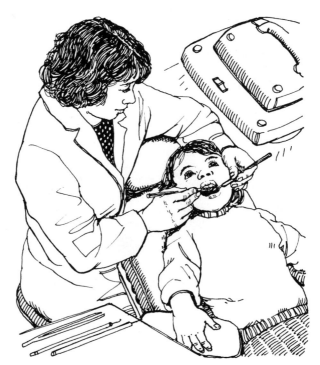

Dental care is important for all children

A speech and language therapy session, communication through signing

A child responding to a toy discrimination hearing test

Activity

Obtain a current immunisation schedule from your local health centre or surgery. In which circumstances would it be unsafe for immunisation to be carried out?

Dental care

Dental care is offered by the family or community dentist. Specialist dental care is provided in a hospital dental clinic.

Therapy services

Many children with special needs require either physiotherapy, occupational therapy and/or speech and language therapy. Therapists assess and help children in their homes, child development centres, clinics or schools.

Aids and equipment

Equipment such as wheelchairs, special seating, standing frames and hearing aids are available either on loan or free of charge. Radio hearing aids are not necessarily free. In some areas health and social services have joint equipment stores.

Prescriptions and medication

Children with special needs may require long- or short-term medication. Drugs and medicines are free of charge. They can be in liquid or tablet form, injections,

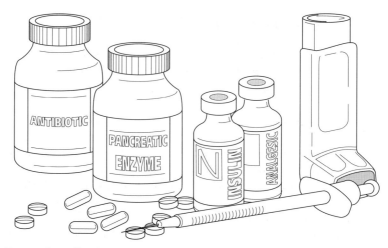

Types of medication

inhalers or suppositories. Certain special dietary foods are also free on prescription.

GOOD PRACTICE

Never give a child an injection or a suppository without prior training and parental permission.

Respite care

The health service provides respite care for children with serious health problems and substantial medical and nursing needs. It should be in small, home-like, locally-based settings – for example Honeylands (see page 137, chapter 5). Children's hospices and paediatric wards may offer respite care for children with complex disabilities or teminal illness.

School health service

School health service provision (in ordinary and special schools) includes health checks, vision and hearing testing, dental care, physiotherapy and speech therapy.

PROGRESS CHECK

1 What special equipment might children with special needs require in their own homes?
2 What is the function of a child development centre?
3 What benefits does a child development centre offer to a child and his family?
4 Why might a child be referred to a child guidance clinic? What is the aim of the child psychiatry service?
5 What do you understand by health promotion?

Social services systems and support

Social services departments (SSDs) are part of local authority provision. At central government level they are responsible to the Social Services Inspectorate and the Department of Health.

SSDs DUTIES

In respect of children with special needs, social services departments, under the Children Act 1989, have a duty to:
- provide a range of support services, including daycare, which will promote and safeguard their welfare, minimise the effect of the special need and allow children to be cared for within their family
- work closely with local health services, including the primary health care team, and be aware of local policy and practice in child health promotion
- work closely with the local education authority including offering information or advice about a child known to them when a statutory assessment or a statement of special educational needs is being prepared
- register and inspect childminders and all voluntary and private sector settings which offer continuous childcare facilities for more than two hours per session.

GOOD PRACTICE

Services should:
- be flexible, locally accessible, culturally and racially appropriate
- provide information and choice
- recognise the importance of partnership with parents.

SOCIAL SERVICE SUPPORT AND PROVISION

Social service support and provision includes the following.

Social service professionals
See chapter 1, page 29.

Family centres
Social services departments provide family centres as a support service to a wide range of families including those with children with special needs.
Family centres can provide:
- daycare and playgroup sessions
- child health clinics
- counselling and help with parenting skills
- toy libraries
- 'after school' clubs.

A daycare session in a family centre

A centre may require specialist advice to make it accessible to children with special needs. Family centres may operate an 'open door' policy or families can be referred from the local education authority or health or social services.

Centre-based daycare services
Centre-based daycare services include day nurseries and combined nursery centres. All settings are inspected by the social service department and must comply with:
■ Health and Safety standards
■ adult to child ratio regulations.
A statement of special educational needs for children under five years may recommend daycare provision in a day nursery, pre-school, playgroup or parent/carer and toddler group. While acceptance of this provision is not obligatory most families recognise its value in the overall development of their child.

Day nurseries
Day nurseries provide daycare for babies and young children. A child with special needs may be offered a full- or part-time place. Although the general move is towards integrated and inclusive daycare a specialist nursery for early intervention care may be of greater help to a child with profound special needs. In practice, there are wide variations among local authorities towards integration and parents' feelings also vary.

It is unlikely that a specialist nursery would be available in every neighbourhood. Travelling to another area each day may may mean the child and his parents have little social contact with other local children and their families.

KEY POINTS

- Many children with special needs have remained sheltered and isolated within the home and are unaware of other children and adults in the wider community. A local nursery provides social contact and support for both the child and parents.
- A stimulating daycare environment, with a wide variety of experiences, will extend all-round physical development and enable children to progress in social and independence skills.
- A child may have a key worker in the nursery to provide one-to-one care for his special needs.
- Daycare provision can also be offered to siblings if parents of a child with complex special needs may otherwise find attendance at a hospital or clinic impossible.

An integrated and inclusive daycare setting is described in chapter 2 (see page 46). The role of a key worker in a day nursery is described in chapter 5 (see page 146 to 149).

Activity
1 What do you consider to be the advantages and disadvantages of an integrated, inclusive daycare setting? Think about the care, management, education and social aspects.
2 Find out your local social services policy towards integrated daycare settings.
3 If you are caring for a child with special needs in either an integrated or specialist daycare setting speak to his parents about what they consider to be the advantages and disadvantages of the setting.

Combined nursery centres

Combined nursery centres offer an integrated service of daycare *and* nursery education for all children from a few months old up to five years. They are organised jointly by social services departments and local education authorities. Many also offer after-school care for primary age children plus family support services such as:

- counselling, child and family guidance
- special needs support groups
- welfare rights advice.

The flexibility and child-centred pre-school care that combined nursery centres offer is a valuable contribution to the integration of children with special needs. Children receive not only physical care and supervision of their health needs but also an appropriately planned curriculum.

PRE-SCHOOL CARE AND EDUCATION PROVISION

Local education authority	Social services departments	Voluntary sector	Private sector
Nursery classes (attached to LEA primary schools)	Day nurseries	Pre-schools	Day nurseries
	Family centres	Playgroups	Nursery schools
Nursery schools (separate LEA schools)		Crèches	Kindergarten classes
		Family centres	Independent schools
Combined nursery centres		Parent/carer and toddler groups	Work-place nurseries and crèches
	Private provision		Nannies
	Childminders		

Childminders, voluntary and private sector settings must register with and be inspected by social services departments.

A typical education scene in a combined nursery centre

PROGRESS CHECK

1 How do family centres support a child with special needs and his family?
2 What is the value of day nursery provision for children with special needs?
3 How does a combined nursery centre differ from a day nursery?
4 What family support services are offered in a combined nursery centre?

Childminding services

Childminders are registered and supported by social services. Special training is provided for any particular health care or management needs a child may require.

KEY POINT

Some childminders prefer to care for children with special needs.

Respite care (short term care and accommodation)

Respite care is offered by social services departments (and by some voluntary organisations) to families with children with special needs. It aims to relieve some of the stress and strain of what is often twenty-four hour care and can mean the difference between a child remaining at home or being looked after by a foster carer or in a residential home. However, it is not just a means of giving a family a break – it must always be a positive experience for the child.

Regular and emergency respite care is considered essential by most parents and should be included in the care and support package.

KEY POINT

Respite care must meet a child's needs, even very complex needs, and take account of the child's family background and culture.

Planning respite care

Social services and voluntary organisations prepare a written care plan for any child they propose to accommodate in respite care. Respite carers receive training and are paid according to individual local authority policy.

No young children like to be away from their home at night unless their parents are with them or they are staying with relatives. The same applies to children with special needs and it is not unusual for many of them to experience homesickness and distress in respite care settings. Sensitive planning is needed to make sure the child feels secure with the carers.

Types of respite care

There are four types of respite care where children, who normally live with their family, may spend short or sometimes longer periods of time.

- Family link care: the most commonly used type of homecare where a child is looked after by an approved family or single person in that family or person's home. The carers are police-checked and trained in specific caring procedures such as lifting, feeding and giving medication. A child may spend a few hours a week, a weekend, a week or longer away from home. Initially, the families will get to know each other and then go on to make their own arrangements.

KEY POINT

It may be difficult to find family link respite care for children who are disruptive, aggressive or display challenging behaviour or whose physical needs are great. However, with extra training and appropriate back-up support it can be successful.

- Approved residential accommodation: this might be a children's home, or a hospital ward or unit. Families often prefer to use children's wards for short-term care for their children – particularly if there are considerable medical or nursing needs.
- 'Own home' care: a child is cared for in his or her own home by a trained family aide, or other substitute carer, while the family take a break.
- Children's holiday schemes: these schemes are usually provided by voluntary

A family aide provides 'own home' respite care

organisations and paid for by the family. Many provide one-to-one key workers. Some voluntary organisations arrange family holidays. While not providing parents and siblings with a total break from childcare it does offer a change of scene and the opportunity for some relaxation.

PROGRESS CHECK

1 What do you understand by respite care?
2 Describe the types of respite care.
3 Why is sensitive respite care planning always necessary?

CASE STUDY

Rosie is a happy seven-year-old. She has cystic fibrosis and several times has been very seriously ill, needing admission to hospital. At the moment the condition is well controlled by careful attention to physiotherapy, diet and medication. The local authority social services department has recently put the family in touch with a voluntary organisation which provides holidays for children with special needs and their families. Rosie, her parents and younger brother are all looking forward to a week together at an activity centre. Rosie is to have her own individual carer, experienced in caring for children with cystic fibrosis.

Imagine that for the past two years you have been Rosie's key worker at school and know her and her family very well. You are familiar with Rosie's care and management routines and are trained to give her physiotherapy during her school day.

1 Write a letter to the carer at the activity centre giving details of what you consider are important aspects of Rosie's care and management.

2 Who else would need a copy of your letter?

Residential settings – foster placements and residential care

Foster placements

More children with special needs, who, for a variety of reasons are unable to live with their natural family, are being successfully fostered. Disabled people themselves are actively encouraged to become foster carers so providing children with positive role models.

KEY POINT

Attempts are always made to provide a cultural and ethnic match between a child and his foster carers.

Foster carers

Social services must be satisfied that foster carers can provide:

- any specific care and management routines, for example, physiotherapy for a child with cystic fibrosis, management of an epileptic seizure, caring for a hearing aid (appropriate training will be given)
- adequate privacy for the child especially in the bedroom and bathroom
- appropriate safety. Easy exit from the house in case of fire is important.

Social services

Social services provide:

- necessary adaptations to the home such as moveable ramps or grab-rails in the bathroom
- daycare and respite care
- information for the foster carers about the range of statutory and voluntary service provision for both the child and themselves
- support, advice and help to the foster parents.

KEY POINT

- Foster carers are involved in the normal range of school activities such as helping a child with their school work, attending open evenings and PTA meetings and maintaining the home/school diary. Encouraging their foster child to bring friends home and join clubs such as Rainbows, Beavers and Brownies, where they can make and maintain friendships, lessens the risk of isolation.
- The Foster Placement Regulations require prospective foster carers to agree not to use physical punishment on children they look after. Advice and reassurance about managing difficult behaviour would be offered where necessary.

A child looked after by foster carers needs opportunities to make friends in the neighbourhood

Activity
1 What are the benefits for a child with special needs being looked after by a disabled foster carer?
2 What might be the advantages of accommodating a child with special needs with foster carers rather than in a residential home?
3 How would you organise a recruitment campaign for foster carers for children with special needs in your local area?

Residential care

Some children may not live at home with their natural or foster family either because they require long-term medical care in hospital or because, for different reasons, they need to live away from their family for a period of time in a local authority children's home.

Residential care settings

Residential care settings include the following.
■ *Health care settings* such as hospitals and hospices where medical care and treatment are provided. If a child is in hospital for a long period the hospital social worker will support the family and work closely with the hospital team, the family doctor and the health visitor.
■ *Residential children's homes* registered by social services departments. The homes

should be friendly and welcoming. Children need access to the recreation, living and garden areas. Where necessary ramps, rails, special facilities and equipment are provided.

GOOD PRACTICE

- Privacy is very important, especially for personal care needs such as incontinence, and adequate bathroom facilities are essential.
- Regular fire drills are part of safe practice. Procedures enabling children with physical conditions or sensory impairments to respond to fire alarms must be in place.

KEY POINT

Social services try to accommodate young children with special needs with foster carers rather than in a residential home.

PROGRESS CHECK

1 Why are disabled people actively encouraged to become foster carers?
2 How can foster carers ensure the children they look after make friends in the local neighbourhood?
3 Give an example of inter-disciplinary cooperation where a child with special needs is accommodated in a residential setting.

Toy libraries
Toy libraries may be organised by social services, health services or voluntary organisations. They can be set up in a day nursery, child development centre, hospital, health centre or other suitable accommodation. Toys made of sturdy materials and suitable for different ages and stages of development are available for the children to play with in a safe setting. Many toys are specifically for use as learning aids for children with special needs. Examples include toys which give an electronic response (flashing lights, buzzer or music) when the toy is manipulated in a particular way by the child. This teaches a child the principle of cause and effect. Toy libraries offer a loan service for a small charge. The library also serves as a meeting place for families where ideas and information can be exchanged in an informal and friendly setting. The Toy Libraries Association gives advice on how to set up and run a toy library and offers guidance on suitable toys. It also runs courses for organisers of toy libraries.

Advocacy
Children and their parents may need an advocate to help them access the support and resources they needs (see page 91, 'Advocacy', chapter 3)

Family aide service
A family aide can provide valuable support and practical help to a family caring for a child with special needs. The aide may live with the family for a short time or visit

on a daily basis to assist with the general running of the home. Tasks may include childcare and domestic duties. Training can be given for a family aide to provide 'own home' respite care.

Transport costs
Help with transport costs to visit children living away from home may be provided.

Financial advice and cash grants
Social services departments, as well as the health service, advise families on their financial entitlement and make grants for specific aids and adaptations such as handrails, bath hoists, ramps and ground floor extensions. They may also be provided free of charge depending on individual circumstances. Benefit forms are usually long and difficult to understand. They contain little simple language. Families sometimes appreciate help from the social worker or other professional in filling them in.

PROGRESS CHECK

1 What are the benefits of a toy library for children with special needs?
2 What is the function of the Toy Library Association?
3 For what specific equipment might social services departments make a cash grant?

Education authority systems and support

The Department for Education and Employment (DfEE) is the statutory body for controlling and regulating education provision.

Education is compulsory in Britain for children between the ages of five and sixteen years. It is also a right to which all children, including those with special needs, are entitled. The following are the goals of education, as stated in the Warnock Report.

- To enlarge a child's knowledge, experience and imaginative understanding, and thus his awareness of moral values and capacity for enjoyment.
- To enable him to enter the world, after formal education is over, as an active participant in society and a responsible contributor to it.

KEY POINT

These goals are still the same today but the help that individual children need in progressing towards them will be different.

The Education Reform Act 1988 introduced for the first time in England and Wales a national curriculum which *all* children are expected to follow in state-funded schools. Teaching staff are responsible for ensuring children have access to, and can make progress in, the subjects they teach.

Teachers are aware of individual differences in children. When some or all of those differences affect a child's learning to the extent that the teacher (or parent) is concerned, the procedures for assessment and implementing special educational provision are put in place. Management of a child's education becomes 'special' when his needs are particularly different from his peers. The definition of special educational needs is included in chapter 3 (see page 65).

THE LOCAL EDUCATION AUTHORITY'S DUTY

A local education authority has a duty to:

■ provide education, assessment and, if necessary, a statement of special educational needs, for children with special needs aged five to sixteen years (up to nineteen years if a child wishes it)

■ identify, assess and statement children under five years with special needs attending a maintained nursery school, taking into account the views of the parents. For children under two years parents must give their consent.

KEY POINT

A local education authority does not have a duty to provide nursery education.

LOCAL EDUCATION AUTHORITY SUPPORT AND PROVISION

Local Education Authority support and provision includes the following.

Education service professionals
See chapter 1, page 28.

Education service professionals

Nursery schools (including nursery classes and units)

There is often confusion about the difference between nursery schools, nursery classes or units, combined nursery centres, pre-schools, day nurseries and play-groups. While all these settings provide pre-school care and learning there is greater emphasis and input on education in nursery schools, classes and combined centres with children following the early years curriculum ('The Desirable Outcomes').

Local education authorities may provide nursery, or pre-school, education for children aged three to five years in:

- separate nursery schools
- nursery classes or units attached to primary schools
- combined nursery centres (see also social services provision, page 107).

KEY POINTS

- Pre-school education is expensive and because it is not compulsory state provision it is patchy throughout the country. Private nursery schools and kindergarten departments of independent schools offer nursery education.
- Many parents prefer nursery school provision to that of day nursery or plagroup because of the greater emphasis on education leading to a smooth transition to infant school and Key Stage 1 of the National Curriculum.

Nursery school staff

A nursery school is staffed by qualified teachers and nursery nurses. While each has particular duties there will always be overlaps in the teaching and caring roles. A mutually supportive partnership will serve the best interests of the children.

PROGRESS CHECK

1 What is the difference between a day nursery/playgroup and a nursery school/class?
2 Which curriculum do children in nursery schools follow?

CHILDREN WITH SPECIAL NEEDS IN NURSERY SCHOOL

Introducing a child with special needs into a pre-school education setting requires the same careful planning as introduction into a day nursery. The staff have a responsibility to provide a safe, warm and welcoming environment within which the child feels comfortable and is able to learn. Specific considerations regarding the physical environment include the following.

- Matching the layout of the setting and use of space to individual needs.
- Provision of any special equipment and furniture to aid mobility, balance and posture. Easy access to toilet and washing facilities.

Care and education plans

Information is required about a child's learning needs. Records of previous assessments, identified needs and provision such as daycare, Portage, speech therapy or physiotherapy should be available. The school SENCO is responsible for care and education plans for children with special educational needs. This includes following the Code of Practice five-stage assessment procedure (see page 67) and writing an IEP (individual education plan). A key worker (perhaps a nursery nurse) follows the IEP and may even be involved in drawing it up. Specialist teachers or assistants may provide additional support.

The diagram on page 119 sets out your role in a nursery school. Please cross reference this with the key worker diagram in chapter 5 on page 147 which is also relevant to your work in a nursery school and will help you with the following progress checks.

PROGRESS CHECK

1 What environmental considerations will you need to think about before a child with special needs starts nursery school?
2 Why is it important to make a pre-visit to the child and her family at home?
3 What information do the staff of the nursery school require before the child attends?
4 Which other professionals might be consulted about the health and learning needs of a child?

KEY POINT

■ Children with special needs should have access to the normal curriculum of the nursey school. Where this is not appropriate an individually tailored programme, within the framework of the curriculum, can be provided.
■ A child with a statement of special educational needs will be offered the curriculum and resources identified in the statement.

GOOD PRACTICE

In the early period of a child's attendance at nursery school it is equally important to care for his emotional and social needs in addition to his educational needs.

Communicating with parents

Parents have a right to be involved in the education of their children. Children's experiences at home, including continuation of learning opportunities provided in the school, significantly influence children's learning. Parents need to know the curriculum being followed, how to support their child's learning and to whom they can turn if they have any worries. Effective communication and regular contact between staff and parents is important. Telephone calls can often give instant reassurance and parents usually have easy access to the nursery school teacher. Many settings have a shared record-keeping system in which the teacher, key worker and parents make daily comments.

KEY POINT

A child may be unable to tell his parents what he has done during the day. Make

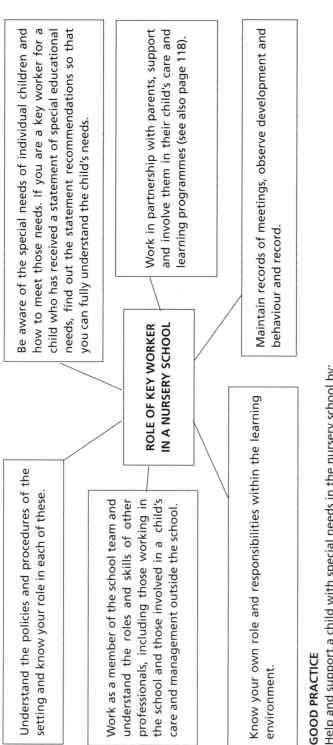

Be aware of the special needs of individual children and how to meet those needs. If you are a key worker for a child who has received a statement of special educational needs, find out the statement recommendations so that you can fully understand the child's needs.

Work in partnership with parents, support and involve them in their child's care and learning programmes (see also page 118).

ROLE OF KEY WORKER IN A NURSERY SCHOOL

Maintain records of meetings, observe development and behaviour and record.

Understand the policies and procedures of the setting and know your role in each of these.

Work as a member of the school team and understand the roles and skills of other professionals, including those working in the school and those involved in a child's care and management outside the school.

Know your own role and responsibilities within the learning environment.

GOOD PRACTICE

Help and support a child with special needs in the nursery school by:
- enabling him or her to feel confident and valued
- promoting language and communication skills
- encouraging independence and social skills
- caring sensitively for physical and emotional needs
- offering praise and encouragement
- being imaginative and creative in finding ways for a child to make full use of materials available.

The role of a key worker in the nursery school

Communicating with parents

sure he takes pictures, craft work or other items home so that his family can enjoy his activities and build up a picture of the school day.

PROGRESS CHECK

1 How can you help and support a child with special needs/special educational needs in a nursery school?
2 Why is it important for a key worker to know the details of a child's statement of special educational needs?
3 How might the normal nursery school curriculum be planned for a child with special needs?
4 Describe how would you help parents to feel valued and supported.

NURSERY EDUCATION VOUCHERS

At the time of writing a nursery education voucher scheme operates nationally. However, it is likely to be replaced or abolished altogether. Currently all parents of four-year-olds are eligible to receive vouchers for nursery education for their children. Children aged four years already attending reception classes in state schools will need vouchers.

KEY POINT

The voucher scheme is not compulsory and parents may keep their four-year-olds at home if they prefer.

What are nursery education vouchers?

Nursery education vouchers are booklets with an exchange value of £1,100 per year. They are exchangeable for: *part-time (up to five sessions) pre-school education for four-year-old children for three terms (one year). A session is taken as 2.5 hours.*

The vouchers may be used in both public and private pre-school settings. Fees in private settings over and above the £1,100 will be met by the parents.

The education settings can be any of the following in the state, private or voluntary sectors, providing they have joined the nursery voucher scheme:

- *pre-schools/playgroups*
- *private schools*
- *day nurseries.*

These settings must all be registered under the Children Act 1989 with their local authority social services department.

Other settings include:

- *nursery schools*
- *nursery classes*
- *reception classes*
- *Portage services* registered with the *National Portage Association.*

Families with four-year-olds are identified through the child benefit centre records system. Application can also be made directly to the agency supplying the vouchers.

Parents will look for a setting that suits the needs of their child in the provision of both care and education. Good practice in health, welfare and safety issues will be a major consideration.

KEY POINT

The voucher scheme does not apply to childminders. Parents who prefer to use childminders cannot benefit from the £1,100 unless their child attends the childminder's home part-time and a group education setting part-time.

Children with special needs

The voucher scheme is for *all* four-year-old children *including* those with *special educational needs* and whether or not the child has received a *statement of special educational needs.*

Under the Nursery Education and Grant Maintained Schools Act 1996 all day nurseries, playgroups, private nursery schools, independent schools and any other establishments, outside the maintained sector of education, which redeem vouchers, have a duty to consider what the Code of Practice says when making provision for children with special educational needs. Local education authorities, the governing bodies of maintained or grant maintained schools (also grant maintained special schools) already have such a duty under the Education Act 1993. The hope is, that by giving all children the opportunity of three terms of nursery education it

Four-year-olds with special needs are entitled to nursery vouchers

will be possible to identify children with special educational needs earlier than might have been the case. However, there are concerns about the scheme as it does not provide extra funding for additional staff or resources that may be needed.

Children looked after by local authorities

Vouchers can be obtained for children looked after by foster carers (if the carers are receiving child benefit in respect of the child) or resident in a children's home.

KEY POINT

Nursery education settings must publish their special needs policy as a condition of entering the voucher scheme and must treat the application from a child with a special need no less favourably than from any other child.

Quality assurance

All nursery education places offered under the scheme are expected to give good value for money. Establishments wanting to register for the voucher scheme have to agree to work towards a set of six desirable learning outcomes (learning goals) defined by the School Curriculum and Assessment Authority (SCAA), an independent organisation. Establishments wishing to register for the vouchers scheme have to prove they are able to achieve these outcomes through the curriculum they offer.

Inspections

Inspections are carried out by the Office for Standards in Education (OFSTED). Areas inspected are:

- planning and preparation of the curriculum, including the curriculum for children with special educational needs
- quality of teaching
- assessment, recording and reporting on children's learning and development
- resources, staffing and accommodation
- links with parents.

PROGRESS CHECK

1 What are nursery education vouchers?
2 In which education settings can nursery vouchers be used?
3 Are children with special educational needs included in the nursery voucher scheme?

CASE STUDY

Early in her pregnancy Edele's mother (a lone parent) contracted rubella and, although only mildly unwell herself, her daughter was born with profound vision and hearing impairment and learning delay. Looking after Edele was exhausting and distressing for her mother whose own family lived abroad and were unable to give practical help and support.

Edele was assessed by a multidisciplinary team during her first year and both Edele and her mother received appropriate care and support from statutory and voluntary agencies. In particular, they found the Named Person (a 'special needs' health visitor) of great help in enabling them to gain access to the necessary provision.

Edele is now two and a half years old and currently attends a local authority integrated day nursery part-time. She will have a statutory assessment of special educational needs when she is three years old.

1 Which statutory service would have been responsible for Edele's assessment in her first year?
2 Where would Edele's assessment most probably have taken place?
3 Name the professionals likely to have been involved in the assessment procedure.
4 Which local authority department would have arranged Edele's admission to the day nursery?
5 Which statutory service will be responsible for Edele's assessment of special educational needs?

6 What particular provision might be recommended in Edele's statement of special educational needs?

7 Would Edele qualify for nursery vouchers if she attended a nursery school?

SPECIAL SCHOOLS

Special schools were first developed in Great Britain in the eighteenth century when Thomas Braidwood established a school for the deaf in Edinburgh in the early 1760s and Henry Dannett founded a school for the blind in Liverpool in 1791. The first special schools for children with physical handicaps were founded in London – The Cripples Home and Industrial School for Girls in 1851 and the Home for Crippled Boys in 1865. Before the middle of the nineteenth century so-called mentally defective children who were in need of care were placed in workhouses and infirmaries. In 1847 the first specific provision for them, the Asylum for Idiots, was established in Highgate, London. Following the Forster Education Act 1870 (and the corresponding Education (Scotland) Act of 1872) state education was introduced and a small number of school boards, out of social conscience rather than as a result of educational legislation, introduced special classes for deaf and blind children. In 1892 the Leicester School Board opened a special class for selected 'feeble-minded' pupils and in the same year the London Board opened a special school for physically and mentally defective children.

The Warnock Report 1978 states:

New provision continued to be made, much of it by voluntary effort and of a pioneering nature. Open air schools, day and boarding schools for physically handicapped children , schools in hospitals and convalescent homes and trade schools all contributed to more varied facilities available to local education authorities and parents. Examples were the Heritage Craft Schools and Hospital at Chailey, Sussex (1903), the Swinton House School of Recovery at Manchester (1905), the London County Council's Open Air School at Plumstead (1907) and the Lord Mayor Treloar Cripples' Hospital and College at Alton (1908). The Manchester Local Education Authority had opened a residential school for epileptics in 1910: by 1918 there were six such schools throughout the country.

The statutory foundation for special education, conferring powers on local councils to provide education in special schools or classes for blind, deaf, defective and epileptic children, was consolidated in the Education Act 1902 and 1921. The Education Act 1944 increased the number of categories of children with special educational needs from four to eleven and many special schools were built to cater for extra demand, although less seriously handicapped children could be educated in ordinary schools.

Activity
Identify the terminology in the above text which is no longer appropriate or acceptable.

KEY POINT

The Second World War destroyed much school accommodation. Building materials and teachers were in short supply during the immediate post-war years. It was easier to expand the use of special schools, by buying large country houses or mansions (often in isolated areas), than providing special education in ordinary schools.

The Education Act 1976 placed a responsibility on local education authorities to provide special education in ordinary schools where practicable. However, although the new legislation would create a move towards integration, the government felt that special schools would continue to play an important role in educating children with special educational needs.

Special schools versus ordinary schools

Special schools are educational establishments solely for the education of children with special educational needs. Their existence is becoming increasingly controversial with many teachers, parents and disabled people's organisations looking for fundamental changes in the education system. They believe inclusive education to be a human rights issue but perceive a lack of will to see it implemented nationally. Ideally, they would like special schools phased out and all children educated in inclusive, mainstream school settings.

KEY POINT

More and more special schools are currently linking with mainstream schools in their area to share facilities, resources such as computers, and social activities.

Both the Centre for Studies on Inclusive Education (CSIE) and the Alliance for Inclusive Education (AIE) believe all children would benefit if those with special needs were brought into mainstream education. The London Borough of Newham is frequently referred to in the debate over inclusive or specialist education. Many of their special schools have been closed and their aim is for all children in the borough with special educational needs to be ordinary schools by 1999.

KEY POINT

For many children, though, particularly those with profound and complex special needs, special schools are seen to provide a safe, protected and adapted environment in which they can develop and gain confidence whilst receiving individual attention and teaching.

Specialist resources and services are thought to be more efficiently used in a single setting than in a range of different settings. All these factors can be particularly reassuring for parents. Resources such as speech therapy are often more readily available in special schools.

Children attending a special school

PROGRESS CHECK

1 Why did special schools develop in large houses in rural areas?
2 Which organisations promote inclusive education?

KEY POINTS

- Education in a special school may be recommended in a child's statement of special needs.
- Children with special educational needs, whether in special or mainstream school, are required to follow the National Curriculum. Through a process known as differentiation the curriculum can be structured to meet individual needs.

Activity
Prepare a talk for your peer group presenting both the advantages and disadvantages of special schools.

Inclusive education
Inclusive, integrated education is the process of educating children, with and without special educational needs, together for all or part of the time. If children with special needs are to take their place in society after school then, it is suggested, the right place to begin integration is in school. For a school to be truly inclusive there has to be a commitment to ending discrimination, removing barriers and welcoming and valuing all children.

One of the gang

KEY POINT

Local education authorities are required to educate children with special educational needs, subject to the wishes of parents, in mainstream schools providing:

(a) appropriate educational provision is available

(b) the interests of other children in the school will be maintained

(c) there is efficient use of the local education authority's resources.

Integration

The move towards integrating children with special educational needs into mainstream schools started with the Education Act 1981. With the requirement under the Education Act 1993 to publish SEN policies schools have to be open and honest about their plans for integration.

Integration is patchy across the country and much depends on where the family lives, what the child's special need is and, often, the persistence of parents.

Activity

1 Prepare a leaflet explaining your nursery or infant school's policy on inclusive education.

2 Think of possible advantages and disadvantages of inclusive education.

Hospital schools

Many children spend periods of time (sometimes long periods) in hospital inevitably missing out on attending school. Hospital schools are run by the local education authority (in cooperation with the health service) for the benefit of children of compulsory school age. The children follow the National Curriculum which is adapted to suit individual needs. Extra help for children with special educational needs is provided. Exams can take place in hospital.

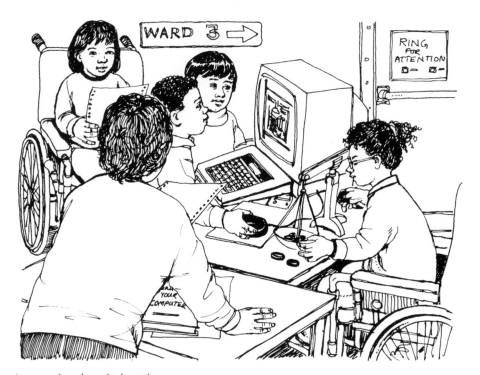

Lessons in a hospital setting

Social security benefits

The Department of Social Security is the Government regulatory body for financial benefits and allowances paid out by the Benefits Agency. Expenses incurred when providing for a child with special needs can be substantial and reduce the family budget very quickly. Parents are entitled to certain state benefits regardless of income or savings. Some benefits are means tested. Claim forms are available from the Benefits Agency. Other parents in a particular support group, the health visitor, social worker or Citizens Advice Bureau staff can give advice about particular benefits and help parents, if necessary, to fill in the forms.

Children with special needs may be entitled to a range of allowances

Activity

1 Research the benefits and grants available for a lone, unemployed parent whose four-year-old child has spina bifida. The child uses a wheelchair for mobility and, as yet, does not have bladder or bowel control.

2 Research as above for a professional couple both in well paid employment. They have a seven-year-old son who is profoundly deaf.

3 Find out about the Family Fund. Who finances it? Who pays out the grants? For what particular provision or help might a grant be given? Are grants means tested?

Financial benefits are constantly changing. It is a good idea to regularly update your knowledge on monies available.

KEY TERMS

You need to know what these words and phrases mean. Go back through the chapter and make sure that you understand:

child development centre

child guidance clinic

combined nursery centre

the Department for Education and Employment

the National Health Service

nursery education vouchers

respite care

social security benefits

Social Services Departments

statutory services

5 CARE SERVICES

> **This chapter covers:**
> - Parents as partners
> - Community-based support services
> - Developing independence in physical care routines
> - The key worker in a daycare setting
> - Voluntary provision
> - A multisensory room and soundbeam
> - Special therapy

The most important thing that happens when a child is born with disabilities is that a child is born. The most important thing that happens when a couple become parents of a child with disabilities is that the couple become parents.   *(R. Wills 1994)*

This chapter emphasises the integral role of parents in the delivery and success of any service provision or care plan. Much can be achieved for children with special needs and their families when there is recognition that parents are crucial members of the multidisciplinary team, not just as recipients of service provision, but as actual deliverers of services.

Community-based integrated provision is essential in order to meet the needs of children and their families. Easily accessible information, link workers for ethnic families, choice and flexibility of services should all be available. Examples are detailed in this chapter.

An important aspect of caring for children with special needs is attending sensitively to their physical care needs. Identification of particular self-care routines and ways to help children develop independence skills are included in this chapter.

Information on the role of a key worker in a daycare setting is both in the general text of the chapter and in table form.

Voluntary provision for children with special needs is wide ranging. The Portage home visiting scheme, befriending schemes and the Handicapped Adventure Playground Association (HAPA) are all described here.

Parents as partners

There is general agreement among childcare professionals that parents know their children best and every effort should be made to keep children with special needs at home with their families. This can be achieved only if sustained, flexible and child-centred services are provided which allow families choice and make it possible for children to be cared for at home. Each family is unique. Considerable extra help may be needed at particular times and at others a small input of help can make all the difference in keeping the family together. Accessible help and support should be available when needed. This gives families the confidence and control they need to shape their own lives.

Parents know their children best

Professional knowledge and ability in caring for children with special needs and their families will vary according to individual training (including disability awareness training), experience and personal qualities.

The MENCAP publication *Ordinary Everyday Families – A Human Rights Issue* by Jo Cameron and Leonie Sturge-Moore, 1990 states:

> *Through lack of knowledge and experience, mainstream professionals and other workers may find themselves in a difficult position as they are confronted with a child with special needs. Some are able to react constructively and find ways and means of helping the child and his or her family. Others, however, may be deterred from offering this help, so that the family miss out on possible support and the professional may be left feeling dissatisfied.*

KEY POINTS

- Children with severe and complex special needs are very dependent on their parents to meet continuing care and management needs. As they grow and get heavier, caring, lifting and carrying become increasingly difficult and tiring. All young children need help with physical care routines such as washing, dressing and feeding but for many children with special needs this need for help does not diminish as they get older.
- Children with special needs may need regular and time-consuming regimes, such as physiotherapy, medication and special diet, several times a day. Some rely on medical equipment, for example, suction or feeding tubes, oxygen and

pain relief pumps. Initially, parents may be very dependent on the professionals for support and reassurance.

The Children Act 1989, the Education Act 1993 and the Code of Practice 1994 give parents a greater say in what happens to their children with a right to be consulted, informed and involved in all planning and provision (health, education and social care).

MULTIDISCIPLINARY CARE

Effective communication between different agencies and departments needs to work smoothly if it is to benefit the child and her family. Professionals should be sure of their own roles and responsibilities and those of their colleagues. This will result in greater understanding, cooperation and efficiency, facilitate better communication with parents and help to establish 'parents as partners'.

GOOD PRACTICE

A partnership between the professionals, the child and her family, built on mutual trust and respect and which recognises the value of the child is essential to the well-being of the child and her family.

KEY POINT

In the past, dependence on professionals often continued for a long time. Today, with the emphasis on a shared and supportive partnership between the parents and the professionals the expectation would be for parents to be more informed and involved in all aspects of their child's care and management needs, confident in their parenting skills and able to make independent decisions.

FINDING OUT THEIR CHILD'S SPECIAL NEED

Whether a special need is identified at birth, or later on when a child is not walking, talking or 'catching up', parents have to try and come to terms with the fact that their child is in some way 'different'. Support for them must aim to reduce stress and anxiety and boost their confidence in their own ability to care for the child.

Initially, parents may be confused and bewildered, with the demands of their child's special needs seemingly beyond their ability to cope. They look for an accurate and early diagnosis of what is wrong. Usually, they prefer the truth, however painful and distressing, to not knowing what is wrong. Having a name or label for their child's special need gives them a starting point from which they can begin to understand and adjust. There may not be definite answers to all questions and concerns, but a sensitive assessment of possible problems and likely health and developmental progress should be given.

KEY POINTS

- Parents' concerns about their child's health or development should never be ignored, they are usually right. Sometimes, they may have to insist there is 'something wrong' or 'not quite right' with their child in order to get a second opinion.
- It is often difficult to decide what, if anything, is wrong with children who are not quite achieving their developmental norms. Much depends on their home environment and how their overall needs are met. A child who is not making progress, though, should be assessed to find out the help required.

PROFESSIONAL GOOD PRACTICE

The Scope template of good practice (produced by a working group led by Scope) recognises the *value of the child, respect for parents* and the importance of *communication skills among professionals.* These three template principles (taken from *Child Health in the Community: A Guide to Good Practice,* published by the NHS Executive) can be implemented by the following means.

- Parents being together when informed of the diagnosis.
- Recognising the need for privacy, while avoiding segregating the parents (without asking them) from other parents.
- Keeping the number of professionals to a minimum, ensuring at least one of them is known to the family.
- Being honest with parents and openly acknowledging the limits of professional knowledge.
- Ensuring that discussions about the child have a positive focus.
- Responding to parents supportively and openly – for example, ensuring continuity with primary health care by contacting the family doctor.
- Providing families with all the information possible about their child's condition and about services and welfare benefits.
- Following up with written notes of the initial meeting and giving advice about practical help – for example, voluntary organisations providing family support.

KEY POINTS

- More than anything parents want to be listened to and involved in meetings about their child. Helping parents to take part in planning and decisions can ease the transition from distress and sadness to acceptance and adjustment.
- As well as professional offers of appropriate support and provision parents should be asked questions such as: 'How do *you* think we can best help your child and family?' 'What particular provision would make life easier, more comfortable/stimulating/enjoyable for your child and for your family?'
- No parents should leave an assessment or follow-up appointment dissatisfied and with questions unasked or unanswered.

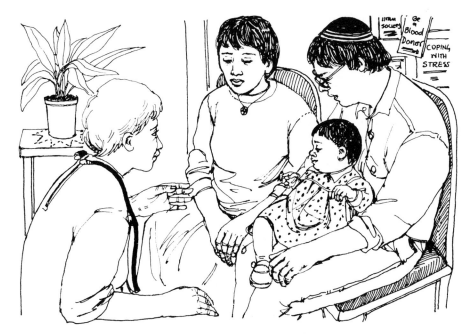

'Is there any other particular help we can offer Miriam and yourselves?'

Activity

Think of an occasion when you listened to what the parents of a child with special needs were saying about their child. Where did the conversation take place? Did the parents share any particular concerns with you? How did you respond to their concerns? How effective do you consider you were in listening and responding to the parents? How did you feel about this conversation?

PROGRESS CHECK

1 Why might some professionals be deterred from offering constructive help to children with special needs and their families?
2 In what ways are children with severe or complex special needs dependent on their families?

At recognition and assessment

When a need is recognised and assessed families should be offered:

- care and support
- a Named Person, for example the health visitor or social worker as a key worker and a link between the family, statutory and voluntary agencies
- professional counselling
- well coordinated service provision

- opportunity to be involved in making decisions that feel right for them (a counsellor or other professional supporters should not try to impose their own solutions).

GOOD PRACTICE

Sensitivity to cultural and social differences and requirements must be reflected in the total care plan.

CARE AND SUPPORT PROGRAMMES

Care and support programmes must be flexible and effective to meet both the needs of the child and her family. In the early years the main care providers are likely to be **health** and **social services**. Later, **educational provision** will be the responsibility of the local education authority.

Social services: early years daycare provision

Through the Named Person, parents have the opportunity to learn about and discuss possible care and management, including goals and long-term objectives. They can be helped to understand their own role as partners and develop skills for managing their child's needs – for example, the best way to hold or position their child for feeding (particularly a child with oral or facial malformations or poor muscle control such as in cerebral palsy), bathing and dressing routines and ways of communicating and playing with her. As partners with the professionals they are enabled and encouraged to become effective care-givers. Early successes in their child's health or development encourages them towards greater participation in care and management routines.

KEY POINT

Not all parents have the immediate confidence or desire to be actively involved in care and management routines, particularly if they are still grieving for their 'lost' child or there does not appear to be any significant progress.

GOOD PRACTICE

Helping parents to feel confident and find pleasure in their child is an essential part of professional support.

PROGRESS CHECK

1 How can society help children with special needs to remain at home and be cared for by their families?
2 What does current legislation say about the rights of parents of children with special needs?
3 Why do parents prefer a 'label' for their child's special need rather than not knowing what is wrong?
4 On what *three* principles is the Scope template of good practice based?
5 What do you understand by the term 'Named Person'? What are his/her functions?

Community-based support services

One way of offering support to children with special needs and their families is through community-based family support units, three of which are described below.

HONEYLANDS

Honeylands is a well-known and frequently described family support unit in Exeter combining local health, education and social services. Honeylands, and other similar units, recognises the need for children with special needs to be cared for in a community rather than a hospital setting. Parents are valued as partners with other care providers and involved with them in all aspects of their child's care, assessments and medical provision. Honeylands provides services according to the needs of the child. Its aims are:

- to provide parents with support and information about their child's special needs
- to help parents come to terms with their own feelings and acquire the special skills needed to increase their confidence and competence in caring for their child
- to provide flexible day and short-term residential support
- to relieve family stress, strain and exhaustion by offering the family day or night support.

Services

Services available at Honeylands include:
- respite care
- daycare facilities
- carers' groups
- health care including physiotherapy, speech and occuptional therapy
- counselling
- a weekly boarder scheme.

Children with special needs are vulnerable to abuse. Where there is ready access to a range of coordinated services such as at Honeylands their vulnerability is reduced.

WANDSWORTH EARLY YEARS CENTRE

Wandsworth Early Years Centre in London is a 'one-stop shop' providing accessible multiservice care and support for children with special needs and their families. A key worker enables families to access appropriate services. Following assessment and identification of needs in the day unit, the centre can offer:
- support and advice from a paediatrician, clinical psychologist and social worker
- physiotherapy, occupational therapy and speech therapy
- the Portage home visiting service
- specialist play activities and toy library facilities.

CHEVIOT'S CHILDREN'S CENTRE

Cheviot's Children's Centre in Enfield is funded by the local social services department. Its aim is to 'Keep children in their families, and make sure that children with disabilities can be included in mainstream life'. Cheviot's homecare team helps families in their own homes by providing:
- skilled babysitters
- parents' help at breakfast or bedtime
- school holiday playschemes.

PROGRESS CHECK

1 What are the advantages of community-based support services such as those described above?

2 In general, what services do such centres offer to a child with special needs and her family?

Activity

Try and arrange to visit, either individually or in a group, a community-based centre in your area similar to those described above. Planning the visit will require a considerate approach to the staff of the centre. Find out about the services offered and, if possible, talk to the children and parents using the facilities.

Developing independence in physical care routines

Children with special needs may take longer to achieve independence in physical care routines than other children. A knowledge of child development and the sequence of emerging independence skills is necessary in helping children move from one level to the next. Gross and fine motor skills and hand–eye coordination are particularly important for tasks such as feeding, dressing and toileting. The level of help needed will vary acording to the special need. Children with cerebral palsy, Down's syndrome, brain injury or complex multiple needs are likely to have difficulties in these areas.

GOOD PRACTICE

Helping children with their physical care routines provides you with the opportunity for close personal contact with them. Do not rush these times. Sensitivity to a child's feelings will be especially important when she is at the age when her peers are able to manage their care without help.

Learning to be independent can be tiring and stressful for a child especially if you try and rush her into achieving. So remember to:
■ allow plenty of time for a child to attempt or complete a task
■ remain relaxed and supportive
■ break the task down into small manageable steps and make sure she knows what you want her to practice and achieve.

KEY POINTS

■ You may find it tempting to take over and dress or wash a child quickly your-self but that will not help her to become independent.
■ Repetition is important in helping a child to remember and retain a skill so

give her the opportunity to repeat over and over again what she has learnt. Obviously, there is a limit to the length of time a child can concentrate and remain interested, and sensible breaks are necessary.

GOOD PRACTICE

Give children lots of praise and encouragement and tell them how well they are doing.

The following lists offer suggestions for helping children with special needs to develop independence skills.

Mealtimes
- Offer the child implements she is used to using at home. Familiar cutlery and crockery is particularly important for a child with visual impairment.
- Remember that in some cultures eating with fingers is usual.
- Wide-handled spoons and forks, high-edged plates with non-slip bases and non-slip mats to hold cups and plates securely in place are available. Plastic, flexible straws help children who cannot hold or drink from a cup. Make sure clothing is protected.
- Eating or assisted eating may take a long time and patience is needed.

Eating independently

KEY POINT

Children with severe or profound language and communication difficulties can be at risk from undernutrition and dehydration. They may not be able to indicate they are hungry or thirsty. Until you get to know a child you may be unsure if she has had enough or you may remove her plate, bowl or cup too soon. Offer regular drinks during the day, also snacks if necessary.

GOOD PRACTICE

Find out from the parent what signs a child uses to indicate she is hungry, thirsty, has had enough or would like some more.

The principles of safe practice must be observed.
- Check the temperature of feeds and the rate of milk flow.
- Check the temperature of food.
- Check chicken and fish for bones, and fruit for seeds and pips.
- Cut food up into manageable pieces.
- Never 'prop' feed a baby or leave children alone during mealtimes.
- Broken and whole nuts must not be given to young children under four years or to any child over that age who has difficulty in chewing and swallowing.
- Children with cerebral palsy may have difficulty swallowing crumbly foods such as biscuits.

Dressing and undressing
Children's clothes must take account of the child's special need allowing the child as much independence as possible in putting clothes on and taking them off.

'I can put my coat on by myself'

Clothes may have to fit under, over or around braces, callipers, harnesses and tubes. Clothes need not be dull and drab. It is possible to make, buy, adjust and adapt colourful, fashionable clothes in a variety of fabrics. Some voluntary organisations have a mail order service or will give advice in a factsheet or newsletter.

Clothes should be practical and pleasurable to wear

- Clothes should be strong, durable, unfussy and appropriate for the weather. They must also wash and wear well.
- They should be comfortable, allowing freedom of movement. Easy or stretchable neck openings, large armholes, front fastenings, Velcro fastenings instead of buttons are all sensible.
- Ensure clothes are suitable for children with restricted mobility who enjoy rolling and crawling around.
- They must be easy and quick to put on and take off especially for toileting needs – children with incontinence (unable to control bladder and/or bowel) require frequent nappy changes. Larger size top clothes, a large ring on a zip, elasticated waists on skirts and trousers all make clothes easier to pull up and take down.
- Clothes should be enjoyable to wear. Children with special needs will enjoy choosing and wearing a variety of colours and fabrics.
- Protective clothing will be needed. Children with cerebral palsy may need extra padding to prevent injury. Knee and elbow padding may help a child with haemophilia following a joint bleed. Helmets may be necessary for children with epilepsy and brain trauma in preventing injury from falls or knocks to the head. Children with severe eczema require protective gloves when using art and craft materials. Children with Down's syndrome, eczema and sickle

cell condition may need reminding to put on an extra jumper or a tracksuit and gloves in the cold weather.

KEY POINT

Footwear, including socks, must also be comfortable and well fitting particularly for children with diabetes. Unless children with special needs wear prescribed boots or shoes, trainers and shoes with Velcro fastenings are probably the easiest to put on and take off. Children with disorders affecting movement, posture, balance and coordination require well fitting and supportive footwear.

Personal hygiene
Personal hygiene routines are an important part of physical care. Keeping a child clean will:
- help to prevent infection
- keep her comfortable
- promote confidence and self esteem.

KEY POINT

Children usually enjoy these times of close contact and feel reassured by a cuddle or hug from their carer. However, not all children want such closeness. You will need to look for signals and signs from a child which indicate the level of contact she likes.

Routines include:
- 'topping and tailing' – washing a baby's face, hands and bottom only
- bathing
- handwashing
- hair, nail and dental care.

KEY POINTS

- Most children enjoy water and water play. You will quickly find out what children can and cannot manage in washing their hands and face and cleaning their teeth. Long-handled taps will be easier for children with poor manipulative skills to manage than the more usual rotating types.
- Special bath seats which protect and support a child are available.

GOOD PRACTICE

Always make sure your practice is safe. Never leave children alone near water and always check the temperature.

Children will need variable amounts of help with personal hygiene routines

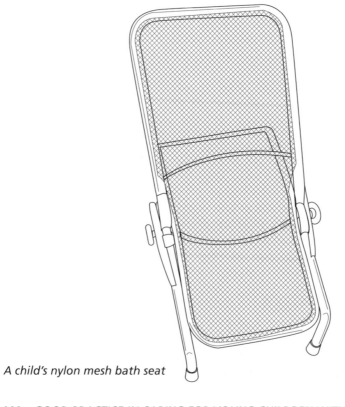

A child's nylon mesh bath seat

Toileting

Control of bladder and bowel is always a major achievement on the road to independence. Many children with special needs are likely to be delayed in this area of development. There are no short cuts towards being potty- or toilet-trained. Children will be clean and dry in their own time. The principles of helping children towards control apply equally to children with special needs as to other children. Watch for signs that a child might be ready:

- dry when waking up from a sleep
- dry for longer periods during the day
- indicating by words or gestures that she is wet.

Have a potty within easy reach, dress her in simple clothing, remain calm, expect accidents and wet and soiled floors. Special potties and toilet seats are available.

Potty-training is covered in detail in most childcare books.

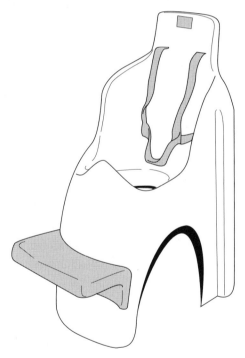

A three-year-old's plastic toilet seat fits over a standard WC, supporting the head and back

KEY POINT

Some children will never learn bladder and bowel control because of their particular condition. Children with spina bifida or those who are paralysed from the waist down may be permanently incontinent (see chapter 9).

Children who are not yet toilet-trained and those who wear incontinence pads will need regular care during the day to keep them fresh and dry and prevent soreness.

KEY POINT

Children must be treated with respect and sensitivity at all times. You will be washing, changing and toileting older children who need a great deal of assistance. Always make sure children have adequate privacy.

PROGRESS CHECK

1 What principles would you follow when helping children with special needs to develop independence in their physical care routines?
2 What types of cutlery and crockery are particularly beneficial for children with special needs?
3 What important factors do you need to remember about clothing and footwear for children with special needs?
4 For which children might protective clothing be important?
5 What do you understand by 'incontinence'?
6 Which conditions are likely to cause incontinence?
7 What particular good practice must you follow when caring for children with special needs who are not yet toilet-trained or who wear incontinence pads?

The key worker in a daycare setting

Attending a nursery may be the first time a child with a special need has mixed with other children outside her family circle. She may have been overprotected in the home with little opportunity for stimulation and learning. Children with physical conditions may have been unable to exercise perhaps because of lack of space in the home or their condition is particularly limiting. Outside the home they may meet people and children who stare and are less sensitive and supportive than her family.

KEY POINT

As a key worker, with special responsibility for one child, you will be a valuable point of contact for both the child and her family and a link with the daycare staff and others providing professional care and support both inside and outside the setting.

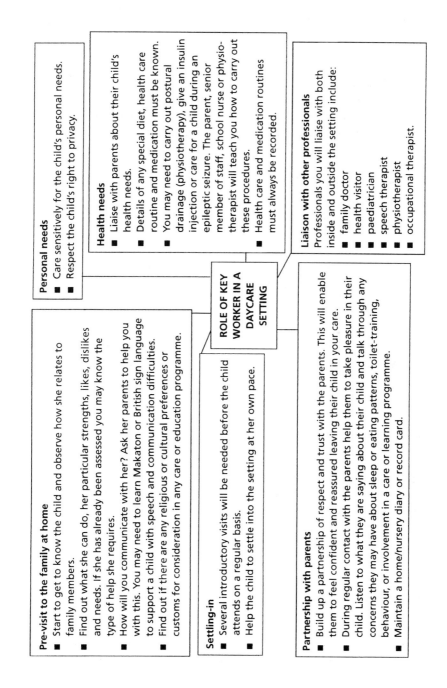

Pre-visit to the family at home

- Start to get to know the child and observe how she relates to family members.
- Find out what she can do, her particular strengths, likes, dislikes and needs. If she has already been assessed you may know the type of help she requires.
- How will you communicate with her? Ask her parents to help you with this. You may need to learn Makaton or British sign language to support a child with speech and communication difficulties.
- Find out if there are any religious or cultural preferences or customs for consideration in any care or education programme.

Settling-in

- Several introductory visits will be needed before the child attends on a regular basis.
- Help the child to settle into the setting at her own pace.

Partnership with parents

- Build up a partnership of respect and trust with the parents. This will enable them to feel confident and reassured leaving their child in your care.
- During regular contact with the parents help them to take pleasure in their child. Listen to what they are saying about their child and talk through any concerns they may have about sleep or eating patterns, toilet-training, behaviour, or involvement in a care or learning programme.
- Maintain a home/nursery diary or record card.

Personal needs

- Care sensitively for the child's personal needs.
- Respect the child's right to privacy.

Health needs

- Liaise with parents about their child's health needs.
- Details of any special diet, health care routine and medication must be known.
- You may need to carry out postural drainage (physiotherapy), give an insulin injection or care for a child during an epileptic seizure. The parent, senior member of staff, school nurse or physiotherapist will teach you how to carry out these procedures.
- Health care and medication routines must always be recorded.

Liaison with other professionals

Professionals you will liaise with both inside and outside the setting include:

- family doctor
- health visitor
- paediatrician
- speech therapist
- physiotherapist
- occupational therapist.

ROLE OF KEY WORKER IN A DAYCARE SETTING

The role of a key worker in a daycare setting

A key worker in a daycare setting

THE KEY WORKER AS A TEAM MEMBER

A key worker is an important member of the multidisciplinary team, receiving and sharing information about a child. To be an effective team member you need an accurate knowledge of other professional roles. This enables you to understand and draw on their expertise and experience and take a more effective part in formulating care plans for a child's overall needs. Never hold back from seeking specialist advice or help – it is a sign of professional competence not weakness.

You will be involved in preparing observations and reports and attend meetings both with the staff in your setting and with the wider team.

KEY POINTS

- Encourage parents and help them to reinforce efforts in their child.
- Parents for whom English is not their first language or who have communication or sensory difficulties should have access to information through an interpreter or ethnic link worker, on tapes, in large print and in Braille.
- Information you receive or share must be accurate and up-to-date. Check carefully whether information is confidential and from whom you require permission before you release it.
- Always make sure the records and reports you make are accurate, clear and objective. They are necessary for professional use and parents have a right to read them. Parents should be invited to attend meetings which directly affect their child.

Activity

Alice is four years old and for the last two years the family (Alice and her parents) have been living in hostel accommodation. Alice displays persistently difficult behaviour including temper tantrums, head-banging, wetting and soiling and disturbed sleep. There has never been any real structure to her daily life and few opportunities for play and stimulation. Alice's parents finally agreed to an appointment with their family doctor who, in addition to recognising her emotional difficulties, found her to be below her expected weight and height. She was referred to a child guidance clinic where family therapy has been arranged. A day nursery place has been secured for Alice and you will be her key worker.

1 Write an overall care and learning plan for Alice which will neet her individual development needs, particularly her emotional needs.
2 Which other professionals would you probably liaise with during your time as Alice's key worker?
3 Why will a variety of observations and accurate record keeping be an important part of your plans?

You may find the section 'Emotional and Behavioural Difficulties' in chapter 8 helpful in carrying out this activity.

KEY POINTS

- Through observing a child's play, behaviour and interaction with those around her you are able to contribute towards a programme which starts with what the child can already do, extends her learning and supports her individual developmental pattern.
- While activities and learning plans should be designed to promote thinking and independence they must also be enjoyable. Like all children, those with special needs learn quickly if they are given the right tools.

GOOD PRACTICE

The demands of care and management routines and the focus on developmental progress should not be so excessive as to limit loving and meaningful relationships being established between the child and members of her family and her friends.

A key worker

A key worker is particularly necessary for children with:

- physical conditions or sensory impairments which limit mobility and access to the environment and equipment
- severe or profound learning difficulties limiting play opportunities and experiences
- speech, language or communication difficulties.

CARING FOR PERSONAL EQUIPMENT

Find out how children's specific aids such as hearing aids, callipers, wheelchairs, standing frames and so on work and how they should be used and cared for. Battery-operated equipment such as wheelchairs must be in working order and recharged as necessary – this is usually done overnight at home. Spare batteries for hearing aids can be kept in the setting. Clearly mark equipment with the child's name. Encourage children to take responsibility for their own equipment and teach all children in the setting to respect it. Equipment that is badly cared for or damaged is of no use to a child.

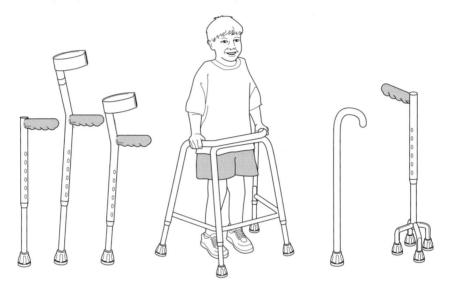

A variety of mobility aids: elbow crutches, walking frame, walking stick and tetrapod

PROGRESS CHECK

1 Which children with special needs would particularly benefit from a nursery key worker?
2 What is the value of making a pre-visit to a child with special needs at home?
3 As a member of the multidisciplinary team how could you contribute to the overall care of a child with special needs?
4 How would you build up and maintain a positive relationship with the parents of a child with special needs?

Activity
This activity should be carried out as a written assignment.
1 Plan an outing for a group of children with special needs in an infant school setting. You will need to consider parental permission, adult to child ratio,

access to the venue for children using wheelchairs and other mobility aids, mode of transport to the venue, toilet facilities, eating arrangements, change of clothing/nappies and safety arrangements at the venue.

2 Take the children on the outing.

3 Review the outing. Your review should reflect the adequacy or otherwise of your arrangements (including safety), the benefits to the children of the outing and anything you would do differently another time to enhance the comfort and pleasure of the children.

4 If you are unable to carry out this particular activity, think of a previous outing you arranged for a group of children with special needs and write up the assignment accordingly.

Voluntary provision

VOLUNTARY ORGANISATIONS

Voluntary organisations are a valuable additional source of help for children with disabilities and special needs and their families, supporting the work of health, education and social service departments. Many of their initiatives have arisen out of lack of statutory provision. With continuing limited statutory resources the contribution of voluntary provision is essential.

Parents have always played a major role in voluntary organisations, often setting them up and being involved in the day-to-day running and management. Voluntary organisations recruit staff and volunteers with a wide range of experience and ability who are able to be innovative in a less rigid and structured environment than a statutory agency. The care and support they offer is flexible and positive.

KEY POINT

National organisations frequently have local groups which offer care and support to children with special needs and their families.

Services provided by voluntary organisations
The range of services provided by voluntary organisations includes:
- daycare and education facilities
- developmental assessment, care and management programmes
- advice and counselling (including genetic counselling)
- information through seminars, workshops, conferences, leaflets and fact sheets
- home assessment facilities by trained health and social work professionals
- respite care
- financial assistance (such as grants for special equipment) and advice on benefits.

Names and addresses of many voluntary organisations are listed throughout part two of this book.

PORTAGE HOME TEACHING SERVICE

The Portage home teaching service, an early intervention programme, was developed in Wisconcin USA in the 1960s. It is a valuable early learning resource for children with special needs providing a home-based daily teaching and learning programme for pre-school children with learning difficulties and physical conditions. For example, a toddler with Down's syndrome or cerebral palsy or a pre-school child with language delay could be helped by Portage, including learning Makaton sign language. Portage visitors come from a variety of backgrounds such as teaching, nursing, nursery nursing, playgroup work or they may be parents whose own children have grown up. They receive special training and focus on what a child *can* rather than *cannot* do, believing in the principle of 'one step at a time'.

KEY POINT

Portage home visitors work closely with parents who are actively encouraged to implement the programme themselves and, in effect, become their child's teachers with the visitor assuming the role of consultant and supporter. Progress and achievement can be enjoyed by parents, siblings and extended members of the family.

Weekly visits are made to the child's home. Both the Portage visitor and the parents assess the child's development through a planned programme of constructive activities and play (tasks). The programme particularly concentrates on gross motor and fine manipulative skills, language, congnitive development, self-help skills, stimulation and socialisation. Each task is broken down into stages so that the child achieves new skills in small steps. A Portage kit is kept at the child's home containing record charts for monitoring progress as well as activity cards for each step towards each task. The cards are colour coded according to developmental area and degree of difficulty. The benefits of the programme are evaluated by the Portage visitor and the parents. Toys and books to develop particular skills are provided through a loan scheme operated by Portage.

The National Portage Association is a small charitable organisation whose visitors are usually employed by local health or social services departments or the local education authority. The provision may be patchy in some areas.

The following series of pictures show Steven, aged twenty months, with his Portage home visitor who visits once a week. In the first photograph Steven is learning to sign. Two other photographs show Steven developing manipulative and cognitive skills. In addition to Portage, Steven attends a day nursery twice a week.

Steven learning to sign

'Yes! The round object fits in the round hole'

Manipulative skills

PROGRESS CHECK

1 What is the function of the Portage home teaching service?
2 On which developmental skills does Portage particularly concentrate?
3 In what ways are parents involved in the Portage programme?
4 What is the guiding principle of the Portage programme?

Activity

Invite a Portage visitor to talk about his/her work at a staff development session in your setting. In particular, ask about the importance of parental participation in the programme and the evaluation process.

PLAYGROUPS

The Pre-school Learning Alliance

The Pre-school Learning Alliance offers opportunities for play and learning in pre-schools for children aged two years and nine months to five years (in some areas three to five years). It is committed to a policy of integrated and inclusive day care. Parents are involved in helping the supervisors to run the groups. The Alliance receives an annual local government grant. Included in the Alliance are opportunity playgroups, playgroups in hospitals (on wards and in out-patient clinics) and specialist language groups. Speech therapists, physiotherapists and other health professionals attend the opportunity playgroup in order to visit young children in their care.

Play activities in a pre-school

Parent/carer and toddler groups

Parent/carer and toddler groups are usually organised and managed by parents/carers and other members of the community. They are often situated in a church or community hall, sometimes in a health centre. Babies and young children attend, always accompanied by an adult who stays for the duration of the session. The groups offer play facilities and social contact.

Adventure playgrounds

Many children's playgrounds are inaccessible to children with special needs. Special adventure playgrounds grew out of the need for children with special needs to have somewhere to play and be adventurous with access to activities other children enjoy. The playgrounds provide opportunities for freedom, challenge and stimulation in a safe and supervised environment. Age ranges vary, but typically a playground would cater for children aged five to fourteen years.

KEY POINT

Many children with special needs have little access to physical space or opportunities to choose what they would like to do. An adventure playground offers the children both these facilities.

HAPA (Handicapped Adventure Playground Association) is a well known charity set up over twenty years ago to provide play opportunities for children with special needs. It runs five adventure playgrounds in London. Its first and late President Lady Allen of Hurtwood said:

> All children need a place to play. They need space, informality, freedom to run around and make a noise, to express themselves, to experiment and investigate. Children and young people with disabilities need this freedom even more than others. In surroundings that stimulate their imagination and challenge them to face and overcome risks, they will be helped to build their self-confidence and independence.

Among other adventure playgrounds are Thames Valley Adventure Playground, Taplow and the North Staffordshire Special Adventure Playground.

A typical playground

A typical playground would include the following.
- A large outdoor area with access everywhere for wheelchairs.
- Handrails for children with mobility difficulties.
- Boat, tyre and bed swings. Rubber moulded swing seats give good support for children with balance and coordination difficulties.
- An aerial runway with harnesses.
- Timber structures with ramps, ladders and poles.
- Sand and water play equipment.
- Slides which are wide enough to take a child and accompanying adult or other child.
- A garden area for digging and planting activities. A sensory garden with herbs and aromatic plants.
- Assistance for children with visual impairment by use of: bright coloured marker lines around the swings; textured surfaces for different playground areas, changes of level or an obstacle near by.
- Indoor soft play equipment and facilities for art and craft activities.
- Some adventure playgrounds have a multisensory room and soundbeam.

Special swings

A slide for a child and acompanying adult or other child

A safe adapted roundabout

A large ball to push and climb on promotes posture and gross motor skills

A variety of outdoor and indoor equipment for children with special needs

GOOD PRACTICE

One-to-one care and support is provided as necessary at the playground and medication and therapy routines are implemented.

KEY POINTS

■ The siblings of children attending the playground are also welcome. Special school groups may have use of the facilities during the school term. Many adventure playgrounds organise holiday play schemes.

- Like many care and education settings, special adventure playgrounds are looking to the future when all playgrounds will be integrated and inclusive.

PROGRESS CHECK

What are the advantages of adventure playgrounds for children with special needs?

Activity
Using the information above, plus further research, design and draw a plan, or make a model, of a typical adventure playground. You should include indoor and outdoor facilities. Make a list of all the safety factors you have included.

BEFRIENDING SCHEMES

Volunteer befrienders are well-informed, experienced parents who have been through their own personal experience of having a child with special needs and have faced their own feelings before reaching the stages of acceptance and adjustment. They are not professionals, therapists or counsellors but have received training in listening and counselling skills. They are able to draw on their own experiences to help and support families who feel lonely, isolated or stressed. A one-to-one relationship is built up between the parents and the befriender before they meet with other families, who are facing a similar experience, in a mutually supportive group setting. Many families value the support they recieve from parent befrienders and eventually become befrienders themselves.

Face to Face
Face to Face is jointly funded and managed by Scope and Mencap. It offers a support service for parents or carers who have difficulty in coming to terms with their child's special need.

Homestart
Homestart befriending schemes offer a home visiting support service for parents who find it difficult to cope with young children. The visitors (parent volunteers) listen to their concerns and enable them to make use of community resources such as parent/carer and toddler groups, toy libraries and playgroups.

Other befriending schemes include: the Parent Support Link Service in London; and Parent-to-Parent Befriending set up by Mencap in Wales.

PROGRESS CHECK

1 What is a befriending scheme?
2 What experience and training is necessary to become a befriender?

A multisensory room and soundbeam

A MULTISENSORY ROOM

Relaxation and stimulation in a multisensory, or white room, are particularly beneficial for children with special needs. The room decor is white – floor, walls, hammock and seating. There are no windows. Equipment includes multicoloured lighting, water-filled bubble tubes, fibre optics, aromatherapy tubes, different textured collages (at a child's handrail height), taped music, wall and ceiling pictures and a wind machine. Some rooms have a water bed. All the equipment is specifically designed to offer a range of sensory experiences (sound, highly visible, textured and perfumed clues) to children who find it difficult to explore, discover and understand their environment. The combination of light, sound, touch, smell and movement creates a calm and peaceful learning environment.

Children, accompanied by their parents or carers, are encouraged to use and experience the equipment. Vibrations are felt when touching and holding the bubble tubes. Bright colours are a stimulus for children with visual impairment (although children with albinism tend to be light sensitive) and coloured balls rising and falling in the tubes help to develop vertical tracking skills. Changing the colours, sounds, smells and pictures in the room by pressing different knobs and levers gives children a sense of being in control of their experiences, as well as developing manipulative skills. The wind machine and collages help children who are tactile defensive. Children with emotional or behavioural difficulties can be calmed by the total experience of the room.

THE SOUNDBEAM

An ultrasonic, adjustable, invisible soundbeam provides music through a cause and effect principle. It can be operated by children who are virtually immobile through the slightest movement of a finger, hand or eye across the beam so activating a keyboard. Children moving through the beam or a child rocking in the beam can produce different sounds of varying tones and intensity. Like the multisensory room it has a pleasurable and peaceful effect on children with special needs.

KEY POINT

Multisensory and soundbeam provision is not exclusively for children with special needs. Any child would benefit from the unique and calming experience. The equipment is expensive to buy and fundraising projects are often the only way of purchasing it. Special schools and adventure playgrounds may provide these facilities for the children.

PROGRESS CHECK

1 Describe how a 'white room' provides multisensory experiences for children with special needs.
2 In what ways can children with special needs activate a soundbeam?

Special therapy

PATTERNING

The British Institute for Brain-Injured Children (BIBIC) is a charity whose work with brain injured children is based on the practices of a Philadelphian psychologist Doman-Delacato. The aim is to assist children's mobility – walking, balance and coordination – through a series of exercises which 'teach' the undamaged part of the brain to take over the functions of the damaged part. Exercises, called 'patterning' and 'cross patterning' are used. Children who cannot voluntarily move their limbs are given intensive, frequent and repetitive rhythmic stimulation (patterning) to their limbs by a team of helpers for up to eight hours a day. Cross patterning involves the helpers moving opposite arms and legs to prepare the child for balanced, coordinated walking. The therapy, which is controversial, can be exhausting and distressing for the child. While many parents and carers have found the commitment to the programme time-consuming and tiring they are rewarded by their children's achievements.

CONDUCTIVE EDUCATION

Conductive Education is a therapy programme designed for children with cerebral palsy and is briefly described in chapter 9 (see page 360).

CASE STUDY

Leonie and her twin sister Petra, now aged two years, were born at thirty-two weeks gestation and sustained brain injury during a difficult birth. They had severe motor and learning difficulties. The family were very new to the area and were trying to settle in as part of the community.

Caring for Leonie and Petra, was exhausting and time-consuming. The children's mother, in particular, was at the end of her tether. She visited the local health centre, registered with a family doctor and made an appointment to see him the next day.

1 How can the family doctor help the family, especially the mother?
2 Which other member of the primary health care team is likely to be immediately involved with the family? What help and support might be offered?
3 What would your role be as key worker for Leonie and Petra in a day-care setting?
4 Which voluntary organisations have particular knowledge, facilities and resources that may be supportive for the children and their family?

KEY TERMS

You need to know what these words and phrases mean. Go back through the chapter and make sure that you understand:

adventure playgrounds
befriending schemes
community-based services
incontinence
multisensory room
parents as partners

Portage
role of a key worker
Scope template of good practice
soundbeam
therapy programmes
voluntary provision

PART TWO
Introduction

The second half of this book covers information to ensure good practice in caring for children with the more commonly occurring conditions. Part two can be used for quick reference for a specific piece of information or to gain wider knowledge. We hope it will help you to work with young children safely and effectively, meeting any particular needs a child may have, with confidence.

An introduction gives a brief background to each condition, including the frequency of occurrence, severity of the effect and any specific sex or race implications. The following headings give more detailed information about each condition.

WHAT HAPPENS: how a condition first shows itself – the signs that something may be amiss – and what to look for if you are worried about a child's development. Patterns of inheritance are described, including a description of how a condition usually progresses and develops.

DIAGNOSIS: which tests or examinations may be used to confirm a child has a certain condition.

CARE: immediate care and priorities of management are covered including all aspects of a child's physical, emotional and social well-being. If applicable specific first aid measures are described and any special medication discussed.

ONGOING MANAGEMENT: longer-term issues concerned with a child with a chronic or possibly life limiting condition are described. This section looks at preparation for care in wider settings away from the home, including nursery, and primary school.

GENERAL IMPLICATIONS: wider, possibly ongoing, issues are raised.

ADDITIONAL DEVELOPMENTS: any recent, specific developments and thoughts about children and their care and management are discussed – not all sections have recent developments.

At the end of chapter 7 information is given about the management of medicines in schools, nurseries and playgroups – essential information for safe practice.

RESOURCES: the specific voluntary organisations associated with each condition are included at the end of each section for your further research. (Wider, more general organisations are included in 'Useful addresses' at the end of the book.)

KEY POINTS

- Even though individual conditions are explained and discussed much of this knowledge will be transferable to children with complex and varied disabilities. For example, a child with behaviour difficulties may also be deaf or have eczema; a child who has cerebral palsy may also have a visual impairment – you may need to read several sections for a holistic approach.
- Always remember that each child is an individual and will respond to stress and distress in different ways. Care and management issues are for guidance and general care principles only.

When a child is born with a special need parents and, later, children themselves, usually want to know why this has happened. Access to this information is a basic right. Knowledge about the reasons for a disability and its associated special needs, can sometimes give relief from uncertainty and help families plan and focus on the future. Often, following this information, families wish to take genetic counselling.

Professionals working with families need to work as a cohesive and sensitive team, valuing and understanding the parents' knowledge of their child and the specific anxieties about him and his individual special needs.

KEY POINTS

- If you have information regarding a child's medical condition this must remain confidential and should not be shared with others without permission from the parent
- Medical records should always be stored within a locked cabinet and accessed only by those with permission.
- Some children with these conditions will require a statutory assessment and statement of their special educational needs (see page 71, chapter 3).
- Many of the principles of care, described in the following chapters can be used when caring for children with other less well known conditions.

6 PHYSICAL CONDITIONS

> **This chapter covers:**
> - **Epilepsy**
> - **Asthma and eczema**
> - **Diabetes mellitus**
> - **HIV and AIDS**
> - **The coeliac condition**

In this chapter we look at a range of physical conditions that affect children. These require some medical supervision and the use of medicines to control and minimise the condition's effects. Even though there may be an acknowledged term for a specific condition, remember each child will respond and be affected differently.

Epilepsy

This is the most common serious neurological condition affecting 100,000 children in the UK. The brain is a highly complex structure comprising millions of nerve cells or neurones which are responsible for a wide range of functions including consciousness, awareness, movement and posture. In epilepsy there is an interruption in the chemical activity in the nerve cells and a 'fit' or seizure is the result.

Seizures can occur that are not epilepsy. In very young children, under two, these are often triggered by a high temperature and rarely lead to epilepsy.

About six in every thousand children have epilepsy and 80 per cent attend mainstream schools. Slightly more girls than boys have epilepsy.

WHAT HAPPENS

Electrical changes in the brain neurones may occur because of intrinsic factors – something in the brain itself – and the reasons are usually unknown but can include:
- ante-natal infections
- family history
- jaundice
- some drugs taken in pregnancy.

Or, external factors – something affecting the brain from outside – may be the reason, including:
- a temporary lack of oxygen, perhaps caused by an injury or birth damage
- susceptibility to flashing or flickering lights (photosensitivity)

- severe infections often with associated brain infections
- certain severe diseases.

There are several different types of seizure, usually classified as either generalised seizures or partial seizures. They need to be managed in different ways.

Generalised seizures

Tonic/clonic seizure

The tonic/clonic seizure used to be known as 'grand mal'.

- The start is sudden and may occur at night. About one third of children experience auras (see coloured lights, taste or smell something specific) which often occur with subsequent seizures.
- The next stage is the tonic or spasm stage. The child's entire body becomes stiff and he falls to the floor losing consciousness. His face may be pale and distorted, with eyes fixed in one position, often rolled back. The back and neck may arch, with arms flexed and hands clenched. He may utter a piercing cry, be incontinent (pass urine or stool) and bite the inside of his cheek during the first spasm. Frothing at the mouth and difficulty in swallowing the saliva, may occur. This stage leads into the clonic phase.
- In the clonic phase the child starts to twitch, sometimes just involving the face, sometimes the whole body, lasting from a few seconds to several minutes. This is followed by the post convulsive stage.
- In the post convulsive stage the child is usually sleepy and may complain of a headache, he may appear dazed and have a memory loss of the convulsion.

Absences

Other generalised seizures can occur and are all much less dramatic in presentation. The most significant to be aware of are 'absences'. Here there is a brief interruption of consciousness without any other signs, except perhaps for a fluttering of the eyelids. This type is especially common in children and used to be known as 'petit mal'. It occurs most frequently in children from three years onwards.

Partial seizures

Simple partial seizures

Consciousness is not affected and the seizure is confined to rhythmical twitching of one limb or part of a limb or to unusual tastes in the mouth, or a sensation such as pins and needles in a specific part of the body (this can be similar to the aura that may precede a major tonic/clonic seizure.)

Complex partial seizures

Consciousness is affected and the child shows 'semi-purposive' movements such as fiddling with clothes or objects, wandering around or appearing confused. These types of seizure occasionally lead to other forms of generalised seizures.

DIAGNOSIS

A child is said to have epilepsy if he or she has repeated fits from a cause triggered internally or externally. Confirmation of the decision is made by looking at the electrical impulses of the brain on an electroencephalogram. Electrodes are attached to the head and a moving record of the brain's activity is recorded – this is a painless and harmless procedure.

CARE

Major seizure

There is little complex treatment required during this time. Basic first aid is all that is required and carers can be reassured that mostly children with seizures need a 'watching brief'. Follow the procedure below.

- Stay calm, a low quiet voice is reassuring, and keep onlookers away.
- Ensure there is nothing around the child which could damage him, such as hard furniture.
- Remove any spectacles if necessary.
- If possible put something soft under his head.

When the spasms have finished proceed with the following.

- Turn the child onto his side and place him in the recovery position.

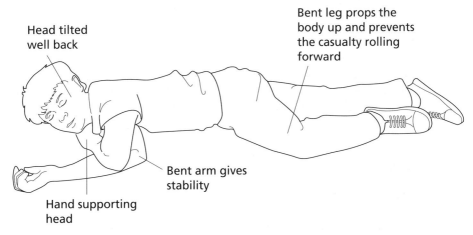

Head tilted well back

Bent leg props the body up and prevents the casualty rolling forward

Hand supporting head

Bent arm gives stability

The recovery position

- Check, with sensitivity, if the child needs changing.
- Encourage him to return to his usual activities when he feels ready.
- If the child fell during the fit, ensure he hasn't hurt himself.
- Maintain a matter-of-fact approach.

- During a seizure never try to force anything between the teeth – you may push a tooth down the throat and cause choking.
- Do not try to restrain the child.
- Keep a record of how long the seizure lasted.
- Seek medical help if this is a first convulsion.

KEY POINT

Your own responses to a major seizure are important to the individual child and other children. Your reactions show the child and his friends how you view epilepsy. Feelings of fear, anxiety and panic are easily transmitted and you may unconsciously increase a child's feelings of embarrassment and guilt and even make him sad or depressed. Remember, too, he may be upset if his peers saw that he soiled himself. This is more likely if a child has only recently mastered the skill of bladder and bowel control. The child may have no recollection of the seizure, only sensing what happened from the people around him.

Non-convulsive seizures

As these seizures vary in type and intensity the response needed may differ – the main principles are as follows.

- Gently guide a child away from obvious danger.
- Keep onlookers away.
- Speak gently and calmly to the child to help him remember his surroundings as quickly as possible.
- Remember, he may be confused for some time after the seizure and it is better to leave him alone than to overcrowd him – discreetly observe him.
- Stay with the child until he resumes his normal activity.

ONGOING MANAGEMENT

Epilepsy can usually be successfully controlled by medication, but the success in this depends on several factors:

- the type of epilepsy
- the accuracy of diagnosis
- the accuracy of treatment
- the child's response to the medication
- additional problems.

With appropriate drug treatment seizures can be completely controlled in about 80 per cent of children with epilepsy. Occasionally seizures diminish as the child grows, however it is usually recommended that anti-epileptic drugs continue for several years even after seizures stop.

A child needs to become involved in the management of his own treatment and see medication as a positive part of remaining healthy and not as part of an 'illness'. He can be especially affected by negative images of this condition from peers and surrounding adults which are the results of fear and ignorance.

For the young child minor adjustments to routine safe practice will be needed.

- Doors should open outwards and locks positioned so that they can be operated from inside and out. You would need to reach him easily if he had a seizure.
- Provide routine supervision at mealtimes, outings and bedtimes – potentially dangerous times for any child.
- Use special anti-smother pillows.
- Check that all your climbing equipment is secure and stable – in case of falls.
- Monitor the condition of toys – check there are no loose pieces to be torn off and inhaled.
- Ensure safety surfaces in playgrounds are in good condition.
- Be aware of any situations which might trigger a seizure.

The disabling effects of epilepsy can be substantially lessened if there is good communication between professionals, parents, the child and his peers. A teacher or other carer must have full information on:

- the type of epilepsy
- the frequency of seizures
- the speed of recovery
- the most appropriate management for the child
- how he feels after a seizure
- how positive he is about his condition
- information about triggering factors, if known
- details of medicines, including any possible side effects.

KEY POINT

The teacher needs to feel confident and so requires information about the child and his condition.

PROGRESS CHECK

Imagine a child has a major seizure when you are involved in playground supervision in the nursery class.
1 How would you manage the child who is having the seizure?
2 How would you manage the other children?

Telling other people

The other children in a class may feel fearful if a seizure occurs and they are unprepared. This can result in myths and stereotypes being reinforced. It may be constructive to include information into general classroom planning before the admission of a child with epilepsy and before any seizure happens. The amount of information disclosed to the class about a specific child must be agreed between the parents, teacher and child and the decision respected.

Consider too the importance of sharing information in other childcare situations – playgroups, childminders and with parents and carers or friends.

KEY POINT

Hiding epilepsy does not limit the risk of seizures – but confidentiality must be respected.

> ### Activity
> Plan a health education information programme about epilepsy for a group of children of infant age. Include information about the brain and its role in controlling functions of the body, perhaps suggesting the idea of the brain as the body's computer. Design a poster for use with the whole class.

Generally the child should develop and grow in as 'normal' an environment as possible. Each child will have different needs depending on the degree of control by his medication. As with any child, normal discipline and risk taking are part of learning and must not be avoided. It is almost unheard of for routine discipline of a child to promote or trigger a seizure.

Children with epilepsy need a normal environment

KEY POINTS

- Over-protection will affect the child's self-esteem, his learning opportunities and eventually his ability to assess danger himself. He should not feel he can never be alone.
- As the child grows he needs appropriate information regarding his condition and its control. Answer questions honestly.

- Activities such as swimming or climbing in high places need not be avoided, but care should be taken to ensure supervision is present from someone confident in seizure management.
- An identification bracelet helps provides useful information, especially if a seizure occurs in an unexpected situation or new staff are involved in care.
- If medication is given at school ensure storage is secure and dosage is always checked and possible side effects known.

Additional help must be sought in the following situations.
- The child has injured himself badly in a seizure.
- The child has trouble breathing after a seizure.
- One seizure immediately follows another or the seizure lasts longer than five minutes and the carer is unaware of the usual length.
- The seizure lasts longer than usual (often a card is carried to indicate length of seizure).

GENERAL IMPLICATIONS

Can epilepsy affect progress?

Occasionally teachers, nursery careworkers and other staff have low expectations of children with epilepsy and may unconsciously treat them differently. If the seizures are well controlled and there are no other associated disabilities there is no reason for underachievement or any unacceptable behaviour in such children. Behavioural problems that sometimes occur, can often be caused by tension and anxiety from carers causing low self-esteem in the child.

Epilepsy should not be used as an excuse for attention-seeking and unacceptable behaviour, as this can result in isolation and effect the child's development of strong peer and social relationships.

The following are some possible causes of why children might underachieve.
- Frequent major seizures may lead to poor school or pre-school attendance. This is made worse if the child is unnecessarily removed every time a seizure occurs. In addition, absences from pre-school and school can affect a child's confidence in making social relationships.
- Frequent 'absence' seizures which may be difficult to detect and can hinder learning.
- Children with especially severe epilepsy may have periods of disorganised brain activity, not enough to cause seizure but which may affect performance and learning.
- Incorrect or excessive drug treatment can cause sleepiness.
- Children who are going through periods of rapid growth may need adjustment of their drugs more frequently.

KEY POINT

Behavioural difficulties should not always be put down to drug effects.

ADDITIONAL DEVELOPMENTS

Epilepsy and surgery

If the epilepsy is caused by a specific structural problem in part of the brain, possibly from a form of head injury or following an infection (e.g. meningitis) and scarring of the brain has occurred, surgery is sometimes undertaken. This may be considered if the child is otherwise fit and medication has proved to be unsuccessful. This is only ever undertaken after extensive investigation involving special brain (MRI) scanning and other procedures to ensure areas responsible for speech, sight, movement or hearing are not close to the affected area.

Specific stimulation, via a nerve in the neck, is offered at present for older children in some hospitals throughout the UK. A small battery-operated device is programmed to send a mild stimulation to the brain. It is only suitable for certain types of epilepsy which do not respond well to medication. This is not yet widely available.

Mostly, however, children manage their epilepsy effectively through medication.

CASE STUDY

Jane was what her mother described as 'dreamy' – she often seemed to disappear into a world of her own. This dreaminess increased when she started infant school and sometimes her teacher complained that she did not appear interested in what was going on in the classroom – she frequently stared blankly ahead and gradually became labelled as 'not interested'. Usually she was outgoing and had friends and many interests.

She failed to make the expected academic progress of which she was thought capable. When she started to learn to read she seemed to find it difficult and would often appear to have forgotten several pages of the stories associated with a book she was reading. Even at home when watching television she missed major parts of the 'plot' of a programme.

Her mother became worried and took her to the family doctor who referred her to a neurologist for special tests.

Jane was diagnosed as having a type of epilepsy known as 'absences' – she was losing consciousness for very brief spells of time, not long enough to fall or show any obvious signs, but sufficient to affect her continuity of learning. She was missing some of the main teaching points or the essential linking material.

Jane was prescribed medicines to help limit the absences but it was not yet fully effective.

1 How could you, as a nursery nurse, help to make up the missing periods for Jane?

2 What knowledge do you need about Jane's medicines?

RESOURCES

British Epilepsy Association
Anstey House
Hanover Square
Leeds LS3 1BE

FABLE (For a better life with epilepsy)
18 Joseph Road
Sheffield S6 3RZ

The National Society for Epilepsy
Chalfont St Peter
Gerrards Cross
Bucks SL9 0RJ

Asthma and eczema

Asthma, eczema and hay fever are conditions that are linked, about half occurring in families with a known history of allergy. In a typical family, for example, one child might have asthma, another eczema, the father may have hay fever and the mother be fit and well.

Asthma

Asthma is a recurrent and reversible condition of the lungs which means that the narrowing of the tubes that happens is temporary and is caused by specific factors. A child with asthma responds to specific triggers and irritants by having breathing difficulties – another child without asthma, exposed to the same triggers, does not react.

Asthma is thought to be increasing in frequency and severity with one in seven school-age children now having the condition, and approximately six children being daily admitted to hospital in the UK.

Breastfeeding is often encouraged in 'atopic' or allergic families. It is helpful in delaying the onset of asthma, but not necessarily preventing it. Smoking in pregnancy also increases the chances of a child developing asthma.

WHAT HAPPENS

A 'trigger' or irritation causes a temporary obstruction in the tiny tubes of the lungs – the bronchioles. These bronchioles go into spasm and produce extra secretions and coughing. Because the airways are in spasm the air passages narrow, causing difficulty in breathing in and out. A wheezing noise is produced. The child fights for breath and can become frightened.

Asthma often has no set pattern of occurrence or severity of symptoms. Up to 30 per cent of children under five years wheeze but never have further symptoms. Many children 'grow out of asthma'.

DIAGNOSIS

There is no single cause for asthma. It is usually divided into the following types, depending on what is found to stimulate a child to produce asthmatic signs.

Extrinsic asthma
The trigger factors for extrinsic asthma can be:
- infections, especially coughs and colds
- pollen, feathers, household dust mite, animals, mould and certain foods
- cold and, occasionally, humidity.
- chemicals
- pollutants especially carbon monoxide, cigarette smoke and fuel and paint fumes, sprays from cleaners and perfumes
- exercise – thought to be a trigger in about 50 per cent of asthma
- emotional factors (in a child with an existing allergic response).

Intrinsic asthma
Here no specific sensitivity or trigger can be found.

Very young children often have troublesome coughs, especially at night or following colds or exercise. If these persist over a period of time asthma may be diagnosed. This diagnosis is helpful as a child can then receive effective monitoring and treatment.

Allergy tests may be undertaken to find if a specific allergen can be identified and removed or its contact with the child limited. However, children often have many responses to these tests and it would be impracticable for all the allergens to be eliminated.

KEY POINT

Baby asthma or wheezing is rarely triggered by allergy, but follows colds and chest infections.

Degrees of asthma
- Severe asthma can result in sleeping difficulties – the child coughs and wheezes more at night – and poor feeding – the child is too breathless to feed effectively and loses weight. General lethargy results, the effort to play and get involved in usual activity is too great – too much energy is spent forcing air in and out through reduced airways. Occasionally the child's lips go blue.
- Moderate asthma is waking at night coughing, and in the day, coughing and difficulty in running around and playing without wheezing.

■ Mild asthma means only coughing and wheezing but not to an extent that playing or feeding is disrupted.

KEY POINT

Healthy children rarely cough except with a bad cold. Many young children with dry irritating coughs may have asthma, even though they never wheeze.

CARE

Medicines

Although asthma cannot be cured, with effective management symptoms can be reduced and usually controlled, allowing children to lead full and active lives.

Almost all asthma medicines are given in some form of inhalers, even to very small babies. Given this way means that correct doses of medicine can be sent straight into the lungs.

There are two main types of medicine and it is important to know what they do as they will be needed in different situations.

Preventers (often in brown, white or red inhalers)

These protect the lining of the airways and make them less likely to narrow when triggered by a specific irritant. They reduce the airway's response to allergies and act specifically on the tubes in the lungs. Usually they are taken morning and evening and must be taken regularly, even if the child is well. Many need to be taken for fourteen days before becoming fully effective. A child can remain fit and well and be completely symptom free on these types of inhalers. They allow the child to use his whole lungs. Unfortunately parents and carers often stop using this type of treatment precisely when it is most effective – the child seems completely well. When these are stopped an attack may occur.

Relievers (often in blue inhalers)

These make breathing easier by relaxing the tiny muscles surrounding the narrowed airways and allowing them to open up; they do not prevent the narrowing occurring again in the future. As well as being effective for symptom relief, they may also be used immediately before exercise (if this is known to be a trigger). A child learns to recognise this type of inhaler which gives him almost immediate symptom relief.

Other medication

Other medication is used if a child fails to respond to inhalers. Steroid medicine is usually given for a short period of one to five days to counteract a severe attack. The child then continues with his spacers and puffers.

Complementary medicines

Complementary medicines are sometimes used in conjunction with the traditional approach if this is wished by parents and carers.

HOW MEDICINE IS GIVEN IN ASTHMA

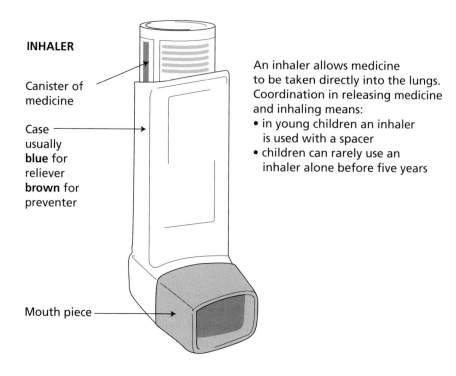

INHALER

Canister of
medicine

Case
usually
blue for
reliever
brown for
preventer

Mouth piece

An inhaler allows medicine
to be taken directly into the lungs.
Coordination in releasing medicine
and inhaling means:
• in young children an inhaler
  is used with a spacer
• children can rarely use an
  inhaler alone before five years

SPACER

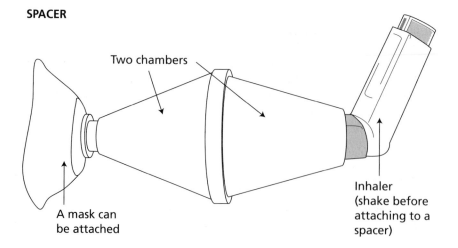

Two chambers

A mask can
be attached

Inhaler
(shake before
attaching to a
spacer)

A spacer fits the aerosol inhaler – medicine is puffed into the spacer via
the inhaler, one puff at a time. The child breathes via the mask.
This allows the medicine to be directly sent to the lungs to dilate the
bronchioles and allow breathing to ease.
Keep spacers clean – wash regularly and air dry.

Using inhalers (puffers) and spacers

Make sure you know how to use the inhaler or spacer – information and demonstrations on how to use one effectively can come from school nurses, pharmacists, family doctor and hospital staff.

When caring for a child with asthma check the following:

- the type of inhaler the child uses, whether a preventer or reliever
- the inhaler is full, and shaken before use, or attached to the spacer
- the inhaler is cleaned and replaced as necessary.

Check you know how many puffs the child takes and how the inhaler is used (usually the child exhales before taking an inhaler, holds his breath following the inhalation and keep his lips shut for ten seconds after).

The following are other points to consider.

- How to administer to a child who is not cooperating because he is frightened. (If a child is distressed he will still be able to get this medicine quickly even when crying, through his spacer.)
- If a young child is having difficulty, use the inhaler yourself (without filling the spacer with medicine) and try to make taking it a game.
- Keep in contact with the health visitor or school nurse over new developments in asthma management.
- Know the school or nursery policy regarding children's medicines. Does it take into account the urgency of access to inhalers for children with asthma?
- Is there a special policy for children with asthma in the school?
- Remember to include a general reminder in letters to parents/carers about taking inhalers on school trips and outings.
- Young children can be given medicines via spacers while asleep.

GOOD PRACTICE

Relieving inhalers should be readily to hand and not locked away in cupboards. Preferably they should remain with the child – remember it is his condition for him to manage, he should feel in control. Obviously very young children will need help in using their spacers.

KEY POINTS

- Research tells us that a significant number of people fail to use their inhalers correctly, making them less effective.
- Treatment is aimed at the prevention of the appearance of symptoms.
- If another child got hold of an inhaler and used it, it would not cause any damage.
- A child cannot 'induce' an asthma attack – asthma is a physical reaction of the lungs to a variety of triggers not an emotional reaction. Not being able to breathe easily is frightening and can induce panic in a child, reducing his already limited lung capacity.
- Quick and calm response is important.

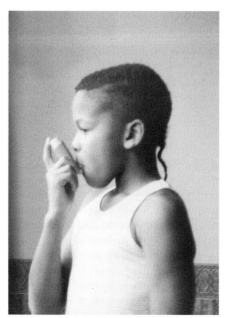
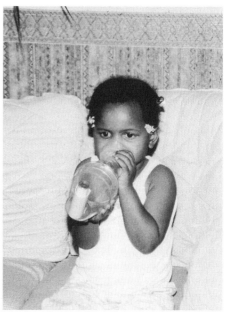

The correct use of an inhaler
for an older child

A younger child finds a spacer easier

ONGOING MANAGEMENT

Childcare workers need to work closely with parents and carers so everyone is aware of known triggers and can try and eliminate them. All involved in care should understand the importance of the management of a child's particular asthma and its special implications for him.

The aim should be to help the child remain symptom free so he can be fully involved in all activities at home, playgroup or school. The child learns to recognise situations which might make him wheeze and develops confidence knowing his symptoms are controlled by his inhalers, he then can forget his asthma. When very young he may need a reminder to take an inhaler before exercise. Check the child's inhalers are with him when he is on outings and trips.

Making the environment asthma 'friendly'
- Dust mites are a common allergen – rooms will need regular vacuuming, including mattresses and curtains.
- Regularly wash cotton bedding and use non-allergenic pillows.
- Keep good ventilation especially in bedrooms.
- As a smoky environment usually makes wheezing worse, a diagnosis of asthma is often the spur families need to give up cigarettes.
- Wash any soft toys regularly. Freezing toys in a plastic bag overnight kills any dust mites. They then need defrosting and washing to remove mites and droppings.

Asthma may be triggered by a pet with a furry coat, exercise or cold weather

■ Check the family, school or nursery pets, as guinea pigs, hamsters, birds and rabbits are often triggers. Try letting the pet have a 'holiday' with a friend and see if the child wheezes less. Perhaps just not handling the animal and certainly stopping the pet sleeping on a bed may be enough. If the pet is the cause try and find an acceptable alternative, perhaps a snake or fish – one without a hairy or feathery coat.

Exercise

Moderate exercise is good and each child will have different amounts he can manage and will learn to pace himself. Nearly all children with asthma become wheezy during exercise and a dose of a dilator or reliever prior to starting to run and jump is often very helpful. He may need a gentle reminder to take the inhaler.

It is important for a child to remain fit with all the benefits of lung expansion, prevention of infection and the opportunities of challenge and adventure that outdoor exercise provides. However if the weather is particularly cold or foggy watch that his breathing remains easy. Asthma is often worse during cold dry days than warm humid ones. Long spells of exercise are more likely to set wheezing off than short bursts.

Grass pollen during late May and July can be difficult for a child allergic to flowering grasses and he will need to stay away from such places during this time.

Swimming is a particularly valuable form of exercise for children with asthma, rarely provoking wheezing if the water is not too cold or heavily chlorinated.

- When joining in school games a child's inhaler should always be near to hand.
- Never force a child to continue to exercise if he is wheezing and uncomfortable.
- Be aware that some children are uncomfortable with taking an inhaler in front of their friends; check if privacy is required.

Diet and asthma

A special diet may be of help for the following children:

- those with clear family histories of food allergy
- those with eczema as well as asthma
- those whose wheezing started when weaning began, or when cows' milk was introduced.

Close liaison with medical personnel is essential before applying a limiting diet to a child. This is especially so for a baby, who is growing and developing and needing a wide variety of foods to meet his needs.

If it is felt that a special feeding regime is required the following advice is usually given.

- Mothers should breastfeed for as long as possible avoiding foods to which they are allergic.
- Especially formulated milks will need to be prescribed by the doctor. Soya milk is almost as likely as cows' milk to cause allergy and sheep and goats' milks are unsuitable for babies.
- Introduce one new food to a baby at a time and watch closely for a few days to assess the results. If the baby becomes snuffly, wheezy, colicky or develops a rash, stop the new food.
- Continue to add new foods one at a time – try and maintain variety.
- Gradually introduce different drinks, one at a time. Avoid fizzy drinks and squashes for at least eighteen months.
- Avoid eggs and cows' milk until the baby is one.
- Avoid fish, nuts or wheat flour for at least the first year if there is a family history of allergy.

KEY POINTS

- If a child has a fever it is the result of infection **not** an adverse food reaction.
- Children who do not have dairy food or a recognised baby milk after stopping breastfeeding will need a calcium supplement prescribed by their doctor.

Activity

To help explain asthma to children of infant school age blow up balloons with a pump. Explain to the children the balloons are like lungs. Give them out to the children and under supervision, ask them to deflate them while restricting the amounts of air released by squeezing and stretching the necks. Tell the children this is how air has problems in leaving the lungs of a child with asthma.

Compare how quickly the air leaves if the neck is not squeezed. Compare the noises the escaping air makes when restricted and when free.
Always closely supervise children with balloons.

Good practice in managing an acute attack

During an asthma attack coughing, wheezing or breathlessness worsens quickly until breathing becomes difficult. Some children become too breathless to talk or feed during an attack. Attacks can take anything from a few hours to a few days to develop. Regular observation is important.

Asthma attacks can occasionally be life-threatening. The following danger signs indicate that routine management is not controlling the condition.

- A reliever needs to be repeated before three hours.
- The child is too breathless to feed or talk and is becoming very distressed.
- The child becomes pale and blue around the lips.

If this happens the following steps should be taken.

- Call for help immediately – it may be quicker to take the child in a car to the nearest accident and emergency department.
- Give the reliever treatment straight away, repeating this treatment every five to ten minutes until the child's breathing improves or help arrives. Check he is taking the reliever treatment correctly.
- Give any other prescribed medicines reserved for such occasions, often steroid tablets.
- Hold or sit the child in a comfortable upright position. He may like his hand held, but do not put an arm around him as this may feel restricting.
- Reassure him and remain calm yourself – the child will be frightened.
- Loosen tight clothing around the neck.
- Sips of tepid fluids can help with a mouth dry from rapid breathing.
- Contact parent/carer.

Often simple breathing exercises are given by physiotherapists to help children with asthma use their lungs effectively. Generally the emphasis is on fully exhaling rather than trying to increase inhalation, together with the use of additional muscles i.e. the abdomen to help increase chest capacity. Occasionally these exercises can stop an attack developing and lessen the severity. They also help a child feel more in control.

PROGRESS CHECK

1 Has a child in your care been given such exercises?
2 How can you support and encourage the child in the use of exercises?
3 When and how should the exercises be used?

GENERAL IMPLICATIONS

The number of children with asthma is increasing, doubling in the last twenty years. Luckily, treatments are increasingly effective even in children seriously affected. Most children do eventually grow out of their condition or the intensity of the symptoms settles over time. However, a recent survey found childcare workers had little training in managing asthma and a campaign has been launched to increase awareness.

CASE STUDY

Aaron had been a sturdy four-year-old boy who regularly attended playgroup. Normally he was active and energetic but recently he seemed to have difficulty in shaking off a persistent cough. This was made worse when he was running and climbing in the outdoor area and seemed to trouble him even more during a particularly cold spell. He began to lack his normal enthusiasm and even fell asleep in the story corner.

After discussion with his mother it was realised that Aaron's cough had persisted since his attack of measles the previous winter. It was worse at night and was causing him sleeplessness.

Aaron had several courses of antibiotic medicine to try and cure the cough but all to no avail. On his next visit to the family doctor he was given further tests. These included measuring his breathing capacity and listening to his chest after he had been running around. The doctor decided he probably had asthma and Aaron's mother confirmed that when she was a child she too had breathing difficulties.

Aaron was prescribed inhaled medication which gave him immediate relief and made him feel much more comfortable, returning him to his usual energetic self. He will continue with his spacer and be regularly checked.

1 What were the three triggers that could have stimulated Aaron's asthma?
2 What precautions should the nursery take in future to ensure Aaron can be fully involved in playgroup activity?

Eczema

This is sometimes called atopic eczema, infantile and childhood eczema and dermatitis.

KEY POINT

Eczema is not a disease but more a reaction of the skin to certain triggering factors. One person in ten has a degree of eczema at some time. The severity of the symptoms varies widely.

WHAT HAPPENS

Usually the skin is very dry with an overwhelming itchiness. The skin may become inflamed, crack and split leaving the child vulnerable to infections and with painful areas or limbs.

In babies the areas affected are concentrated on the head and body, but the eczema may spread and cover the whole child. Even on children not severely affected, patches can often remain and be seen especially in the creases of the body, behind the ears, knees and under the arms. The irritation is made worse when the child is warm, it can disrupt his sleeping and lead to tiredness and irritability. Different parts of the skin can be at various stages of eczema at the same time. These stages can range from a red rash, to dry scalings or cracks and to bleeding or infected skin with pustules and crusting. Typically of eczema there are times when the skin flares up and is badly affected yet at other times is completed cleared.

DIAGNOSIS

Although a significant number of children come from families with an allergic history the cause is not always known. Diagnosis is made from observing the skin which may react to certain triggers – setting off lesions or sore and irritating patches.

Triggers can be:
- bacterial, viral or fungal infections
- specific contact irritants such as perfumed soaps, washing powders and paints
- environmental factors, such as temperature (especially heat) and humidity, and inhalants
- certain foods, especially dairy products and those containing dairy products
- emotional or physical stress
- drugs.

KEY POINT

Each child may have a different trigger or react to a combination of triggers.

CARE

The aim is to keep the skin in good condition, lessening the chances of skin infections and reducing the painful and irritant effects for the child. For the very young child there are several things that help.
- Emulsifiers or emollient ointments are vital as they help limit dryness and reduce irritation. They are mild, easily obtained and do not contain steroids. They must be used freely and generously. Put them in the bath water and liberally spread onto the skin after washing. A toddler who is distressed and scratching can be helped by having 'his' cream applied. It needs to be easily available, day and night.
- For bathing use only warm water as heat irritates. Try an aqueous soap substitute. Do not use perfumed soaps or bubble baths as they dry and irritate the skin.
- Change the child's nappies frequently and maintain good skin condition. A sore nappy rash will make the eczema much worse, so watch this area especially. Leave the nappy off for part of the day.

- Check the skin creases: underarm, behind the ears, in the groins etc. Pat the child dry thoroughly. Do not use powders as they cake and dry the skin further and they may be a focus for bacteria to multiply.
- Keep nails short and hands clean to lessen the chances of secondary infection.
- Use non-irritant fabric for clothes – natural cotton is best. Avoid wools, non-absorbent nylons and clothes with 'pile'.
- Use mild non-biological soap powder in laundering clothes as they may be greasy from the effects of the emulsifying ointments.
- Keep the child cool. Make sure a bedroom doesn't become overheated, as it is at night that scratching is most likely. Use light bedding, no feather duvets or wool blankets. Cotton cellular blankets are ideal.
- Limit damage to the skin by providing all-in-one sleep suits at night, with cotton mittens and socks. This helps reduce the extent of easily exposed skin.
- Dummies are helpful as night time pacifiers and can be valuable as a distracter, better than a thumb which can become sore and cracked, so increasing the child's distress.
- Toddler anger and frustration often sets off intense irritation of the skin. Distraction management is helpful, so try to anticipate his needs.

Diet
Breastfeeding lessens the severity of eczema and should be encouraged.

Babies who are unable to tolerate cows' milk can be provided with a special replacement formula obtained from their doctor. Goats' and soya milks are found to cause similar skin reactions to cows' milk.

Tests can be undertaken to show which foods produce skin reactions, however they are more likely to show what irritants in the environment make the skin worse, for example animal hair or pollen, rather than a specific food. The most effective way of finding an unacceptable food is by 'exclusion and challenge'.

Here foods are removed from the diet for two to four weeks and the condition of the skin observed carefully. The food is then reintroduced to check if the skin worsens. It is then excluded again, for a second time to see if any improvement is continued. This is undertaken under the supervision of a specialist paediatric team including a dietitician.

Which children are most likely to show a skin reaction to a specific food?
- A child from a family with a known family history of food intolerance.
- The younger the child, the more likely food is to be a trigger.
- A child with eczema who also has other symptoms such as rashes, loose stools and a runny nose.

Foods possibly likely to provoke a reaction include eggs, cheese, cows' milk, chocolate, nuts, wheat cereal, orange juice and additives.

GOOD PRACTICE

Restricting children's diets must never be undertaken unless in conjunction with qualified registered dieticians. Severely limiting children's food can be dangerous if not carried out correctly and may cause long term nutritional problems, including delayed growth and development. Excluding cows' milk from a child's diet reduces his calcium intake by 75 per cent.

Also reintroducing food at home to which a child is strongly intolerant, without medical supervision, may produce asthma attacks.

KEY POINT

If you are working with a child on a restricting diet, emphasise the food he can eat, not the food he cannot.

PROGRESS CHECK

1 What are the most common triggers for eczema?
2 What makes the skin irritation worse?
3 In what circumstances might a special diet be advised?
4 How could you help a toddler whose skin was causing him intense irritation?

Medicines

The skin is maintained with the moisturising of emulsifying ointments. Local lesions are also treated with very mild steroid creams. These are effective and quickly heal any sores but, unlike the emulsifiers, they must be applied sparingly and only as prescribed.

If a child with eczema has enormous difficulty in sleeping due to constant irritation then antihistamine tablets are sometimes given. Antihistamine creams are not used as they can cause an extra skin reaction. Antihistamine tablets reduce irritation and help the child to sleep; however the effects can make the child sleepy the following day as well and may affect his ability to take full advantage of play and learning. Correct dosage is important.

If a child's eczema becomes infected then often antibiotic medicines are prescribed to treat this. Very occasionally a child is admitted to hospital, for a short period, if his eczema is not responding to treatment.

Chinese medicinal plants are increasingly being used in the control of eczema and research continues into their development. However the combination mixture currently used as a medicine, should not be taken by children under two years of age or any child with a history of liver or kidney disease.

PROGRESS CHECK

Which creams must be applied liberally and which type sparingly?

Activity
Plan a day's routine for a two-year-old boy with eczema. Include in your plan of activities things that will give him quick release of tension if he is frustrated.

- It is unhelpful to tell a child not to scratch a severe itch – try not scratching yourself when you have intense irritation!
- Encourage the child to use pressure on the area or gently rub in a circular movement.
- Always keep the child's nails short and clean.

KEY POINTS

- Eczema is usually controlled and has few long lasting physical effects, very rarely causing scarring. However to many parents the good appearance of their child's skin is a sign of being a 'good carer' so great distress can be caused by the condition.
- Ensure everyone knows that eczema is not catching and is not caused by neglect or poor hygiene.

ONGOING MANAGEMENT

The skin dries more quickly in hot, dry atmospheres such as schools or playgroups so it is important that a child can use his emulsifiers regularly during his school day. An application at breakfast will not last all morning, more will be needed to limit irritation and keep the skin in good condition.

Signs of discomfort include the child's:

- wriggling
- lack of concentration
- red and flushed skin
- irritability.

The table on page 185 gives suggestions on how to cope with the various potential stresses that may occur in children.

The family pet may make eczema worse

ECZEMA

Potential stresses for child	Coping suggestions
Soaps, detergents and paper towels can cause irritation.	Arrange for child to have their own aqueous soap substitute and access to cotton towels. (Parents/carers may wish to bring these in.)
Classroom is hot and dry, making irritation worse.	Position child away from radiators and sunny windows, have damp flannel available to cool down overheated limbs. Tights and woolly trousers increase itching. Keep emollients to hand, younger children may need help applying them.
Seating arrangements can increase irritation e.g. plastic chairs, story time on a carpet with pile.	Provide cotton squares for chairs, temporarily cover carpet area with cotton sheet.
Messy activities provoke a skin reaction e.g. sand, water, paint, dough and clay.	Encourage the use of cotton or even light plastic gloves. In an emergency tape plastic bags around wrists. Try to avoid stopping a child's involvement in an activity if possible. Liaise with parents/carers.
School meals are unsuitable, there is limited choice. Poor nutritional balance of 'allowed' foods.	Liaise with kitchen staff. Check everyone is aware of any dietary restriction. Suggest packed lunches if agreement cannot be reached. Monitor the suitability of any snacks given e.g orange or milk drinks. Try and offer acceptable alternatives.
Swimming, especially in chlorinated pools, may dry and irritate the skin.	Encourage the use of emollients before swimming. Shower chlorine off after swimming then reapply emollient. Allow privacy and additional time for this.
Child appears listless, sleepy and lethargic during the day.	Liaise with parents/carers, this may be the effect of antihistamines. Provision of additional rest facilities might be needed for occasional short term management.
Child continually scratches.	Try distraction activities: involve the child in small tasks, suggest a brief physical exercise. Remind the child to apply pressure and try not to scratch. Suggest finding a quiet space to apply emollient. Check nails are short and not increasing damage to skin. Is the child wearing too many clothes?
Child appears to be losing confidence, embarrassed about appearance of skin,, reluctant to expose body (e.g. changing for games or swimming).	Challenge any teasing or name calling. Give physical contact e.g. holding hands with child which publicly reaffirms condition is not infectious. Check you are providing an easily available private area for changing, applying ointment etc. so child is not singled out. Do not always comment on skin condition with parents/carers. **Key point:** Put the child before the eczema.
There is chicken pox, cold sores or impetigo in the nursery/school.	Liaise with parents/carers and the school nurse. These conditions can cause serious complications if contracted by a child with eczema. Maintain routine measures for the prevention of infection e.g. encourage effective hand washing for staff and children. Ventilate classrooms well. Keep environment clean, especially the furniture, lavatories, toys and teaching materials.
Developing fine manipulative control is painful and difficult with sore hands and fingers. Emollients leave greasy marks on paper and can cause slipping when holding pens etc. Learning to write or paint activities are not going well.	Eczema is constantly changing and there are often good periods when the skin is clear. So if the skin is sore and cracked leave practising fine manipulative skills and associated activities for a while. Frustration over failure to achieve can make eczema worse. Re-introduce fine skill development when the skin is improved. Offer an alternative new challenge. Keep a calm matter-of- fact response. Note: computers and word processors are valuable aids as the child grows.
Handling the hairy or fluffy nursery pet makes the irritation worse.	Unfortunately it may be better to leave that specific animal alone, encourage involvement with other live creatures such as feeding the goldfish or developing a wormery.

PROGRESS CHECK

1 Look through your chosen outline plan of the week for your nursery or play-group. Identify possible triggers in the chosen activities.
2 How could these activities be adapted?

GENERAL IMPLICATIONS

It is important for a child with eczema to remain positive. Symptoms can usually be controlled and often diminish with age. Managing his condition himself, helps promote the child's own self-esteem, as he learns that he can help control his condition rather than the condition controlling him.

DEVELOPMENTS

New developments in the treatment of severe symptoms include possible forms of phototherapy.

CASE STUDY

Jenny was four. She had had mild eczema since she was six months old. At times her eczema appeared as only minor with red scaly patches behind her knees and ears, but occasionally there were periods when several areas of her body were affected and bled after being scratched. These patches had sometimes become infected, once requiring admission to hospital. She used a variety of emollients to control her condition. However, she constantly woke at night with extreme irritation. She disturbed her two-year-old sister who shared her bedroom and woke her mother who slept in the next room. All the family, as a result, were exhausted and were finding it difficult to function effectively the next day.

Jenny attended a dermatology clinic and a meeting was arranged to reassess the effectiveness of her treatments.

As Jenny appeared most distressed at night this problem was discussed. It was suggested changing her bathing routine to exclude the use of the bubble baths that both sisters normally enjoyed together, lowering the water temperature and changing from nighties to using cotton pyjamas. The temperature of the bedroom was to be reduced and the central heating turned off overnight. Jenny was to stop using a duvet and to sleep under cotton sheets and blankets.

A strict policy of not allowing the family cat to sleep on the bed when Jenny was at nursery was introduced and Jenny was prescribed antihistamine medicine for use when her irritation was especially distressing. However, the procedures introduced for bedtime greatly reduced her night-time scratching and were rarely required.

Her mother had recently joined the Eczema Society which she found very supportive.

1 How could you ensure Jenny's skin was kept in good condition?
2 How could you reduce the chances of Jenny developing secondary skin infections?

RESOURCES

Junior Asthma Club
Providence House
Providence Place
London N1 0NT

National Asthma Campaign
Providence House
Providence Place
London N1 0NT

National Eczema Society
163 Eversholt Street
London NW1 1BU

Diabetes mellitus

This is usually known just as diabetes. Most children with diabetes will have the insulin dependent variety. Diabetes is thought to run in families, affecting about 1.4 million people in the UK. About 5 per cent of these are children, although it is rare in children under one year.

The condition is caused by a failure of the body to manage and control its use of carbohydrate and to a lesser extent fat and protein. Carbohydrates are found in starchy foods, such as bread, potatoes, pasta, cereals and sweet foods such as cakes and pastries. All types of carbohydrates are broken down, during digestion, into glucose. Glucose is also made in the liver.

Diabetes cannot be cured, but it can be controlled effectively.

WHAT HAPPENS

The pancreas fails to work effectively. This organ, hidden underneath the stomach, has two main jobs.
1 To produce chemical enzymes that are released into the gut to break down food.
2 To produce insulin, a hormone that controls the amounts of sugar released into the bloodstream. This sugar, or glucose, usually enters the cells and is used by the body as fuel.

A child with diabetes loses the ability to produce insulin. This is because the cells in the islets of Langerhans in the pancreas (see page 188) have lost their ability to work.

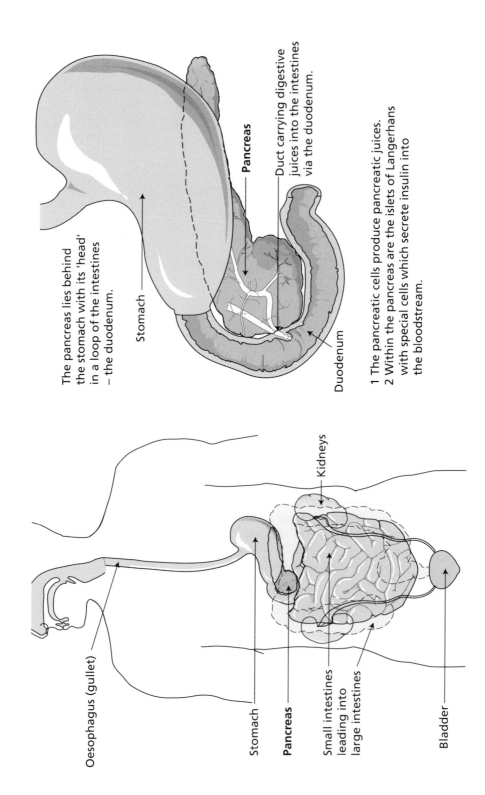

The pancreas lies behind the stomach with its 'head' in a loop of the intestines – the duodenum.

Stomach

Pancreas

Duct carrying digestive juices into the intestines via the duodenum.

Duodenum

1 The pancreatic cells produce pancreatic juices.
2 Within the pancreas are the islets of Langerhans with special cells which secrete insulin into the bloodstream.

Oesophagus (gullet)

Stomach

Pancreas

Small intestines leading into large intestines

Bladder

Kidneys

Without their beta-producing insulin the child's body cannot use glucose and the blood glucose level rises. The kidneys work hard to get rid of the excess glucose in the urine losing, in the process, large amounts of fluids. Without insulin the body cannot use the glucose so the child loses weight and becomes listless. If the situation is not noticed he continues to lose fluids, becoming dehydrated and drowsy. In order to maintain his energy levels his body begins to break down fat causing keytones in the urine which smell of pear drops. Coma, leading to death, will result if medical aid is not sought.

DIAGNOSIS

Signs that might indicate a child has diabetes:
- thirst and dry mouth
- frequent trips to the lavatory
- weight loss
- tiredness
- bedwetting, especially in a child who was previously dry at night
- irritation around the genital area
- dry skin
- frequent urinary tract infections
- in young babies a failure to thrive (remember diabetes is rare in babies under six months).

A final diagnosis is made by blood and urine tests.

CARE

The aim of management is to control the blood glucose level so that it does not rise too high – the term for this is *hyper*glycaemia. (The term for the blood glucose level being too low is *hypo*glycaemia.) Control is achieved by replacing the missing insulin by injections and by a special diet. Managing one of these areas without the other is ineffective; they are interlinked.

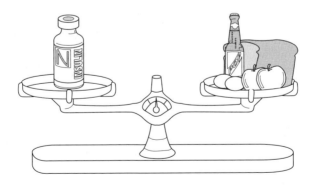

Keeping the scales of food intake and exercise evenly balanced with insulin given is the key to a healthy future for a child with diabetes

Insulin
Children with diabetes need regular insulin injections, usually twice daily, often before breakfast and the evening meal. Injections are needed as insulin is a protein so it cannot be taken by mouth – it is digested and neutralised by the stomach.

From about six years old, a child can be taught to give her own injections with a syringe or pen device. This encourages her to feel in control of her diabetes. These injections are accompanied by testing the blood glucose levels, usually by a simple finger-prick blood test. The blood is put onto a prepared reactive strip which shows the level of glucose in the blood. The amount of insulin given may then be varied to meet individual need.

Good practice in managing injections
Inevitably the younger the child the more difficult is the idea of the dependence on daily injections, for the maintenance of life. This is true for parents/carers and child. Frequent finger pricks, too, may initially be distressing. How can you help her to adjust and adapt?
- Always tell her what is going to happen; you will promote trust.
- Never surprise an unprepared child with a syringe.
- Always reward after an injection with a cuddle or praise.
- Understand her distress and encourage her to talk about it if she wishes.

KEY POINTS

- A child will get used to these procedures, especially if managed efficiently, calmly and as a regular part of a daily routine.
- As she grows she will be able to make the link between her injections, her diet and feeling well.
- She will recognise the signs her body tells her when her insulin or diet are out of balance with each other.

Activity
Let a toddler practise her 'injections' on a teddy.

Practical issues
Insulin should be stored in the fridge, the type and amounts to be given carefully checked prior to each injection. Shake the phial as insulin has crystals that need dispersing.

If a pen device is used the insulin is contained within a cartridge and the dose dialled with a mechanism at one end of the pen so there is no drawing up of the insulin required. Needles are attached to the pen.

Injection technique will be taught at the special diabetic clinic for children and their carers. You may be required to support and help in the home, possibly giving the injections. In school these are mostly organised before or after lessons.

There are areas to consider when giving or supporting children having insulin injections.

- Timing of injections: these are arranged with the medical team, but usually happen twenty to forty minutes before a meal so the insulin starts working in the bloodstream at the same time as the carbohydrate from the meal.
- Too late (less than fifteen minutes) before a meal means that the blood glucose levels may be too high after the meal because the insulin was not available to help use it. But each child is an individual and her schedule will be arranged for her particular needs.
- Air bubbles in a syringe: these should be removed (by flicking it with your finger) as bubbles take up insulin space. This can cause inaccuracies in dosage.
- Safety: secure a toddler firmly, in your arms, if you are involved in helping another adult.
- Cleaning the skin at the injection site: out of a hospital environment normal hygiene measures are usually all that is required. Of course, wash hands before handling any equipment.
- Injection areas: usually a child rotates these around the body from upper thighs and arms to tummies and buttocks. Also moving around within these areas is helpful in limiting 'fatty lumps' at injection areas.
- Angles and areas: the small, half-inch needle is inserted under the skin (subcutaneous) at an angle of 90 degrees. Lifting the skin slightly helps this.
- Bruising or slight bleeding at the injection site: this only means a small blood vessel has been punctured – it is harmless.
- Disposal of needles and syringes: the usual procedure is to keep all used equipment in a strong, plastic box (sometimes provided by the health authority). The hospital or health centre will arrange collection and disposal.

KEY POINTS

- *Never put syringes and needles into the dustbin.*
- *Never use other people's syringes or needles.*

PROGRESS CHECK

How would you respond to a four-year-old child who does not wish to have her injection today?

Diet

A specialist dietician will plan a child's diet in liaison with parents and carers taking into account personal likes and dislikes and cultural and religious preferences.

Each child will have her own diet plan, involving the eating of the correct amounts as well as types of foods. Usually this means a healthy balanced diet that is low in sugar and saturated fat and high in fibre. The diet should have variety and be designed to meet her growth needs from regular meals and snacks. Snacks are important as they prevent her blood sugar falling too low between meals.

Carbohydrate intake is controlled, especially those found in sugary foods – these quickly raise the blood glucose levels. Starchy carbohydrates take longer to digest and help maintain blood sugar levels so are included more freely in the diet e.g. bread, pasta, rice, potatoes and cereals.

Fibre-containing foods especially oranges, lentils and beans are all valuable in a diet for diabetes.

Foods containing polyunsaturated fats are included (fish, olive oils, etc) but the amount of animal fats is limited. Trimming meat and removing the skin from chicken helps reduce fat content.

Promoting the habit of healthy eating is important. Encouraging the child not to develop a sweet tooth will be valuable in the long term. Remember, the diet is for life.

KEY POINTS

- If a child is hungry on her diet tell the parents/carers and dietician.
- Sweets and crisps can be eaten occasionally, but not too much or too often and within the overall diet plan.

Sweets and crisps should be eaten only occasionally

- It is better to have an occasional treat than to regularly eat 'diabetic' jams, sweets and chocolates. They have no nutritional advantage and are expensive.
- A key factor in good management of the condition is the planning of a diet that a child enjoys – this helps her keep to the regime.

Food refusal

Any child, especially around two to three years old, will have periods of exerting her independence over food and mealtimes. With diabetes where regular food intake is essential this can be an especially challenging time. Mealtimes can easily become a power battlefield if the tension from carers is transmitted to a determined toddler. The following are helpful suggestions.

- Never force a child to eat.

- Try to ensure she eats in company.
- Check her meals are attractive and the environment appealing.
- Frequently offer foods the child likes. Keep a list of favourites from her diet. Try to rotate through the most nutritious.
- Only offer foods at snack and meal times.
- Do not overload plates in the hope she will eat 'something'.
- Never withhold puddings if a first course is refused, instead offer a second pudding.
- Always give drinks.
- Praise her when she eats, remove uneaten food without comment. Concentrate on the positive. Try to remain in control!
- Ensure all adults involved in her care are following the same policy.
- The dietician will always be available to offer advice on the telephone.

Hypoglycaemic and hyperglycaemic attacks
If the balance between insulin given and food eaten is wrong, in the short term, a hypoglycaemic attack will occur. The causes may be:
- too much insulin
- insufficient food, missed snack or meal
- strenuous physical activity without an adjustment to the carbohydrate intake
- sometimes illness.

The signs of an attack are:
- hunger
- pallor – especially of the face, recognisable in all skin colours
- shaking
- dizziness
- sweating
- tingling around the mouth
- dilated pupils
- mood changes
- irritability
- loss of concentration
- crying easily
- vagueness.

First aid
Immediately give a fast-acting carbohydrate such as a glucose tablet or a carton of sweetened fizzy drink. If the child is uncooperative and this is not possible try rubbing jam or a glucose gel onto her gums. Usually this will be effective in five to ten minutes.

Then follow up with a starchy carbohydrate to make sure the glucose level doesn't fall again – fruit or milk is ideal. Mild 'hypos' can occur often in some children and are easily managed without the need for outside help. However, ongoing liaison with the specialist team for diabetes is important in preventing serious hypoglycaemic attacks. These can be especially dangerous in children under eight and can result in seizures as well as coma.

The signs of a hyperglycaemic attack are similar to those the child had when her diabetes was first discovered. The onset of a hyperglycaemic attack is much slower and is generally less common than a 'hypo'. Occasionally these attacks can be triggered by illness.

Check that the child's insulin injection wasn't overlooked and seek advice if you are worried.

PROGRESS CHECK

What are the signs of hyperglycaemia?

GOOD PRACTICE

- If a child shows any symptoms of a 'hypo' and you are unsure if her blood sugar level is low, treat as for a confirmed hypoglycaemic attack. She will not be placed in danger from this.
- Good communication between childcare workers and parents/carers mean a child's individual signs of low blood sugar are familiar to all involved in her care.

ONGOING MANAGEMENT

In the home

Care is the same as for any other child while maintaining her diet and insulin treatment. Allowing diabetes to become an excuse for giving in to all demands and leaving attention-seeking behaviour unresolved is unfair to the child. Although a sensitive approach to possibly unpleasant procedures is important, a child's social and emotional development is helped by the security of understanding the acceptable rules and routines of the family. Learning to live with her diabetes is important.

Physical care

Make sure good skin-care routines develop, as a child with diabetes may heal slowly and become vulnerable to infection. Check she has a daily bath and develops good hand-washing habits.

Watch to make sure clothing does not rub and shoes fit well. Keep nails trimmed regularly and liaise with medical staff if cuts and grazes appear not to be healing. Encourage regular visits to the dentist.

GOOD PRACTICE

Encourage all children with diabetes to wear some identification bracelet or necklace.

Care in the education environment

To help a smooth transition from home to school or playgroup some planning is needed. Remember parents need to feel confident that you understand their child and her condition.

Before admission

Sharing and exchanging information is important and pre-visits vital. It is helpful for parents/carers to give written information about their particular child on:

- hypoglycaemia: the signs and individual symptoms
- meal and snack times: what should be eaten, and when
- exercise and activity: what preparation is necessary before and during any physical activity
- emergency contacts' names and numbers.

Organising the exchange of information before a child is admitted allows time for the childcare workers to update their own knowledge on diabetes.

Discussion about the following will also be needed:

- where fast-acting sugars are kept and replenished
- how to manage a child with hypoglycaemia
- the importance of full involvement of the child in all activities
- how you will prepare the other children.

Recording information

A child with diabetes will need an individual record card with information on managing her condition. This is essential in any setting where staff are changing and may be unaware of procedures. This card should include medical contact numbers.

Diet

The diet plan from the hospital dietician must be available for staff involved in providing meals. Stress the importance of regular meal times.

Arrange facilities for eating any packed lunches. If having school meals she will need to be served first or go to the top of any canteen queue. Check all staff and children understand the reasons.

The importance of snacks will need to be reinforced, these may have to be eaten in class or during a group time. Decide how you will manage this.

Physical activity

In order to fully involve a child with diabetes in all aspects of a school or playgroup, preparation or anticipation about the effects of certain activities will be necessary.

Extra glucose will be needed before vigorous games and occasionally after as well. A younger child may need reminding to take hers.

Trips and outings

On day trips out, remember to take glucose tablets and arrange for 'usual' meal breaks or snack opportunities – plan for any delays with sandwiches etc. Liaise with parents/carers regarding any special arrangements they feel will be necessary.

An older child involved in staying away overnight will need special arrangements for insulin injections and a wider sharing of information regarding food management.

Remember she may need extra glucose after physical exercise

PROGRESS CHECK

How could you give confidence to the mother of a five-year-old child with diabetes, who is to enter your reception class, that her child will be 'safe in your hands'?

GENERAL IMPLICATIONS

Children with diabetes run greater risks of health problems in later life. These include damage to eyes with cataracts, kidney diseases, increased risks of strokes, heart attacks and gangrene.

These dangers are considerably lessened if a child's diabetes is well controlled when young. So your support, understanding and encouragement in helping her stick to dietary restraint and her insulin regime, is important. All children are resentful and rebellious at times, not wanting to be different from their peers, but with sensible management this is usually short-lived. Children find it difficult to think of themselves as 'old' and so telling them they might get ill later, if they don't 'follow the rules' will not be helpful. Praise her for being in control of her condition now.

CASE STUDY

Junior was an active sociable seven-year-old boy who managed his diabetes effectively with insulin injections twice daily, before and after school.

His mother was pregnant and went into labour early one morning before Junior left home. The household was excited and anxious, but even in labour his mother supervised his early insulin injection before asking the neighbour to take him to school. Junior, in all the upheaval, had only a slice of toast, much less than his usual breakfast.

Later at school Junior refused to join in with another group of children and snatched work from his close friend and then sat silently at his table. The teacher was a supply teacher who commented at breaktime in the staff room upon Junior's 'difficult' behaviour. The permanent staff were surprised as this was out of character, then another colleague casually mentioned Junior had diabetes. The supply teacher immediately gave Junior a drink of sweetened orange juice, followed by a sandwich.

1 What signs of diabetes was Junior displaying?
2 How could this situation be avoided in the future?

RESOURCES

The British Diabetic Association
10 Queen Anne Street
London W1M OBD

HIV and AIDS

HIV (Human Immuno-deficiency Virus) attacks the human immune system which is the body's defence system against infection. HIV was first recognised in America in 1981. Currently, in the UK, no other condition appears to provoke more fear or misunderstanding than HIV or AIDS (Acquired Immune Deficiency Syndrome). For children affected there is, in addition the added distress of possibly having a parent also with the virus. On average two young children are orphaned for every woman killed by AIDS.

It is very difficult to accurately assess the numbers of affected children with the virus. Currently, in the UK, approximately 600 children under fourteen years are known to have HIV and 190 children have AIDS. These children were affected by contaminated blood products used in the treatment of haemophilia before the introduction of increased safety procedures, or from blood transfusions abroad in at-risk countries.

It is impossible to assess how many children, in addition, are currently affected by HIV transmitted from their parents.

KEY POINT

In some African countries children have had whole families die from the effects of the virus.

What is the difference between HIV and AIDS?
A person who has contracted the HIV may feel completely fit and well, with no signs

of ill health. In time he may develop a particular rare illness or cancer because his immune system is weakened. When this happens he is said to have AIDS.

At risk in Britain are:

- children who have HIV positive mothers
- children of fathers who are HIV positive (often where the father has haemophilia)
- children born in certain areas of Africa and, increasingly, India
- where parental HIV status is unknown
- children who have one, or both, positive parents
- children who have an 'at risk' sibling e.g. injecting drug user.

WHAT HAPPENS

HIV can affect various parts of the body's immune or defence system. The most important is the damage to special white blood cells known as CD4 or T-helper cells. These are found in the lymphatic system – in the glands and fluids circulating around the body. These cells are designed to trigger the immune system to protect the body when pathogenic or harmful organisms enter to cause disease.

In HIV the CD4 cells mount a defence against the HIV virus, often successfully for many years, but never fully destroying it and it continues to attack the CD4 cells. Eventually the number of these CD4 cells fall and the numbers of the virus rise. This may not happen for up to ten years or longer and one in twenty people affected are thought never to become ill.

When it does happen though, the child becomes vulnerable to a variety of infections, which would not affect someone with a healthy immune system. In a depleted immune system tumours, severe diarrhoea, rare pneumonia, skin cancers, damage to many organs and other serious conditions can occur – these are described as opportunistic infections or tumours.

In addition the virus can attack the cells directly in the brain, affecting its working.

KEY POINT

When a child has one or more of these opportunistic diseases, tumours or brain disease he is said to have AIDS.

Remember, though, a person can just be 'ill' during this period. Not all opportunistic illness are part of the AIDS definition – someone may just have a simple cold or flu.

PROGRESS CHECK

What is the difference between having HIV and having AIDS?

How does infection take place?

A sufficient amount of HIV must enter the bloodstream for a child to contract HIV. The virus is significantly contained in only:

- blood
- sperm and seminal fluid
- vaginal fluids, including menstrual fluids
- breast milk.

KEY POINT

Although HIV is present in other body fluids such as saliva, sweat or urine they do not contain enough virus to cause infection.

Even if HIV is present in a person's body fluids it is still difficult for it to enter another person's body easily. In addition the virus itself is fragile and will not live outside the body. It can enter the body:
- directly into the blood stream e.g. through dirty injection needles
- organ transplant or blood transfusion, *but* remember this no longer happens in Britain
- transfer through the mucus membrane – the rectum, vagina etc.
- very rarely through the eyes, mouth or throat.

PROGRESS CHECK

Which body fluids are most likely to cause infection to children?

HIV and pregnancy

In the UK the risk of HIV being passed from a positive woman to her baby either during pregnancy or at birth is about one in seven. It is higher in areas of the world where obstetric care is limited due to poor facilities and poverty. Transmission can also occur from a positive mother to her baby during breastfeeding.

GOOD PRACTICE

Remember, HIV *cannot* be transmitted through:

- intact external skin – so cover all cuts and grazes with a waterproof dressing.
- airborne routes – so coughing, sneezing and kissing are all safe.

DIAGNOSIS

HIV is usually diagnosed by a blood test known as an HIV antibody test. The test looks for antibodies formed by the immune system if HIV is present. However there is a gap between when infection occurs and when antibodies are formed – this can last from a few weeks to three months.

KEY POINT

If antibodies are present a person is considered 'HIV positive' and although well can transmit the virus.

In babies under eighteen months maternal antibodies will still be present in the child's bloodstream so an antibody test will not tell if the baby has been infected. A test known as a Polymerase Chain Reaction (PCR) will be undertaken on babies thought to be at risk of HIV – this detects the presence of the actual virus in the blood.

- It is thought that a third of infected babies will develop AIDS before their first birthday.
- 80 per cent will show symptoms by thirty months old.
- A baby born with HIV rarely lives longer than eight years of age.

CARE

The decision about who to tell about HIV status either for themselves or their child is a major one for parents. This is often influenced by society's ignorance and fear about AIDS and HIV rather than what would be best for the child or family. If you are told a child in your care has the virus confidentiality must be respected.

Normally childcare workers will have contact only with a child with HIV; you are less likely to be caring for a child with AIDS as often specialist nursing care is required.

GOOD PRACTICE

- A clean environment with good hygiene measures should be routine in all childcare establishments. This is for the benefit of all – staff and children.
- If sensible procedures are followed parents should feel confident their children are safe.
- Consider your own policy regarding health and safety in your childcare establishment.

KEY POINT

The HIV virus is fragile and does not live outside the body, when exposed to air.

Good practice
Good practice for all, with or without HIV, means the following.
- Keeping to routine procedures for the disposal of blood and other body fluids such as:
  - all spills to be cleared up with very hot water or a bleach solution
  - use gloves so you can stand the high temperature
  - dispose of soiled napkins, vomit or urine or faeces accidents, into plastic sealed bags
  - clearly mark mops or cloths for use in mopping floors
  - dispose of cloths used to wipe up body spills.
- Keeping your own skin in good condition, cover any sores or cuts with waterproof dressings.
- No sharing of tooth brushes.
- Cleaning toys by regularly washing them, especially if sucked.

Encourage healthy habits

- Encouraging all children to develop healthy habits especially hand-washing after using the lavatory and using tissues.
- Making sure everyone knows if there are outbreaks of infection in the establishment – chicken pox and measles might be very serious for a child with a damaged immune system.
- Excluding obviously infectious children and staff.

In addition a child with the virus will need:

- love, security, stimulation and opportunities to play, develop and learn
- regular medical checks
- routine immunisations but only following discussion with medical staff involved in care ('live' virus immunisations will be avoided e.g. poliomyelitis)
- good dental care
- observation of any changes in his condition.

PROGRESS CHECK

How long may a child with HIV remain symptom-free?

Areas that might need additional consideration

Occasionally a frustrated toddler will bite another child – this really does not pose a risk as blood has to be exchanged for infection to be transmitted.

Ear piercing should always be undertaken by a reputable establishment – do not share children's earrings.

Using public swimming pools is safe – the virus cannot survive in chlorinated water.

Demonstrate that a child is not infectious by routine hand holding, kissing and cuddling as with any other child.

ONGOING MANAGEMENT

Unlike those with many other serious conditions children who are HIV positive may also have ill parents, themselves anxious and fearful for the future. Worries they have about their child are to be expected, including what will happen when they die and what care arrangements, permanent or temporary, will be needed if they become ill. This is especially difficult when a very young child is involved. Always be ready to listen and respond to his times of distress, provide plenty of activities for him to release tension or talk about his worries.

A sensitivity and awareness from you, together with a knowledge of support networks and statutory services available will be essential. Develop effective communication with all involved agencies.

Activity
Design a series of information posters, for the parents in your establishment, on how general infections are spread. Give examples of how specific illnesses may be spread; include HIV as one of your examples. Include a section on myths associated with the spread of ill health.

How can you make your posters catch and hold interest?

GENERAL IMPLICATIONS

Stigma, ignorance and fear regarding HIV and AIDS remain widespread. Parents are often reluctant to seek support from neighbours or friends and cope with the condition in secret. This particularly affects people from African and Indian communities, where the virus is prevalent. In addition they may also face racism and rejection.

For a child to be asked to keep information about HIV and AIDS secret places him under great strain and can isolate him from him peers.

Cultural factors and different child-rearing practices will all influence how parents reach major decisions about how much information to disclose. Support and advice will be available from within the caring specialist team. However, the final decisions made by the parents must be respected and supported.

Consider too, that you may have to prepare the child for possibly losing a parent, even becoming ill himself, and be ready to answer questions about death.

KEY POINT

For a child in such a situation, the security of a normal routine, in a playgroup, nursery or school will be vital – it may be the only area of stability when many changes and worries are happening in the home. Allow the child to be 'normal' – naughty, active and energetic – but always applying the same rules of managing behaviour as with any child.

ADDITIONAL DEVELOPMENTS

At present there is no cure for HIV. Medical developments are concentrated on producing a vaccine to prevent transmission of the virus. The three drugs currently used have been most effective at prolonging full and valuable life for people with the virus and research continues.

Bonnie's Poem

I do not like having HIV
Because sometimes it stings me like a bee.

I do not like it being a secret
But I promised I would keep it.

When I play I want to say I have HIV
But no – it's a secret
And I keep it to myself.

Bonnie died of AIDS at twelve years old, infected after her mother was given a contaminated blood transfusion during her pregnancy. Bonnie's poem appears to show that keeping the secret, for Bonnie, was almost as stressful as being HIV positive.

The poem is printed with the kind permission of Bonnie's brother Joshua Handel.

RESOURCES

Children with AIDS Charity (CWAC)
2nd Floor
111 High Holborn
London WC1V 6JS

Terrence Higgins Trust
52–54 Gray's Inn Road
London WC1X 8JU

The coeliac condition

This condition has been known under a variety of names for centuries and until the mid-1950s was thought to affect only children. It is now known to occur in both adults and children, happening at any age and affecting one in 1,100 to 1,500 people.

The condition produces a sensitivity to gluten – a protein found in wheat and rye and a similar reaction to substances in barley and possibly oats. This means foods such as bread, rolls, buns, biscuits, pastry and pasta must be excluded permanently from the diet.

The coeliac condition can 'run' in families although a genetic pattern has not yet been identified. It cannot be cured and is lifelong, but it is effectively controlled by a special diet.

WHAT HAPPENS

Gluten, a protein found in certain cereals, damages the lining of the small intestine, so reducing the amount of gut available to absorb nutrients. The signs do not become obvious until gluten has been introduced to a child's diet – usually at the time of weaning at four to six months. Up until that time the child is thriving, alert and interested. Then he:

■ begins to refuse food
■ fails to gain weight
■ is lethargic, irritable and listless

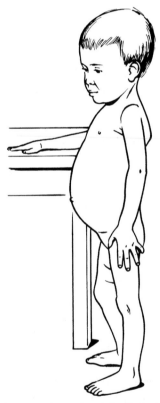

A child with the coeliac condition is typically lethargic with a distended stomach and wasted buttocks

- passes abnormal stools that are usually large, pale and offensive or loose and diarrhoea-like
- may vomit
- begins to have increased body-wasting, especially the buttocks, and his stomach protrudes
- has severe illness and dehydration may appear.

In the older child the following may also appear:
- poor appetite
- anaemia – pallor, breathlessness and tiredness
- growth failure
- colicky stomach pains.

DIAGNOSIS

A simple test, not requiring admission to hospital, is undertaken. Under sedation a biopsy capsule is passed through the mouth, with X-ray control, into the upper part of the small intestine and a biopsy sample is taken.

The cells will appear abnormal. A second biopsy may be taken later to confirm the diagnosis and if the results are positive then a gluten-free diet for life is recommended.

CARE

The basis of care is to remove all gluten-containing food from the diet for life. After diagnosis the following may also be recommended for a few months.
- A diet with a reduced fat intake, to allow 'healing' of the gut.
- Extra vitamin D, folic acid and iron.
- Occasionally, sugars are limited as they can stimulate diarrhoea.

KEY POINT

These three measures are usually only advised for a short period.

In a young baby choosing gluten-free baby foods is simple, all commercial products are clearly identified. A benefit to introducing this diet early is that a baby will develop tastes for foods that will not damage his health, rather than have to change formed eating patterns later in life.

When following the diet, a baby with coeliac condition will have gradually improved health, growth and weight. Usually by a year, he will no longer have the offensive and bulky stools, have gained weight and will be thriving. There will be no return to the signs of the condition if the diet is maintained.

How do families avoid foods with gluten and also possibly, barley and oats?
The Coeliac Society produces a regular list of foods that contain gluten and so must be avoided – this list should be taken on every shopping trip as products frequently have their ingredients changed.

Gluten-free flours, breads and cakes can be obtained, often on prescription from the family doctor and traditional recipes can be easily adapted with a little practice. Many foods readily available are in fact gluten-free.

KEY POINTS

Most plainly prepared natural foods, apart from wheat, rye, barley and oats, can be eaten.

Plainly prepared natural foods that can be eaten include the following.
- Gluten-free flour, potato, rice and soya flours and arrowroot.
- Sago, tapioca, maize, buckwheat and rices.
- Butter, fats and oils, eggs, milks, cheeses (unprocessed) and natural yoghurt.
- 'Pure' herbs.
- Pure fruit and vegetable juices, raw or frozen fruits and vegetables.
- Meat, poultry and fish – care is needed only with products involving processing, stuffing and coatings.
- Nuts.

In addition many other foods can be included but their contents must be checked on the packaging against the Society's list.

KEY POINTS

- Foods containing the following ingredients are unacceptable: cereal binders, starch, food starch, edible starch, modified starch, rusk, stabilisers, cereal fillers and cereal protein.
- Remember too that flour is an ingredient in many tinned and processed foods as well as in ready-prepared meals.

The pre-school child
Useful ways of managing the child's diet within the family can include the following.
- Removing all flour from family cooking – gluten-free alternatives may be included if wished.
- Offering the same food to all the family and visitors.
- Accepting invitations out, but let the child take his own 'gluten-free' biscuits with him if he wishes.
- Do not blame every minor stomach upset onto the child's 'condition'.
- Clearly explain to all involved in the child's care what he can have.
- Always tell the child why certain foods are not allowed and link your explanations to his remaining healthy – be matter-of-fact.
- Do not discuss the child's symptoms or his diet routinely before him – he must learn to accept it as an integral part of his life.

It is often easier for a whole family to follow a gluten-free diet rather than isolate a child from sharing family foods as a gluten-free diet is essentially a healthy diet for all.

PROGRESS CHECK

What are the physical and emotional advantages of cooking gluten-free food meals for all the family rather than producing special foods for the child with coeliac condition?

'Are the ingredients gluten-free?'

KEY POINT

Many children are also not offered foods that are harmful to a child with coeliac condition, for example biscuits, ice creams and carbonated drinks. This helpful practice has the benefit of reducing the isolation of the child with the coeliac condition from his peers.

ONGOING MANAGEMENT

A child who is diagnosed with the condition as a baby will have considerable knowledge of his own diet by the time he needs school dinners. He should be empowered to control his own diet and support must be given to allow this.

All involved in his care, including dinner supervisors as well as teaching and care staff, will need to know what is acceptable.

It is always preferable for a child to be the same as his peers, so if they all take packed lunches that will be fine for him, but if school dinners are the norm then he should not be excluded because of his dietary needs. Some authorities cope better than others with special diets, but it must be emphasised that a child with this condition will be healthy, fit and active providing he adheres to the gluten-free diet. He will have no external signs of his condition.

Special awareness will be needed for:

- parties
- school trips and outings
- changes of staffing at dinner times
- when the child is is unwell. He may show signs of intolerance, by fatty stools or diarrhoea but this does not mean necessarily he has been given gluten.

GOOD PRACTICE

If he inadvertently takes gluten he may have diarrhoea or stool abnormalities – this may happen within twenty-four hours or up to two or three weeks. No long-term harm occurs, providing the incident is an isolated one.

Activity
Plan a cake baking session for a group of five-year-olds. Identify all your usual learning outcomes for a cookery activity. Ensure your recipe is gluten-free – what 'flour' could you use instead? Research any changes needed to the method for the cake to rise successfully.

Take a group of children with you to buy the ingredients. Look for the contents of the packages in your supermarket visit – how easy did you find it to discover if gluten was included?

GENERAL IMPLICATIONS

A matter-of-fact approach to the coeliac condition is helpful, coupled with an awareness that the condition is for life.

ADDITIONAL DEVELOPMENTS

Gluten content is usually clearly identified on packaging. In the recent past the symbol 'the crossed grain' has been used to indicate a product is gluten-free; this however has now been withdrawn.

CASE STUDY

Conor was a four-year-old boy, the middle child with an older sister and younger toddler brother.

He had always been more demanding than his siblings and was noted to be sickly. He often had periods of stomach upsets and this was the reason his parents gave for his poor appetite, slimness and short stature.

After he started at playgroup he began to have more frequent bouts of diarrhoea, his stools became offensive and he also developed sore buttocks. An infection going around the nursery was blamed. However Conor continued to appear 'off colour' and eventually the family doctor decided he needed further investigation. A biopsy was taken from his intestine and coeliac condition was clearly identified. He started a gluten-free diet immediately.

Several months later Conor had gained weight, his stools were normal and he was much more outgoing and relaxed. He still remained short in comparison to his peers, but as both his parents are also small this was thought to be related more to their stature, than his coeliac condition.

1 Why do you think discovery of the condition took so long?
2 What other common illnesses may the coeliac condition be confused with?
3 How will Conor's height and weight be measured to monitor his progress?

RESOURCES

The Coeliac Society
PO Box 220
High Wycombe
Bucks HP11 2HY

KEY TERMS

You need to know what these words and phrases mean. Go back through the chapter and make sure that you understand:

'absences'
AIDS and the transmission of
   the virus
asthma
atopic
coeliac condition and gluten
   intolerance
diabetes
epilepsy

eczema
gluten
HIV
hypoglycaemia and hyperglycaemia
preventers and relievers
spacers and inhalers
tonic/clonic seizures
trigger factors

---

7 CONDITIONS WHICH DISCRIMINATE

In this chapter we look at certain physical conditions which discriminate, that is they only affect specific types of children, for example certain sexes or racial groups. These conditions are genetically transferred – inherited by a child from his or her family – and are caused by faults in specific genes.

Sickle cell and thalassaemia conditions

These are the names given to a group of lifelong blood disorders that affect specific racial groups.

Sickle cell

This is a genetically inherited condition, commonly found in people of Afro-Caribbean (i.e. African or West Indian) descent. It also occurs in people from the Eastern Mediterranean, the Middle East, India and Pakistan.

Sickle cell is a lifelong condition affecting children from birth. It is thought that one in 500 live births worldwide will have sickle cell condition. Currently there is no cure.

The sickle cell condition is a term given to a group of blood disorders in which abnormal haemoglobin is produced. Haemoglobin is a special protein found in the red blood cells and is responsible for carrying oxygen around the body. Sickle haemoglobin is one of a number of types of haemoglobin. Under certain conditions called 'crisis' the red blood cells in the body change shape. Children with sickle cell condition have low haemoglobin levels because the red blood cells do not last as long as normal blood cells.

WHAT HAPPENS

The sickle cell condition can affect children in two main ways: they may have the sickle cell trait which means that they are carriers, but healthy, or they may have the condition of sickle cell anaemia.

Sickle cell trait

Genes come in pairs. Each characteristic will have a gene from both mother and father e.g. colour of hair and physical features. One of these pairs of genes determines haemoglobin – sickle cell trait means that one haemoglobin gene from one parent carries the sickle cell gene which is HB AS (see page 212).

If a child has the trait it means that she is a healthy carrier and will never develop the condition.

However, it may have implications for her own children. If her partner does not have the trait then all her children will never have the condition. One in ten Afro-Caribbeans have sickle cell trait which means although perfectly healthy they are carriers of the condition.

Sickle cell condition

If two carriers have a child, there is a one in four chance that the child will have sickle cell anaemia.

A baby initially appears fit and well with no apparent problems often until four to six months of age. The baby then shows signs of being anaemic:

- lacks energy
- is listless
- has poor circulation to hands and feet
- is vulnerable to minor infections such as coughs and colds.

DIAGNOSIS

Prenatal diagnosis is available if both partners are carriers. Sickle cell condition is easily detected at birth by examining a sample of the umbilical cord blood. This allows important preventive measures to start early. These can limit the triggers which promote crisis.

A crisis causes:

- pain
- possible damage to vital organs.

Children in the steady state (between crises) are anaemic due to rapid destruction of the red blood cells, but not from lack of iron. Iron tablets are not recommended and may in fact be harmful. Occasionally the anaemia can deteriorate rapidly and then urgent blood transfusion may be required.

Sometimes parents find it difficult to accept their baby has a life threatening condition when the baby appears so well.

CARE

Sickle cell is characterised by crises in the condition. These happen when the abnormal haemoglobin changes shape from the usual round one to that of a sickled or crescent moon. The cells become rigid and 'sickling' – clumping together. These sickled cells then get stuck in the small blood vessels, often blocking the blood supply to tissues. This can happen anywhere in the body causing severe pain and often slight fever and damaging the affected area. The severe pain associated

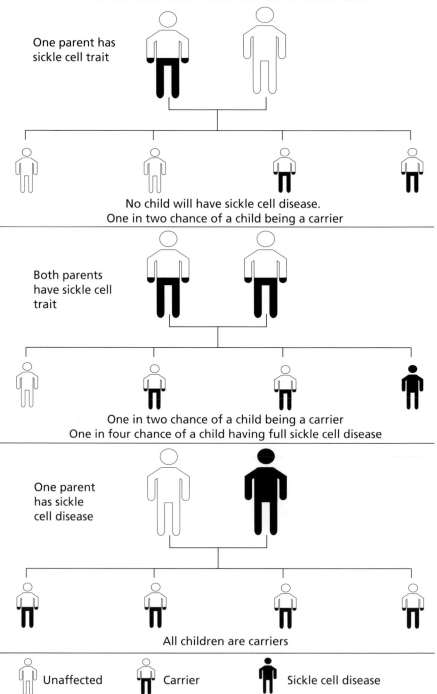

SICKLE CELL TRAIT - HOW INHERITANCE IS PASSED

One parent has
sickle cell trait

No child will have sickle cell disease.
One in two chance of a child being a carrier

Both parents
have sickle cell
trait

One in two chance of a child being a carrier
One in four chance of a child having full sickle cell disease

One parent
has sickle
cell disease

All children are carriers

Unaffected   Carrier   Sickle cell disease

NOTE: In each of these examples these chances happen with <u>every</u> pregnancy with crises is frequently in the limbs, back and abdomen. Sometimes these crises happen often and sometimes only once in several years.

What can trigger a crisis?
- Infection from minor coughs and colds, to common childhood infections such as measles, chicken pox, etc.
- Dehydration (lack of fluid) such as inadequate fluids in sudden heatwaves.
- Extremes of cold such as cold swimming pools, unheated classrooms and bed-rooms.
- Stress or distress such as staring a new school, divorce in the family or worries over academic success.
- Strenuous physical exercises: even normal school games or energetic games with peers.
- No obvious cause.

Strenuous activity may trigger a crisis

KEY POINT

In a crisis pain during these times can be exceptionally severe.

GOOD PRACTICE

While waiting for medical advice the following may be helpful:
- Support painful limbs and position carefully.
- Local heat or massage may be comforting.

- Give medication if prescribed.
- Songs and stories may give useful distraction.

Children in crisis are initially treated in hospital with oxygen, fluids, blood transfusions, painkillers and often antibiotics.

ONGOING MANAGEMENT

- Maintain good health with freedom from as many infections as possible.
- Protect by routine courses of immunisation.
- Provide a balanced diet, love, security, stimulation and association as with any child.
- Check that you are using positive images of children from a variety of backgrounds in your displays and educational material.
- Assess the cleanliness of your environment (see cystic fibrosis page 223 and follow the progress check).
- Consider that children will need frequent drinks and as a result may need more changes of nappies or visits to the toilet.
- Check the skin remains in good condition.
- If the child is older and involved in school visits liaison with the parents/carers over sensitive management of enuresis is helpful. Stigma over bedwetting can affect peer relationships and make a child reluctant to sleep away from home.
- Strenuous sports and playtimes in wet or cold playgrounds are best avoided.

GOOD PRACTICE

- Check all staff are aware of the potentially serious nature of the condition and sensitive to the particular anxieties of the parents.
- As the condition affects the blood ensure everyone is aware the condition is not infectious and cannot be transmitted.
- Ensure your knowledge of sickle cell is accurate and current.
- Can you answer children's questions honestly, with knowledge and in accordance with parental wishes?
- Maintain good liaison with all the care team including parents/carers.

KEY POINT

If a child has only rare crises then normal play, schooling and peer relationships should not be affected.

A child who is more seriously ill, however, may feel isolated, especially if there is no other child with the condition in her family or school. She may feel frightened, especially as she grows and becomes more aware that severe complications and possible early death may occur. Previous experiences of severe pain are not easily forgotten and can affect a child's confidence. Frequent absences from school or playgroup may affect developing relationships or academic progress, possibly leading to low self-esteem.

Staff can help by listening, understanding, acknowledging fears and by developing positive relationships with parents.

PROGRESS CHECK

1 What playgroup or school situations might trigger a crisis?
2 What signs tell you a child is having a crisis?
3 Do you have emergency telephone contact numbers readily available?
4 Are these telephone contact numbers updated regularly?

Activity
For children often away from school involve your infant class in making a Class Diary to keep absent friends involved. This can be given or sent to the child in hospital and could provide a useful link to limit feelings of isolation. Include drawings, examples of work, personal messages, tapes and photographs.

GENERAL IMPLICATIONS

Additional health complications
Children with the condition are especially vulnerable to the following illnesses.

- Infections, especially severe ones such as meningitis and pneumonia.
- Strokes (clots in the brain that can deprive vital areas of the brain of blood). About 6 to 9 per cent of young children are at risk of sickling episodes that can result in transient or permanent strokes. Signs of these are weakness in limbs, slurred speech and severe headaches. They are a major cause of disability.
- Enuresis (bedwetting). Delay in gaining bladder control at night is common mainly due to the delay in the ability of the kidney to concentrate large quantities of dilute urine.
- Jaundice – yellowing in the whites of the eyes. This is not infectious.

KEY POINTS

- Various counselling agencies are being developed in areas with high incidence of sickle cell. They offer information advice and support by post and in person. These information sources are especially important when sickle cell affects a child in an area where it has previously been uncommon.
- Remember, too, that more than one child in a family may be affected.

ADDITIONAL DEVELOPMENTS

Scientists in several centres in the world, are currently working on eventually preventing or treating sickle cell. Experimental developments at present include attempting the correction or gene repair of the sickle cell taken from a patient with the condition and the use of bone marrow transplants.

Thalassaemia

This is a general term for a number of inherited blood disorders in which there is insufficient haemoglobin. Specific racial groups at risk are children from southern Mediterranean countries and the Middle East. Occasionally children from Asia and Africa are affected but rarely those from Northern European parentage. As with sickle cell this is a genetic condition, passed from parent to child. It cannot be contracted in other ways.

WHAT HAPPENS

Thalassaemia trait
Children carrying the trait are normally healthy but may have mild anaemia shown by occasional tiredness, breathlessness and pallor. Their life is not shortened.

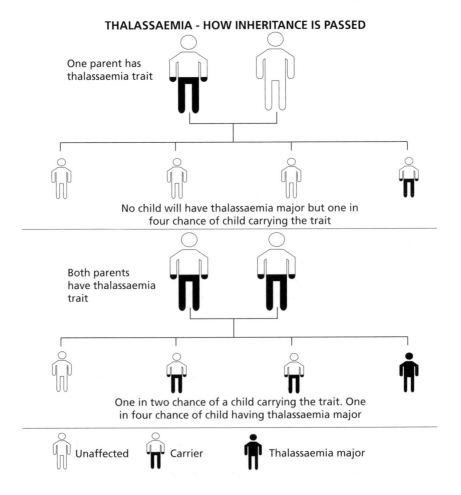

THALASSAEMIA - HOW INHERITANCE IS PASSED

One parent has thalassaemia trait

No child will have thalassaemia major but one in four chance of child carrying the trait

Both parents have thalassaemia trait

One in two chance of a child carrying the trait. One in four chance of child having thalassaemia major

Unaffected   Carrier   Thalassaemia major

Thalassaemia major

In thalassaemia major a child appears well at birth but within months becomes pale and irritable, has a poor appetite and fails to thrive. There is no cure for the condition and without treatment a child would die in infancy.

DIAGNOSIS

As with sickle cell, diagnosis of thalassaemia major can be made prenatally or after birth by simple blood tests.

CARE

Symptoms are controlled by regular blood transfusions. However, as a result of these, too many iron-rich red blood cells can accumulate in the body with possible damage to vital organs like the heart and liver. Regular, often daily drugs, given by injections under the skin, are essential to help reduce this. Children are usually given these drugs at night via a portable pump attached to a needle. This allows the treatment to be given over many hours. This treatment can be unpleasant and difficult for a child to live with. Unfortunately without such treatment a child would die in infancy and so it must be maintained and continued for life. Support for parents and the child may be available, if requested, from one of the specialist counselling agencies.

ONGOING MANAGEMENT

With effective treatment a child can attend and thrive in any childcare setting from playgroup to mainstream school. Check, however, if a child is tired and needs extra rest during a busy school or playgroup session.

GENERAL IMPLICATIONS

In sickle cell and thalassaemia the conditions can be passed on to future generations from carriers who are well in themselves. Genetic counselling regarding the risk for future pregnancies is usually offered.

Points to consider
- Why do you think both sickle cell and thalassaemia, which are genetically passed blood disorders, are relatively poorly understood by the population?
- How can knowledge of these conditions be increased?

CASE STUDY

Jerome was a six-month-old baby brought to England, on holiday, from Jamaica by his mother, to meet his aunts and uncles. The weather was cold and Jerome appeared generally off-colour, unhappy and with a runny nose. He deteriorated and became inconsolable, screaming and crying. His hands and feet became inflamed.

His mother took him to the local hospital and he was admitted for investigation and tests. He was fed by a 'drip' and sedated. His mother was told that he was having a sickle cell crisis. She was unaware that he had the condition and was greatly upset as one of her brothers had died of the condition a few years previously. She was referred for genetic counselling and support.

1 Would Jerome be better returning with his mother to Jamaica, if so why?
2 What special precautions should his mother take during the next few years with his physical health?

RESOURCES

Sickle Cell Society
54 Station Road
London NW10 4UA

UK Thalassaemia Society
107 Nightingale Lane
London N8 7QY

Cystic fibrosis

Cystic fibrosis is a genetically inherited condition affecting two main body systems – the lungs and the digestion. Until about fifty years ago affected children usually died in the first years of life from pneumonia. The condition is now recognised and since the discovery of antibiotics children live longer.

It cannot be cured but the symptoms and their associated damage to vital organs can be limited. Cystic fibrosis must be considered a life-threatening condition.

It is passed from parent to child and affects about one in every 2,000 live births. Approximately one in twenty of Northern Europeans has one of the abnormal genes. This gene is responsible for making secretions in different parts of the body and in cystic fibrosis produces secretions which are much thicker and stickier than usual, containing a high proportion of salt.

People with the abnormal gene are healthy but are 'carriers' of the condition. A child will be affected only if both parents have the carrier gene.

WHAT HAPPENS

Although any organ can be affected by the thicker secretions produced by the abnormal gene the most likely to be affected are the respiratory and digestive systems.

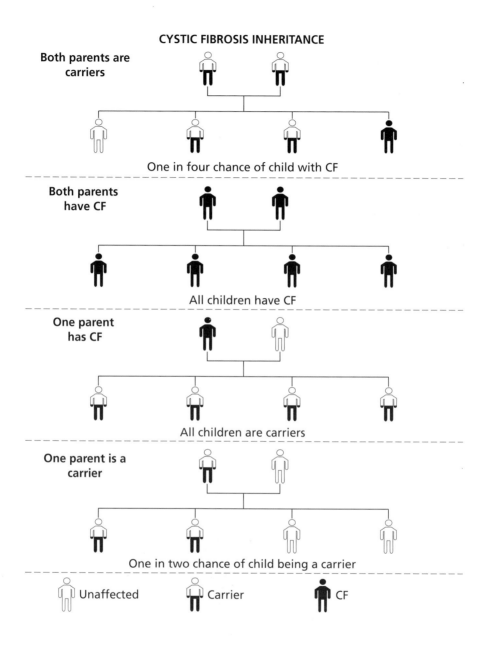

CYSTIC FIBROSIS INHERITANCE

Both parents are carriers

One in four chance of child with CF

Both parents have CF

All children have CF

One parent has CF

All children are carriers

One parent is a carrier

One in two chance of child being a carrier

Unaffected   Carrier   CF

Respiratory system

Damage to the lungs is the most serious worry. The sticky mucus the condition produces is difficult to move to the top of the lungs where, usually, it would be coughed up or swallowed. As a result bacteria build up in the smaller airways, making the lungs liable to infection. The linings of the airways become swollen, and produce more mucus to try and get rid of the increased bacteria.

KEY POINT

Repeated infections can cause scarring of the lungs.

Digestive system

The pancreas, the organ which produces insulin and digestive juices, is affected. In cystic fibrosis the digestive juices are thick and can block the duct system where the juices are secreted into the intestines (see the diagram on page 188)

Sometimes this effect takes several months to become apparent. The lack of digestive juices inhibits a child's ability to use her food, especially fats and to a lesser extent protein. These nutrients are lost and excreted in the stools.

Meconium ileus

In about 10 per cent of children with cystic fibrosis the baby is born with a meconium ileus. Here the duct from the pancreas is already blocked and the baby has a severe obstruction. She is unable to pass her meconium or first stool. This must be cleared to allow the baby to feed and excrete normally.

DIAGNOSIS

It is not always obvious that a baby has the condition. If she has a meconium ileus this is a dramatic and obvious sign of something seriously amiss.

Other signs in the young baby can occur.

- The mother notices her baby's skin tastes salty when kissed.
- The baby coughs and wheezes.
- The baby fails to gain weight, even though she eats well, in sufficient amounts and appears hungry.
- The baby's stools are bulky, passed often and unpleasantly smelly – this may result in a sore napkin area.
- The baby often vomits when coughing.

Sometimes very few signs are evident and a child may just have a cough and fail to gain weight during her first year.

Confirmation that a child has the condition is made by a 'sweat test' at the hospital. She will also have a chest X-ray to assess if any lung damage has occurred.

Recent developments have shown that the abnormal gene can be identified during pregnancy.

KEY POINT

Early diagnosis is important in order that treatment can start immediately to limit the damage to important organs, especially the lungs.

CARE

The prime aims of management are threefold:

- maintenance of nutrition

- prevention and control of lung infections
- physiotherapy and exercises to keep the airways clear.

Nutrition

Even though a child may be eating well her body will be unable to use the food without replacing the pancreatic enzymes. The enzyme is given usually, approximately fifteen minutes before every meal. This replacement has to be continued for life. If not, the child will lose weight, fail to grow and be vulnerable to increased and possibly dangerous, lung infections.

- The diet itself will be high in calories – it is estimated that the child will need a minimum of 20 per cent extra calories than her peers and possibly as much as 100 per cent more.
- The child will require at least three meals daily with two extra snacks.
- The diet will be devised by the paediatric dietician and the paediatrician in conjunction with the parents, carers and the child herself when older.
- The balance between pancreatic replacement and the calorie intake is important.
- Even with enzyme replacement food absorption is not perfect and so the quality of the diet will be important. The child cannot afford to fill up regularly on junk foods or foods with only limited nutritional content. This would leave no room for important body building nutrients such as proteins. The child needs stores of body fat as an insurance policy for when she may have infections and lose appetite and suffer temporary weight loss.
- Usually the child will be given vitamin A, D, E and K replacements to compensate for those lost because of her difficulty in absorbing fat.
- Fat as part of the child's diet is limited only if she continues to have trouble in digestion. This is shown by continuing, bulky, greasy stools, abdominal pain and failure to gain expected weight.

Diet management for particular developmental stages

Babies
- Although breast milk is the ideal milk for babies, in cystic fibrosis it is important that feeds are frequent.
- Small amounts of pancreatic enzyme will be needed.
- If babies are artificially fed, a modified milk higher in energy and protein than the usual formula milks is recommended for up to one year of age.

GOOD PRACTICE

Never mix medicine into a baby's bottle as you may find the baby rejects her milk. If this happened you would not be able to tell how much medicine had been taken.

Weaning
- A baby with cystic fibrosis may be especially hungry and often will need solids from three months.

- The usual weaning practice is followed, with the pancreatic enzyme increasing with the food.

The toddler

The normal food refusal that can occur at this age may make meal times testing for parents and carers. Pancreatic enzymes can be unpalatable and will need to be mixed with an acceptable food such as teaspoons of apple purée or yoghurt – whatever the child prefers.

Food fads normally resolve of their own accord if calmly managed – never withhold food if something is refused. Offer an acceptable 'nutritious' alternative.

School children

Eating away from home means the child is controlling her own diet. All carers need to know:
- the child's special nutritional needs
- the child's need to take enzyme replacement at every meal
- where her medicines will be stored and that there are sufficient supplies
- if the daily snacks – which the child will need – can take place in the classroom
- how her dietary choice and intake will be monitored
- extra food will be needed if the child is involved in physical activity
- extra salt will be necessary in very hot weather or after strenuous activity.

GOOD PRACTICE

A child may feel embarrassed at needing medication at every meal – she may feel the need to be the same as her peers. Try to ensure she has privacy.

PROGRESS CHECK

Why does a child with cystic fibrosis need extra calories?

Prevention and control of lung infection

The main aim is to keep the lungs as free from damage by infection as possible. This is important in extending both life and its quality.

Often children are maintained on continuing antibiotic medicine. Any new infection needs prompt attention. Some children are given medication via a nebuliser or spacer (see page 174). Develop your own observation skills in watching for changes in the child's condition.

You should try to maintain a clean environment by:
- providing good ventilation in the prevention of airborne infections
- the disposal of tissues into covered bins
- encouraging hand-washing after using tissues
- encouraging covering noses and mouths when sneezing – adults and children!
- trying to stop contact with adults and children who have coughs and colds but without becoming over-protective
- keeping the environment from becoming overcrowded

- ensuring everyone involved with the child with cystic fibrosis, including parents and all carers, have current immunisations
- maintaining good levels of general hygiene
- informing parents and carers when there are outbreaks of infections.

PROGRESS CHECK

1 How can you protect a child, vulnerable to infection, without smothering her?
2 How clean is your childcare environment?
3 How free from infection are the staff?
4 Are all staff protected from transmitting infections, by available immunisation?
5 How effective is the prevention of infection routine in your workplace?
6 How often do you reassess your health practice?
7 Have the staff received recent training?

Physiotherapy and exercises to keep the lungs clear
Even if a child appears symptom-free the importance of measures to help clear her lungs remains vital. These measures are essential in helping to keep the lungs clear and expanded. In children the following methods will be used.
1 Drainage – positioning a child to clear different areas of the lungs.
2 Chest clapping – a cupped hand is used to clap the chest firmly.
3 Chest shaking – place your hands on the chest, tell the child to breathe out and firmly shake the chest, squeezing the air out in short bursts and applying the pressure inwards.
4 Breathing exercises.

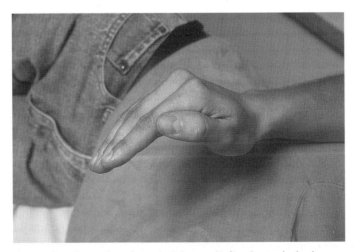

Chest clapping: the chest is 'clapped' firmly to help loosen secretions and encourage the child to cough. Note the cupped position of the hand for chest clapping

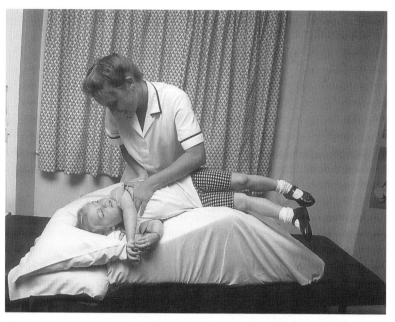

Chest shaking: *while the child breathes out the chest is shaken – pressing and squeezing the air out – so coughing is stimulated and secretions brought up. Note the child is tilted to help drainage*

How often and how long should physiotherapy take place?

- Length: this will vary depending on the number and type of secretions a child is producing at any time but will range from 10–15 minutes to 45–60 minutes.
- Number of sessions: usually two per day when she is well to three or four during times of infections.
- Changes to the above: the carer involved in the treatments will learn by experience the need to change the types and amounts of treatment, by looking, feeling the chest and asking the older child.

KEY POINT

Nursery nurses involved in caring for a child with cystic fibrosis will need to learn these treatment techniques from the physiotherapist involved in the child's care.

Physiotherapy for a baby

It is often easier to develop treatment routines with babies as a mother and child inevitably spend much time together. Usually the baby will enjoy the physical contact involved.

All areas of the lungs will need to be cleared.

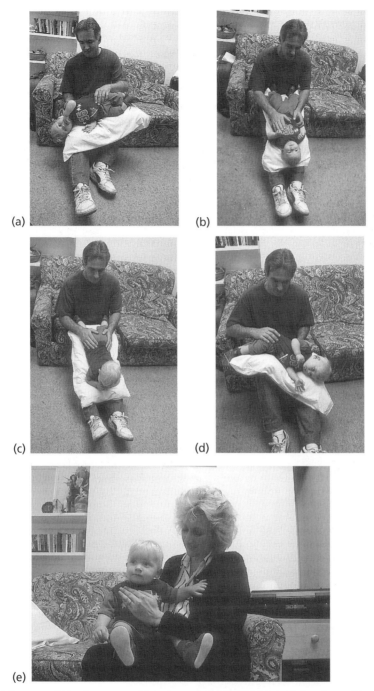

All areas of the lungs must be cleared. (a) Right lower lobe, lateral basal segment. (b) Lower lobes, anterior basal segments. (c) Lower lobes, posterior basal segments. (d) Left lower lobe, lateral basal segment. (e) Treatment in sitting for apical segment of upper lobes.

- Treatments take place before or well after a feed as the baby may vomit.
- Check the baby is comfortably dressed.
- Use your knee covered by a pillow for the baby to lie over – she will be comfortable and her head fully supported.
- When clearing the chest by clapping, allow pauses for her to cough and breathe quietly.
- If you are successful she will cough her secretions into the back of her throat – it does not matter if she swallows them.
- Hold young babies who are unable to sit unaided to clear the upper lobes.

KEY POINT

A moist steamy atmosphere will help the baby clear her secretions – the bathroom may be useful on occasions.

Physiotherapy for toddlers and young children

- When a child is too large to be comfortably placed over the knee, treatment will need to take place over a foam wedge.
- From about two years encourage the child to become more involved in her treatment by introducing breathing exercises such as blowing games with bubbles and steaming mirrors, etc.
- Encourage physical exercise – trampolining is both fun and effective.

Trampolining, huffing and puffing to steam up a mirror and blowing through a cardbord tube are fun ways to help control breathing and clear the chest

Physiotherapy for the young school child

All the above treatments will continue, but the child will increasingly develop an awareness of her own breathing and how to extend her lung capacity. She will be an active participant in treatment.

GOOD PRACTICE

From about five years encourage the child to spit her secretions out, because:
- the mucus can be observed and indicate infection, changes in stickiness, etc.
- swallowing mucus can increase nausea and affect appetite
- it develops good habits.

Breathing exercises

These are an important aspect of managing cystic fibrosis, but they must be taught initially by the physiotherapist. They aim to help the child control her breathing, expand as much of her chest as possible and move secretions. Your role is to encourage and remind.

ONGOING MANAGEMENT

As with other conditions requiring medical supervision, pre-planning before a child starts attending any childcare and education setting will help smooth admission and promote easy transfer. All staff need to be aware of the following.
- The severity of the condition – update your own knowledge.
- The importance of the diet and medicine (see page 221).
- Reminders that the cough is not infectious.
- Time and space for physiotherapy – check who will undertake the treatments.
- The need for good liaison with the school health service.

Parents and carers may find separating from their child especially difficult, worrying that she may contract additional infections.

KEY POINTS

- The child should be offered full involvement in all activities, let her make her own decisions about how many strenuous games and other activities she can manage.
- Generally how much participation she can manage will depend on the severity of her condition at any one time.
- The child needs to make friends and develop relationships. It is important too for her to have success in the areas where she can compete equally with her peers, such as in music and creative activities.

Activity
Create a themed interest table on the topic of everyday sounds and noises. Encourage all the children to participate.

- Always be aware and ready to intervene if a child is teased or picked on. This may be because of her coughing or expectorating, her possible underweight and need for regular medicines.
- She may be away from school with infections. You can help by ensuring she is helped to make up work missed and that she is told of classroom or playgroup developments. Keep a Class Diary as for the child with sickle cell anaemia (see page 215).

KEY POINT

It may be hard for parents and carers to let a child with cystic fibrosis take the normal rough and tumble of a school or playgroup. This is especially so if the child has spent much time in hospital. Both child and parent can lose confidence as a result. You can help by a sensitive and understanding approach.

PROGRESS CHECK

1 What are the two main systems affected in cystic fibrosis?
2 In which system is it more important to prevent damage?
3 Which factors associated with this condition, do you consider might affect a child's body image?

GENERAL IMPLICATIONS

Increasingly more and more children with cystic fibrosis are living full and active lives and reaching adulthood. Sterility in males, however, will occur.

For a childcare worker maintaining the balance of a sensitive approach by demonstrating understanding without over-protecting will help the child take full advantage of the learning opportunities available.

ADDITIONAL DEVELOPMENTS

For some children heart and lung transplants are increasingly being used in treatment for prolonging life. However the condition is not cured by this treatment as the new lungs will continue to be attacked by thick sticky mucus. Also, the availability of suitable donors means not all children can be offered the treatment.

Scientists are researching at present how to replace the abnormal cystic fibrosis gene.

CASE STUDY

Kirsty was diagnosed immediately following her birth as having cystic fibrosis. She was living in an area where all newborn babies are routinely tested for the condition. As a result she was carefully monitored during her first year to prevent chest infections. She coped well and even enjoyed her chest 'clapping' and physiotherapy and kept healthy. She began attending and enjoying a local playgroup at three years.

She developed a faddiness with her food, causing anxiety to her mother. She would only take her enzyme supplement with strawberry yoghurt and seemed to want to eat a diet of only baked beans on toast and yoghurt.

1 Which nutrients, if any, was Kirsty missing in her diet?
2 How would you manage Kirsty's diet?

RESOURCES

The Cystic Fibrosis Trust
Alexandra House
5 Blyth Road
Bromley
Kent BR1 3RS

Haemophilia

This is a general term used to describe a group of inherited blood disorders in which there is a lifelong defect in the clotting mechanism of the blood. Approximately one in 10,000 men and boys have haemophilia. It affects all racial backgrounds. Although haemophilia is hereditary, up to a third of all occurrences appear in families with no previous history of the disorder.

WHAT HAPPENS

A child with haemophilia does not bleed more heavily or faster, but bleeds for a longer time. If untreated, bleeding will cause pain and swelling and permanent damage can occur in the area where it is happening, especially the joints. Haemophilia is termed a sex-linked recessive condition. This means that only males have the condition, except in very rare situations, but it is passed through the female line in the family.

DIAGNOSIS

For normal blood clotting a group of agents called factors are involved. The factors all work together to cause a chain reaction and if a factor does not work the chain reaction cannot take place. In haemophilia there are potentially two factors that might be faulty or missing.
■ In haemophilia A factor 8 is missing.
■ In haemophilia B (also known as Christmas disease) factor 9 is missing.
Haemophilia A is five times more common than haemophilia B.

The symptoms and inheritance patterns are the same for both types but the medical treatment is different.

HOW HAEMOPHILIA IS INHERITED

Genetic instructions are carried on 46 chromosomes inherited from the mother and father. Two of these decide sex : females have two X chromosomes (XX) and males an X and a Y chromosome (XY).

One chromosome from each parent decides a child's sex.

A normal X chromosome carries the instruction to produce active Factor 8 and 9. If the mother is a haemophilia carrier the defective X chromosome carries no such information.

REMEMBER: the normal Y (male) chromosome has no factor 8 or 9 instruction on it, so if a carrier's defective X chromosome is linked with the father's Y the son will have haemophilia.

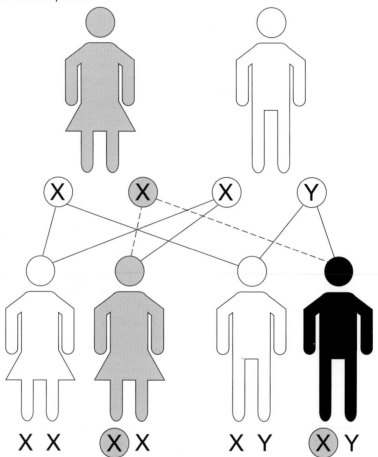

Here the mother is a carrier of the defective X chromosome. This is linked with the father's Y and the son has haemophilia.

Here too the mother has passed her defective X chromosome to her daughter who will also be a carrier.

NOTE: when the mother is a carrier and the father unaffected, there is a 50% chance for *each child* that a daughter will be a carrier and a son will have haemophilia.

CARRIERS OF HAEMOPHILIA

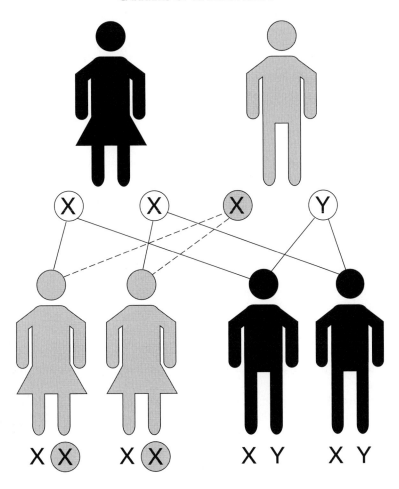

When the father has haemophilia and the mother is not a carrier each daughter *must* inherit the defective X chromosome and will be a carrier.
All sons will be normal because they inherit their father's Y chromosome.
They cannot pass haemophilia on to their children.

What is the range of severity to those affected?

- 1 per cent of haemophiliacs have severe haemophilia where there is frequent bleeding into joints, muscles and tissues. No injury is necessary to set off bleeding.
- From 2 to 5 per cent of haemophiliacs have moderate haemophilia where bleeding is usually related to some injury such as a knock or deep cut.
- From 6 to 25 per cent of haemophiliacs have mild haemophilia where bleeding problems are associated only with tooth extractions, surgery or a severe accident.
- Over 25 per cent of haemophiliacs have a normal range of bleeding for which treatment is rarely required.

CARE

Both types of haemophilia are treated by replacing the missing clotting factor, which is now made in the laboratory. Clotting factors are large molecules and cannot be given by tablets or by injections under the skin. They have to be given into a vein by a nurse or doctor, either as first aid to encourage blood clotting following a bleed – they are effective quickly – or to help prevent bleeding. Here injections are given routinely two or three times a week.

Quick treatment means permanent damage to joints and muscles is avoided and the child can return to routine life quickly.

Boys with mild haemophilia are now treated with a drug which stimulates the body to produce a normal factor 8.

Caring for the young child

When a baby is diagnosed as having haemophilia parents need reassurance that the effects on their baby's lifestyle, growth and development should be minimal and that:

- there will be normal growth and life expectancy
- there will not be a life of pain
- normal play and schooling is usual.

Over-protection is sometimes a response to the diagnosis, however, it is important that usual handling, cuddling and play takes place.

Cots and prams do not need extra padding, but when the baby toddles, dungarees provide sensible protection for knees. Occasionally joints will need additional padding, but it should be removed as soon as possible.

Maintain good dental hygiene to reduce the need for treatment which might provoke bleeding.

KEY POINTS

- Bruises often accompany any child learning to walk, and carers will learn when one bruise is more significant than another. Childminders and babysitters all need reassurance and information about what to watch for.
- Toddlers with haemophilia may have more bruises than their peers. False

allegations of child abuse have occurred in some situations. Free exchange of information helps stop gossip.

GOOD PRACTICE

- If a toddler or older child falls and hits his head, medical advice should be sought.
- Usual safety precautions, as with any toddler should be undertaken:
    - gates at top and bottom of stairs
    - no mats on highly polished floors
    - ensure toys are robust and check for sharp edges
    - keep heavy ornaments out of reach.

PROGRESS CHECK

1 What are the different levels of haemophilia?
2 How will the different levels of haemophilia affect care?

Caring for the older child

All staff need to update their own knowledge of haemophilia and be aware of the treatments required for the individual child.

GOOD PRACTICE

Procedures for the handling of blood (as discussed in caring for children who are HIV positive, see page 200) need to be implemented and applied for all children who bleed in school, regardless of whether or not they have haemophilia.

A boy usually knows when he is bleeding into a joint or muscle before any obvious signs occur. Listen and believe him, so treatment can then start early.

Following a severe bleed, mobility aids such as crutches, splints or a wheelchair may be needed temporarily (see the mobility aids for muscular dystrophy, page 239). A boy with haemophilia may feel especially vulnerable as he will lack the confidence and skills of the experienced user of crutches or chairs.

If a child needs to rest a limb following a bleed, be creative in providing interesting activities to stimulate and occupy him. Active young children find it difficult to 'rest' and not join in with their friends. Remember he will probably feel well in himself which may increase his frustration at forced immobility.

At-risk activities

Most primary school games and sporting activities pose no risk. Exercise helps develop strong joints and muscles, better balance and sharper reactions leading to better avoidance of injury. Swimming is especially valuable, even for a boy with severe haemophilia, as all his joints will be supported. However physical contact games are not recommended and this may include soccer.

Activities such as woodwork and metalwork are fine, providing supervision means all tools are used correctly.

Woodwork is fine, but ensure supervision

GOOD PRACTICE

Treatment should be given as soon as possible for the following.

- Bleeding into a joint.
- Bleeding into a muscle, especially in the arm or leg.
- Injury to the neck, mouth, tongue, face or eye.
- Severe knock to the head and unusual headache.
- Heavy or persistent bleeding.
- Severe pain or swelling.
- All open wounds requiring stitches.
- Following any accident that may result in a bleed.

First aid

The usual first aid measures always apply and the following information may be helpful.

- Blood in the urine is common, frequent and painless: increase fluids.
- Cuts and scratches: apply waterproof dressings and firm bandaging over cotton dressings.
- Eye injuries: seek immediate help.
- Head injuries: seek immediate help.
- Joint bleeds: never leave untreated, if the child complains of pain or inability to move a joint, a bleed may be happening. This is painful so handle carefully, support the limb or joint. Firm bandaging, if the child lets you touch, can sometimes help swelling and limit joint damage. Seek help.

- Mouth, gum and cheek bleeds: seek advice, offer ice cubes to suck.
- Neck and throat bleeds: these sometimes happen after a throat infection or injury. Swelling can obstruct the air passages: seek immediate help.
- Nose bleeds: sometimes spontaneous, often from nose picking. Firm pressure on the nostril or ice pack to the nose bridge.
- Bruises: superficial bruising is common, deep bruising is dangerous. Seek help. If symptoms do not subside following routine first aid, seek help.

KEY POINTS

- Never give aspirin to children.
- Have medical contact numbers readily available.
- Encourage boys with severe haemophilia to wear a 'Medi-alert' identification bracelet.

GOOD PRACTICE

It is strongly recommended that you gain a first aid certificate and update your skills regularly. Ensure you are aware of who manages the First Aid box, what its contents are and how the checking procedure is recorded.

Activity
1 Design a First Aid box for use with a child with haemophilia.
2 What additions to the usual First Aid box do you think might be required?
3 How would you record and assess the range of bumps and bruises that are often gained at school?

ONGOING MANAGEMENT

Boys with haemophilia should be regarded as normal children with a chronic, variable problem which sometimes interferes with their education.

ADDITIONAL DEVELOPMENTS

In the past children have been treated with infected blood clotting factors. This resulted in their contracting the HIV virus (see page 197). All clotting factors are now heat-treated which kills the HIV virus.

CASE STUDY

Kevin and his father were both well-known as haemophiliacs in their local neighbourhood. Kevin was fit and well and having only minor haemophilia was not restricted in his reception class activities. However he became upset and anxious, refusing to go to school, complaining of tummy aches and showing sleep disturbance. His mother visited the school to discuss the situation and try to discover the reason. After discussion it transpired that two other children had been teasing him that his dad had AIDS and was going to die. They had overheard mothers talking at the school gate.

1 How would you help Kevin?
2 How could you counter the rumours?

RESOURCES

Haemophilia Society
123 Westminster Bridge Road
London NW2 5RB

Duchenne muscular dystrophy

This is one of over twenty types of muscular dystrophy. They all cause progressive and relentless weakness as there is a gradual breakdown in muscle cells. All muscular dystrophies are thought to be genetic in origin

Duchenne muscular dystrophy was first identified by a French doctor in the mid-nineteenth century. It is one of the most common and serious muscular dystrophies and is caused by an X chromosome-linked genetic condition. Mothers carry the condition and pass it to their sons. It results from a fault in a single important protein in muscle fibres called dystrophin. About a hundred boys with the condition are born each year in the UK – one in every 3,500 male births.

At present there is no cure for the condition, with the weakness increasing as the child grows and often causing death by late teens or early twenties.

Treatment is aimed at limiting the effects of the condition and providing a full quality of life for the child.

WHAT HAPPENS

- A child appears as any other baby at birth; the first signs of the condition may be a delay in walking between one and three years.
- His gait then, typically, will be wide-based and he will have an increased curve in his lower back – lordosis.
- Climbing stairs may be easier on all fours, however, coming down is usually not difficult.
- He may fall more frequently than other children.
- His difficulties will increase, leading to problems in walking any distance.
- He may need support to stand, be unable to sit up in bed or turn over without help.
- His lower legs appear well formed and muscular, but this is due to an increase of fibrous and fatty tissue while his underlying muscles are small and weak

- About one third of boys with the condition will also have learning difficulties, although these will vary enormously in severity and unlike the weakness, do not increase as the child grows.

KEY POINT

Progress of this condition can often be likened to climbing stairs with steep acceleration and then periods when little changes. Frequently by the age of ten to twelve years a boy will need a wheelchair for mobility.

DIAGNOSIS

As Duchenne muscular dystrophy is inherited families will often be aware of other relatives with the condition. However in almost half of all affected boys the faulty gene has occurred by a change or mutation in the boy himself – skilled genetic examination is required. In the remaining half it is the mother who carries the gene but is unaffected.

Each subsequent son of a carrier has a 50:50 chance of being affected and each daughter has a 50:50 chance of being a carrier. Daughters will usually be completely unaffected although a very small number have a mild degree of muscle weakness.

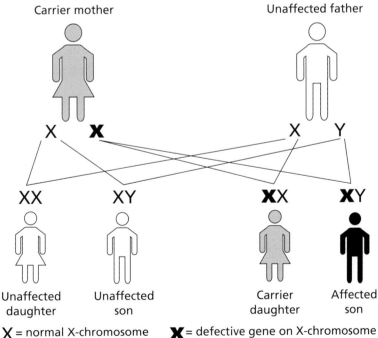

PATTERNS OF INHERITANCE FOR DUCHENNE MUSCULAR DYSTROPHY

Carrier mother — Unaffected father

X **X** — X Y

XX — Unaffected daughter

XY — Unaffected son

XX — Carrier daughter

XY — Affected son

X = normal X-chromosome   **X** = defective gene on X-chromosome

A highly reliable test which examines the levels of creatine kinase in the blood is undertaken. A biopsy, or sample, of muscle tissue is taken for microscopic examination where it will appear abnormal if affected.

Other tests may include measurement of the electrical impulses of the heart as that muscle too will be affected.

KEY POINTS

- Remember these tests are important as there are many other, more common and less serious reasons why a child may be late to walk.
- Confirmation of a diagnosis of Duchenne muscular dystrophy is obviously devastating for families and they will need much support at that time. Worries about other carriers, the effects on future pregnancies and siblings, are all very real and will need addressing.

What to tell the growing child with muscular dystrophy as he grows is difficult for many parents.

- Information needs to be appropriate to his age and developmental stage.
- Answer his questions honestly when he wants more information.
- Never force him into difficult truths, let him set the pace for more information.
- Remember you cannot make him 'better' but you can prevent additional distress. Consider too the immediate situation is often more important to a young child than weeks or months ahead.
- Always check what parents have told a child and what they wish him to know – there is no right or wrong way to manage such a situation.

PROGRESS CHECK

What might be the first indication that a boy may have muscular dystrophy?

CARE

No specific medicines or treatment can halt the progress of the condition but good management can ensure good quality of life for the child and limit associated problems.

- He needs to develop wide social relationships, so involve him in as many experiences as possible.
- Help him to develop hobbies and interests that he can continue long term, even when he may have reduced mobility, such as using computers, collecting stamps, reading and listening to music.
- Support and encourage him in all his academic activities; as his physical strength decreases remember his education will be especially important.
- Physical fitness and good general health should be part of a fun routine and pleasurable for its own sake, not forced on him. Swimming, ballet, gym clubs and horseriding can all be included in his overall care plan, giving his muscles valuable exercise

- Try to ensure he does not become overweight. This can easily occur when he becomes less mobile and so needs fewer calories. Additional health problems can happen if he gains too much weight, so offer a carefully balanced diet. Promote healthy eating habits with not too many fatty, sugary foods.
- A smoke-free environment is important if his chest muscles weaken, making him vulnerable to respiratory infections.

Activity

For pre-school children, help the group create a set of puppets – these need not be complicated. Encourage the children to develop their own puppets' characters in games, stories and songs.

This may be a useful way of helping a child express anxieties about his condition.

Physiotherapy

The physiotherapist will plan a programme of care and you must maintain good liaison with her. The child may require up to four hours of planned exercises a day which you may have to help him implement. Aim to keep him enthusiastic, cooperative and as independent as possible.

Physiotherapy may involve passive movement of limbs – careful positioning to prevent contracture (shortening of muscles) and stretching of any of these already shortened muscles.

Hydrotherapy is often used as valuable and enjoyable exercise – muscles move more freely in water and are less likely to overstrain.

KEY POINT

Use your observation skills to spot any developing weakness or abnormality of the position of limbs or the body, especially the spine.

The following various aids may be required to help the child's posture and mobility.
- Callipers: frames around the legs to support, balance and help him to stand.
- Frames to hold him upright so he can involve himself in activities such as cooking, sewing, drawing and painting and eating his meals with family and friends.
- Crutches to continue mobility.
- Wheelchairs.

GOOD PRACTICE

Always check that aids are comfortable, not rubbing or causing soreness of the skin, in good condition, no parts or bits missing, and no other child is using them inappropriately. Remember as the child grows he may need larger aids.

Aids to prolong mobility

Environmental considerations – a checklist for mobility and good practice

- Are doors wide enough, handles not too high?
- Is the environment clutter-free? Encourage other children to all pick up debris from floors.
- Are spills from water trays, bathrooms, etc. cleared up immediately and are floors non-slip?
- Are floors in good condition, even, with no mats or loose carpets.
- Are extra handrails needed?
- Are wide ramps installed, with gentle slopes?
- Are the desks or tables at a comfortable height for the child, with a good light?
- Can he move easily around with crutches or wheelchair?
- Will a wheelchair go easily into the lavatory and can he reach the taps and towels?
- Do the displays and play materials represent other children in wheelchairs, or with callipers or crutches?
- Are wedges and bean bags available for temporary, additional support if necessary?
- Can the child easily use the equipment in the playground – will additional ramps and rails be needed? Is there a safety surface? Are some bikes fitted with hand pedals and are there some trucks he can sit in?
- Can one of the flower beds be raised for him to garden, touch and smell the flowers?
- Can you organise space for an additional adult helper?

■ Can a parent park a car with good access to the nursery or school for taking and fetching him?

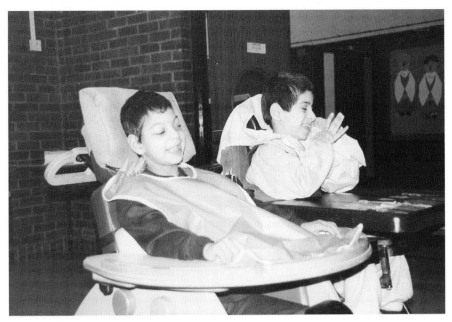

Is your environment wheelchair-friendly?

Good practice is essential in lifting and carrying children

Skills are important not only to protect your own back, but also to ensure a child feels secure and safe.

■ Always wear comfortable, non-restricting clothes and flat shoes.
■ Do not wear jewellery that could scratch and catch.
■ Organise the room so you do not have to carry a child far or twist your body around objects.
■ Always lift in pairs if a child is too heavy for you.
■ Tell the child what you are doing, how you are doing it and what you want him to do. (It can be useful to say 'One, two, three, up we go'.)
■ Bend your knees to the same level as the child you are lifting.
■ Keep your own back straight throughout the whole lift.
■ Keep one of your feet well forward and the other foot comfortably behind you.
■ Transfer your body weight from one foot to the other during the lift.
■ Grasp the child firmly and comfortably using the whole of your hand, not just your fingers, holding him close to your body.
■ Always leave him safe, secure and comfortable.

KEY POINT

Encourage the child to help himself as much as possible.

ONGOING MANAGEMENT

As he becomes increasingly affected by the condition and his mobility and strength decrease, remember he will still be growing and becoming heavier.

Electric beds and wheelchairs can be operated with minimal physical strength. They allow him to sit and lie, as he wants, and move around freely, with little adult interference. Computer technology is increasing in sophistication (see the use of microtechnology in cerebral palsy, page 362).

If other muscles weaken, bladder and bowel control may be lost (see bladder and bowel control in spina bifida, page 340)

The child will become increasingly vulnerable to chest and other infections.

Additional family support and help may be needed. Consider the effects on any siblings and remember they need time and attention too.

PROGRESS CHECK

What are the main principles in safe lifting procedures?

ADDITIONAL DEVELOPMENTS

The voluntary body involved with muscular dystrophy has developed 'muscle centres' which provide comprehensive medical care, advice and support for some families.

New developments are happening all the time holding out great hope for a possible cure of the condition in the future. Recently a specific virus has been found which, it is thought, might carry dystropin genes into muscles and prevent further deterioration. Research is continuing with their development.

CASE STUDY

James was diagnosed as having muscular dystrophy from birth. Now four, he is still unable to walk unaided, but can stand with the help of callipers and has recently been allocated an electric wheelchair from funds from the Muscular Dystrophy Group. He attends and enjoys a local playgroup which is easily accessible to the family home and is all on one level.

The nursery nurse and teacher from the infant school that James is hoping to attend are coming to his home to meet James and his family.

1 What information should James and his family give the nursery nurse and teacher about his condition?
2 What changes may be needed to make access to the old Victorian school possible for James and his wheelchair?

RESOURCES

Duchenne Family Support Group
37a Highbury New Park
Islington
London N5 2EN

The Muscular Dystrophy Group
Nattrass House
35 Macaulay Road
London SW4 0QP

Muscular Dystrophy Group of Great Britain and Northern Ireland
7–11 Prescott Place
London SW4 6BS

Managing medicines in a school, nursery or playgroup

For a child with a condition that requires vital medicines during his school, nursery or playgroup day, planning and cooperation of the staff will be needed. Some establishments feel happier about this area than others, but if a child who needs regular and essential medicine is to learn and develop equally with other children, the following points must be considered.

- Who will be in charge of the medicine and take responsibility?
- Has the parent/carer given written consent for the administration?
- When and where will medicines be given?
- Who will check that the dosage is correct and that it is being given to the right child?
- How will the dose be recorded – where will this record be held?
- Where will the medicines be safely stored?
- Is the temperature correct? (E.g. antibiotic medicines may need storage in the fridge.)
- What side-effects might occur?
- Is there a current contact telephone number available for queries about the condition and the medicine required?
- Which medicines will the child need to access freely e.g. inhalers, powders for cystic fibrosis, and when will the child take responsibility for this herself?

GOOD PRACTICE

Find out the policy regarding giving medicines to children with special needs in your work setting.

KEY TERMS

You need to know what these words and phrases mean. Go back through the chapter and make sure that you understand:

anaemia

bulky stools

callipers and frames

contractures

cystic fibrosis

digestive juices

factor 8

genes

haemoglobin

haemophilia

hydrotherapy

muscular dystrophy and Duchenne
    muscular dystrophy

pancreatic enzymes

passive movement of limbs

physiotherapy

respiratory system

sickle cell and thalassaemia

sickled cells

trait

8 CONDITIONS AFFECTING COMMUNICATION AND CONTROL

> ## This chapter covers:
> - **Dyslexia**
> - **Dyspraxia**
> - **Autism**
> - **Speech and communication impairment**
> - **Emotional and behavioural difficulties**

In this chapter we look at a variety of conditions where children find difficulty in controlling and directing a variety of their functions. These include difficulties with speech, behaviour, relationships and physical movement. Many of these conditions do not have an agreed cause.

Dyslexia

Dyslexia is often included under the term 'specific learning difficulty'. It is sometimes subdivided further into specific types of dyslexia, however we will refer to them all under the umbrella term of *dyslexia: dys* meaning difficulty, *lexicon* meaning words or symbols together.

Dyslexia mainly affects one or more areas of reading, spelling and written language. In addition it can affect other skills including:
- short term memory
- sequencing
- auditory and/or visual perception
- motor skills
- oral language
- occasionally dexterity – a degree of clumsiness can be present.

KEY POINT

In the past, failure to recognise this specific difficulty has resulted in children being perceived as lazy, uncooperative or stupid. Occasionally these difficulties have been put down to late development. It also has been used as a handy cover-all label for children with minor problems of reading and writing. These assumptions can undermine the serious nature of dyslexia.

True dyslexia is thought to affect between 1 and 4 per cent of all children with boys outnumbering girls one to four. It occurs despite normal teaching and ability and affects all social and racial groups. Affected children are often 'quick thinkers and doers' on their own terms – following instructions is more difficult.

WHAT HAPPENS

The condition is not fully understood. Some consider it a brain disorder which happens because there is an immaturity in the neurological system. The processing and transmitting of sensory stimuli – visual and auditory – have been affected, possibly following damage, or as a result of inheritance. Although no genetic patterns of inheritance – faulty genes – have been identified children with dyslexia often come from families where their parents have had similar difficulties with reading and organising words.

Premature babies and those who have had a difficult period immediately after birth, are all thought to have an increased risk of dyslexia.

Whatever the cause, if a child is not helped to cope with his condition he will suffer stress and anxiety and fall behind in his academic work, failing to reach his potential. His social and emotional development may also be affected as a result of frustration and low self-esteem. He may learn to view school with horror as a place where he never achieves success.

DIAGNOSIS

There is no single test to confirm dyslexia. A combination of signs and events may be used to confirm the diagnosis.

Early indications
Some, or all, of the following may be present in one or more of the following areas.

Speech
- Delayed clear speech development.
- Jumbled words and phrases.
- Consistent problems at correctly naming colours.
- Confusion over directional words – right and left, up and down, in and out, etc.
- Pronunciation difficulties e.g. lisping.

Movement control
- Delayed fine motor skills in dressing e.g. tying laces, buttoning, fastening, etc.
- Difficulties in controlling a pencil, crayon, paintbrush, etc.
- Problems over dressing independently e.g. clothes inside out, shoes not on correct feet.
- Frequent tripping, bumping and falling over – general clumsiness.
- Difficulty in games requiring coordination such as catching and throwing or hopping and skipping; problems over learning to ride a bike etc.
- The slightly older child will reverse and invert letters and handwriting will be poor.

Rhythm may be difficult

- Hand preference is late developing (he appears to have no dominant hand).
- Rhythm problems in beating time or clapping to a simple tune.

Memory and sequencing
- Difficulty in remembering rhymes, the names of everyday objects etc.
- Problems remembering time: the routines of a day – when lunch or playtime is – and days of the week, months, years etc.
- Difficulty in learning and remembering patterns and sequences of coloured beads, finding an odd one out, etc.
- Problems over remembering tables and the alphabet.
- When he is older his spelling will be bizarre.
- Inability to develop reading skills or very late achieving them.

Other areas
- He appears bored and lacking attention, especially in reading and reading preparation.
- He appears uncooperative and doesn't follow instructions.
- He may have great pleasure in creative activities.
- He will be alert and interested when personally engaged and talking with others whether adults or children.
- He may show anti-social behaviour and frustration if he is unable to complete tasks or is constantly 'failing'.
- He may be shy and withdrawn.

Do not make assumptions that a child is dyslexic from only one or two of the above signs being present in an individual child. Most children will, at some stage, show some of these areas of difficulties – they will also usually disappear with maturity. However a child with dyslexia will have marked and persistent difficulties in several areas.

Who makes the decision that a child has dyslexia?

Often a parent or carer will feel anxiety about their child's progress – always listen and take their concerns seriously. Following a special assessment by an educational psychologist, a multidisciplinary team will assess the child's signs, including, depending on the age of the child, the child's GP or school medical officer, the health visitor, school teacher, care workers and other professionals.

Hearing and sight tests are always undertaken to exclude any other possible causes.

PROGRESS CHECK

1 What are the main developmental areas in a child, that are affected by dyslexia?
2 Why is dyslexia difficult to diagnose?

CARE

There are two separate schools of thought about the desirability of discovering and helping the child of pre-school age with dyslexia. Some people think that the younger the child the less certain can be the diagnosis, and an incorrect diagnosis may result in problems being created where none exist. They also argue that labelling a child as 'at risk' of having problems learning to read and write and so on may actually cause a child to be anxious and lose confidence.

The other school of thought is that early identification is vital. This argues that starting appropriate activities early can help a child build a firm foundation for formal learning.

Helping the younger child – useful for all children

■ Listen carefully to him, spend time explaining and answering questions. Gently and occasionally (not always) correct errors in pronunciation of words, etc. If you ask him to do certain tasks or jobs get him to repeat any instructions back to you.

■ In your music and singing activities include rhyming songs and use much repetition, reinforced with actions. Help him to clap out rhythms.

■ Read regularly and frequently. You will need to look at your own practice to ensure that you are skilful in holding his attention, making books fun. Show him the way to hold the book, where the words start and which pattern they follow. Have familiar stories he can join in with – reinforce them with tapes and music.

Make books pleasurable and encourage her to choose her own stories

Use actions to accompany your stories. Include poems, rhymes, jingles and nonsense verse. Repeat them regularly.

- Use drama and action where possible and play finger games.
- Encourage games to develop sequencing skills such as making lists of items to use in a painting activity or ingredients for cooking; and counting cutlery for laying tables (emphasising left and right).
- Help his memory with games such as picture lotto. Reduce the numbers of pictures to remember and build up as his skill improves.
- Play sorting games to help his sequencing such as sorting buttons into sizes and colours. Use board games to help in taking turns, counting, etc, such as snakes and ladders and lotto.
- Encourage him to paint, let him use his fingers and short stubby brushes. Explain about the top and bottom of the paper and starting at the left when painting horizontal lines.
- Encourage him in dressing and teach him to manage buttons ties, buckles, etc. Start with simple 'pull-on' clothes, moving on to more complicated ones when he is confident. Give him time and devise schemes to help him remember inside and outside and right and left shoes (these will need to be visual reminders such as stickers or marks).
- Encourage his coordination with large ball games and balancing games. Outside, play action games such as 'Follow my leader' and 'In and out the dusty bluebells'.
- Reinforce time such as days of the week and months of the year.

- Help him recognise and write his own name in lower case letters and teach him the sounds of the letters. Follow this up with teaching and helping him to write his address.

KEY POINTS

- Always extend your activities with appropriate language and use repetition.
- All instructions must be simple, clear and repeated if necessary.
- Try to give him plenty of time in undertaking any activity.

GOOD PRACTICE

- In your choice of materials such as songs, poems and stories ensure some are familiar to the child.
- Are you adequately reflecting his cultural and ethnic background – do you know his particular culture's rhymes, songs and traditional childhood stories?

Develop your technique to hold children's interest

Ensure a child with dyslexia feels he is achieving success in your establishment. He may be very creative, good at construction – make sure he has the opportunities to display his talents.

KEY POINT

Good practice for a young child with dyslexia is also good practice for other children. However, a child with dyslexia will need more one-to-one attention. He will need time and patience and will need to feel able to talk about problems as they happen.

ONGOING MANAGEMENT

As a child grows his special needs should be formally recognised and additional help provided within the educational environment.

This help should be:

- multisensory – developing to the fullest the senses of hearing, touch, sight and smell
- carefully organised and structured
- systematic, with reinforcement at all stages of his learning from all staff within the establishment – this is a continuing programme.

KEY POINT

Ensure you are confident in supporting a child's special learning programme – update your own knowledge. Liaise with the teaching team.

Sometimes a young child with a specific learning difficulty and unmet needs shows anti-social behaviour in school. This can be by:

- tantrums in frustration
- school refusal
- clinging and reluctance to leave parents and carers
- biting and kicking
- bedwetting and sleep disturbance
- becoming the class 'clown'.

Tasks difficult to him seem to be easily achieved by his friends, his words and stories are jumbled and confusing, reading is mechanical not pleasurable and his self-esteem is low. When he is demonstrating some or all of the above behaviour he is showing his distress and anxiety in a very obvious manner.

As the class comedian he is often covering the fact that he is finding some work difficult but, in an attempt to win favour with his peers, he resorts to behaving in a way that both gets attention and makes him popular with his friends.

Consider, too, the child who just withdraws and is good or passive.

To help the child learn the rules of the school you will need to provide him with a framework of acceptable codes of behaviour. Be consistent in what you expect of him. Challenge unacceptable behaviour. However, always acknowledge and reward his efforts and provide opportunities for him to be successful – work to his strengths (see pages 280 and 281).

Support and understand his individual learning programme, remember that, like other children, he will have good and bad days.

Be aware that all the extra effort and concentration he uses in learning may make him especially tired at the end of a session.

KEY POINT

A child with dyslexia should feel learning is fun. You will need ongoing liaison with the educational psychologist and teachers to support the structured learning programmes.

GENERAL IMPLICATIONS

A child with dyslexia needs encouragement to practise his skills otherwise he will lose them. It is an ongoing process where he will learn to compensate for the areas he finds difficult. Often he will take longer to achieve skills and reach goals than his peers. Remember, though, his intelligence is the same and there will be areas in which he can outshine his friends.

ADDITIONAL DEVELOPMENTS

A recent survey undertaken in a variety of childcare establishments found many workers felt the incidence of dyslexia was high. However the childcare workers said they felt they lacked both knowledge and confidence in identifying and developing helpful strategies for these children.

CASE STUDY

Hasan was a seven-year-old boy attending an inner city primary school. He was articulate with strong verbal logic and effective oral reasoning.

He had difficulty in the three areas expected of a boy with dyslexia – reading, writing and spelling. His problems were marked with an apparent total inability to make sense of any written information – in reading he was still unable to recognise flash cards with more than two written words. He was currently being assessed by the educational psychologist.

Hasan had become increasingly anxious over his inability to make progress like his peers, he was reluctant to attempt anything new that he thought would lead to further failure. He was frequently in tears.

His parents were despairing and worried for him.

1 How could you and Hasan's family help improve his confidence in approaching new challenges?
2 What measures could you take to help his recognition of shapes and letters?

RESOURCES

The British Dyslexia Association
98 London Road
Reading
RG1 54U

Dyslexia Institute
133 Gresham Road
Staines
Middlesex TW18 2AJ

Dyspraxia

Dyspraxia is the term given for difficulty or immaturity in the organisation of movement. Sometimes, too, there may be problems over language, perception and thought. It is known under a variety of different terms including developmental coordination disorder, the clumsy-child syndrome and motor learning difficulty.

As with dyslexia it is associated with normal intelligence, again affecting four times more boys than girls. It is suggested that it affects up to a tenth of the population, with a wide range of severity.

Although dyspraxia cannot be cured the effects of the condition can be dramatically controlled and reduced. In addition associated problems of low self-esteem and possible behavioural difficulties may be eliminated.

WHAT HAPPENS

A child will primarily have difficulty over fine and gross motor development. Occasionally it will be in one area alone, but more commonly it affects both. Skills in these areas seem hard to learn and retain and the child appears awkward in his performance. Generally as he grows and develops, certain warning signs may be noticed, depending on his age.

- Lateness in reaching physical milestones – rolling, sitting unaided, crawling and walking.
- Poor balance and frequent falls, slowness and hesitation in action. Hopping, running and jumping are all delayed and difficult.
- Difficulties in managing dressing, particularly with fasteners, zips, buttons and laces.
- Kicking, catching and throwing balls and games needing coordination such as those with bats and balls, are all difficult.

- Lateness in achieving bladder and bowel control.
- Delay in fine motor development with poor control of tools, immature art work and writing skills delayed and laboured.
- Motor skills that other children achieve easily and instinctively, need to be taught.

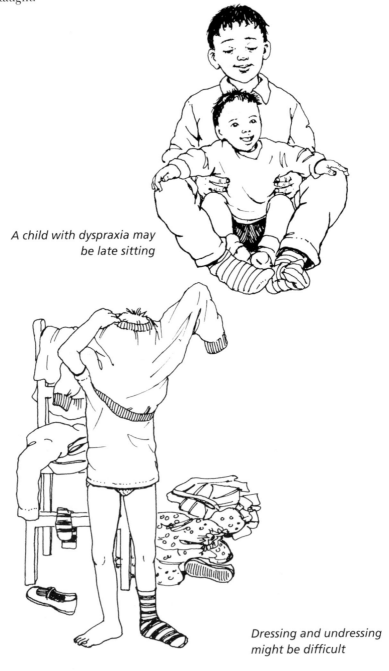

A child with dyspraxia may be late sitting

Dressing and undressing might be difficult

As he grows older the child may avoid physical activity, such as games and PE, and pre-school difficulties remain or even accelerate. His written work appears laboured and immature and he remains poorly organised.

Other developmental areas that may also be affected

Perception
He may show difficulty in linking the messages his senses convey to his action.

Thought
Planning and organising thoughts may be difficult. This will be especially marked in children who, in addition, have learning difficulties.

Language
Poor articulation, unclear or unintelligible speech may be present and speech development may be delayed.

These difficulties may result in limited attention-span, anxiety and distractibility, and confusion over socially acceptable behaviour.

DIAGNOSIS

The condition is thought possibly to be due to immaturity of the nervous system or even damage to the nerve links in the brain that organise the messages received from other parts of the body – the motor sensory system. At present there are no specific tests available to confirm these possible abnormalities.

Diagnosis is made after discussion and assessment from a wide variety of involved adults. The parents and carers are usually the first people to feel something is wrong with their child and often raise these anxieties with their health visitor or family doctor.

Diagnosis follows an accurate history-taking of a child's particular area of difficulty and a full developmental assessment at a child development centre where a paediatrician, psychologists and a range of therapists can be involved. Other conditions will have to be excluded before a final diagnosis is made – these include:
- middle ear infections (which can affect balance)
- hearing and vision damage
- cerebral palsy.

GOOD PRACTICE

Remember, a sound knowledge of the range of normal developmental progress in children is essential for all areas of childcare practice. This information allows you to identify easily and early when a child is not reaching his developmental milestones.

PROGRESS CHECK

1 What are the main areas of development that are affected in a child with dyspraxia?
2 What other secondary areas of development may also be affected?

CARE

KEY POINT

There is agreement by all professionals that the sooner the difficulties associated with dyspraxia are identified the more effective will be the control.

All children need to practise emerging physical skills and this is especially important in a child with dyspraxia. As with any child he will need time and encouragement. For the very young child ensure that the following conditions apply.

- He is given toys and activities appropriate to his developmental level.
- His clothes are unrestricting.
- He has bare feet as much as possible, when learning to walk.
- He is encouraged and praised for attempting new skills.
- Self-help skills are encouraged, even if it means allowing considerable extra time such as when dressing for putting on shoes, cleaning teeth, bathing, etc.
- A flexible yet organised care routine is followed, including a good diet – try not to let him become overweight. Plan for sufficient rest – remember he may use more energy learning physical skills than his peers.
- Encourage speech development, which may be delayed, with stories, rhymes and active listening.

Pre-school activities that will be especially helpful
- Stacking games, using beakers rings, etc.
- Jigsaws – the size and number of pieces at an achievable level.
- Balancing games – swings, seesaws, hopping, skipping, etc.
- Walking heel to toe and along straight lines.
- Threading and lacing activities.
- Dressing dolls, to include buttons, laces, zips and poppers.
- Activities involving turning and screwing lids.
- Action rhymes involving body movements and naming body parts.
- Any type of painting activity.

Balancing games help develop control

Activity

Play a catching game with a group of four-year-olds. Vary the size of the ball or bean bag and the distance. Watch how the children attempt to catch – do they watch you or the ball? How many instructions do you need to give them to help them catch? Do they move their hands and arms or just leave them outstretched? How much complementary activity do they use to concentrate – tongues out, faces screwed up etc. Compare the skill levels of the group – are you surprised by the results?

GOOD PRACTICE

- Encourage walking, not the use of pushchair or car.
- Allow time for skills to be achieved.
- Use distraction when frustration becomes apparent, but acknowledge his feelings.
- Break tasks down into small stages, rather than overwhelm him with the whole.
- Always praise effort – never criticise failure.
- If a child is finding an activity exceptionally demanding or difficult, leave it and consolidate a previous skill – this helps self-confidence and makes him keen to try again.
- Ensure success is acknowledged in other unrelated areas in which he has prowess.

Playing a catching game

KEY POINT

Play and learning should be enjoyable.

Programmes of exercises and activities will be arranged by a variety of involved professionals, including children's occupational and speech therapists and physiotherapists.

Check you understand what they ask of the child, how often and when activity schemes need to be undertaken and how you should support their expertise. It is important for any child's security and confidence that all involved in his care have the same approach – ask if you are unsure.

ONGOING MANAGEMENT

A child in school, with the condition only recently identified, may have additional behavioural or social problems. Often the playground is the area where children achieve status with their peers. For a child who is clumsy with dyspraxia, however, this may be a place to cause him worry, making playtime distressing.

He may cause irritation by dropping equipment, producing messy work and being slow in dressing, undressing and eating and his confidence will fall. Check he is not bullied and maintain careful observations.

Try to watch that he is not excluded, that he is learning to make friends and developing social relationships. Remember he may lack confidence and have low self-esteem.

Research tells us the earlier the diagnosis and implementation of a planned programme to help manage the condition, the less is the occurrence of behavioural problems.

KEY POINTS

- Never label him a 'clumsy' child.
- Acknowledge what he can do, not what he cannot.

With a planned programme of skill enhancement he is likely improve the management of his coordination and help himself cope with some of his difficulties. However this will need to continue throughout his school life.

GENERAL IMPLICATIONS

Although difficulties associated with motor development have always been present, the recognition of the actual condition is still relatively recent. Many professionals do not have current knowledge of the condition or an awareness of how to manage a child with coordination problems. All involved staff will need to update their own knowledge.

ADDITIONAL DEVELOPMENTS

Although controversy continues about the sources and incidence of dyspraxia, there is an agreed feeling about the value of promoting physical skills in management.

Recent practitioners involved in dyspraxia have posited the idea that, as motor sensory skills form the foundation for the later development of abstract and verbal thoughts, improving these motor sensory systems should also allow for higher brain function improvement.

CASE STUDY

Although John appeared as any other baby during the early years of his life he had some minor delay in developing speech. He was an only child with his mother at home as a full-time carer. She identified this as possibly the reason for his delay in gaining the expected skills of independence – feeding and dressing himself and his general clumsiness. Prior to commencing school John was always considered by his mother to be sunny-natured and easygoing. Increasingly he had found school difficult. Dressing and undressing for games and swimming lessons took him considerably longer than his peers, he was considered a messy and slow eater and his peers had begun to avoid sharing the same table with him. John had begun to make excuses for not going to school, he had few friends and was rarely asked to other childrens' houses.

1 What could you as a nursery nurse do to promote John's self-esteem?
2 Where could John be referred for an accurate assessment of his needs?

RESOURCES

The Dyspraxia Foundation
8 West Alley
Hitchin
Herts SG5 1EG

Autism

Autism, sometimes known as a pervasive developmental disorder, is a condition which damages a child's ability for abstract thought. The child appears to lack the ability or need to communicate with others, including her parents and carers. She shows a basic lack of curiosity about the world. She has an inability to understand the meaning and purpose of language and she retreats into ritualistic and obsessive behaviour. She cannot make sense of her surroundings and so the world can be very frightening.

The exact number of children with autism is unknown, but it is thought to affect between two and five per 10,000, possibly increasing to another ten to twenty per 10,000 children if a wider definition is used – it must therefore be considered rare. All social and racial groups can have the condition, with more boys affected than girls in a ratio of about one to four.

About 75 per cent of children with autism also have a learning disability. The degree of severity is wide, ranging from severe difficulties to a small percentage of children with above average intelligence.

KEY POINTS

■ Some children display some of the characteristics of autism but without the accompanying learning disabilities and are in fact of average or above average ability. These children are often considered to have the related condition called Asperger's syndrome.

  Here we consider children with autism and Asperger's syndrome together.
■ There is no cure at present. Careful management strategies with appropriate education and support can help a child improve her communication and social skills so leading to increased independence and fulfilment.

WHAT HAPPENS

A child will demonstrate her difficulties primarily in three areas.

Lack of communication skills
Speech delay may be present and she will often be silent in her play.

However, her communication difficulty is more than her ability to form and use words. She will find it difficult to mix and will appear to prefer her own company. As she grows, making friends becomes problematic and stressful, reinforcing her isolation.

Language seems to develop differently from her peers, she shows constant repetition often of single words and phrases – echolalia. She can remain fixed on a single topic and seem not to listen, constantly interrupting. She often repeats questions back to her questioner – she does not answer. She may avoid eye contact.

She shows inappropriate social behaviour – kissing strangers, asking personal questions of little known adults. She takes no account of age, status or mood when involved in conversation. Interpreting gesture and facial expressions, body language, is difficult – often resulting in her making an unsuitable response. She takes words literally.

Feeding the dog – a literal interpretation

Lack of imaginative play

Unlike other young children, a child with autism will be unable to get involved in imaginative or role play, either with objects or other children or adults. Instead she will spend her time in repetitive activities – arranging and organising objects, even collecting specific items such as bottle tops, leaves, certain containers, etc. She can become obsessive about this and as she grows collections can become a major part of her life. An older child may develop a fascination for certain facts such as types or colours of cars, numbers of buses, and so on.

Obsessive or ritualistic behaviour

Young children usually find security in a degree of ritual and routine. In a child with autism this need for ritual is obsessive and rigid. It is her attempt to try to impose a degree of control over her sometimes frightening world. Changes in any established routine can make her distressed, anxious or angry, often provoking tantrums. Such routines may be dressing and bathing that must follow a certain plan, routes to nursery or school that must always be the same, the road must be crossed at a certain point or she must always sit in the same chair in the same position.

She may show bizarre repeated forms of behaviour such as hand-flapping, flicking her fingers in front of her eyes or walking on tiptoe.

She often tends to focus her attention on a trivial aspect of her environment, such as excessive interest in someone's jewellery rather than the person wearing it, or the wheel of a toy rather than the whole train.

KEY POINT

As with any special need, the degrees of severity of certain aspects of the condition, vary enormously from child to child.

DIAGNOSIS

Autism is now generally considered to be a developmental disorder involving a biological defect in brain functioning. It is no longer thought to be the result of emotional deprivation, or misunderstood genius. Although no affected gene has been identified autism tends to reoccur in certain families. It also occurs with other brain disorders e.g. epilepsy, encephalitis (inflammation of the brain) and maternal rubella.

Parents and carers often worry over the lack of response, delay in smiling and dislike of physical contact that a child with this condition will show and they may have discussed this with their health visitor.

There is no simple test for autism and the diagnosis is made by a multidisciplinary team following a child psychiatric assessment. A child is usually considered to have autism if she shows signs in all of the three areas of poor communication, ritualistic behaviour and lack of imaginative play.

Early diagnosis is important – the onset is thought always to be before three years of age. However accuracy is difficult under eighteen months. A child is often not identified fully until she begins to attend a care or educational establishment and her particular difficulties over relating and involving herself with peers in usual play and relationships, become apparent.

Often a hearing test is undertaken to exclude deafness.

PROGRESS CHECK

Name three significant signs that might lead you to consider that a child of four has autism and will need specialist assessment.

CARE

Drug therapy is not used in the general management of autism. A child is helped by a programme of structured activity and response. These programmes are developed through a multidisciplinary team involving psychologists, speech and occupational therapists and, as the child grows, the wider educational team does too, following formal assessment.

The very young child
Often when a diagnosis of autism is made parents and carers feel a degree of relief that there is some special reason behind their child's challenging behaviour.

KEY POINT

All children with autism will need considerable one-to-one attention in order to fulfil their potential. This may be demanding and require skill and patience.

Managing communication problems
- Speak clearly and directly, using simple words and language, complemented by gesture.
- Try not to use metaphorical speech or exaggeration – remember she will take your words literally.
- Check she is listening and understanding and repeat if necessary – be aware of your own choice of words.
- Use songs and rhymes, especially those to which she shows response. Encourage her to clap and beat a rhythm. Music is often very helpful in developing oral skills.

Children with autism find difficulty in differentiating between objects which are inanimate – toys or furniture – and social, living creatures which are unpredictable and have languages. Consider how confused her world may be as a result.

PROGRESS CHECK

Which professional worker should be able to give expert information and advice on how to develop language skills?

Social interaction
- Encourage her to meet other children regularly, even if she plays passively on her own and doesn't register any emotion – it is part of her learning programme.
- Encourage two-way interaction between child and adult, and later child and child – this is easier than trying to force her into large group involvement before she is ready. Remember the seesaw in the park involves two people as do blowing bubbles between you, pouring sand and water over her and your hands, brushing her hair and yours one stroke each.
- Repeat games she enjoys – this rewards her for demonstrating a response.
- Music with a whole group of children is a good way for her to begin to learn

interaction with larger numbers of children. Musical instruments that involve banging and shaking can be particularly effective.

■ Plan for her development in easy stages, don't overwhelm her.

In group settings it is often helpful to acknowledge to other parents and carers that a child has autism. This explains any apparent unfriendliness or occasional tantrum following an apparently minor frustration or change of routine. It can prevent her being labelled as just 'naughty' or 'spoilt'.

Try to encourage single child-to-child involvement

Safety issues and physical care

A child with autism has a lack of natural caution and this makes her vulnerable.

■ Be vigilant. For example, she may consider all water the same, not discriminating between hot and cold and always expect her food to be of the same temperature.

■ Remember she may display inappropriate behaviour in public such as approaching strangers and wandering off unsupervised.

Toilet-training, developing healthy food habits and sleep management can all pose challenges when caring for a child with autism. Try using a routine to extend her interaction: dressing and undressing; laying the table for meals – placing cutlery in expected places. Try to use any obsessional trait to build on rather than see it as only negative.

A firm, caring consistent approach is important, with expected behaviour clearly and simply explained, efforts rewarded and success praised.

She will respond more readily to the expected and familiar, (remember she is ritualistic) so if you have chosen a certain plan of action, ensure that this is manageable and keep to it. Do not choose areas of conflict that are unimportant and hard to enforce such as saying 'Please' and 'Thank you' but choose those that are vital to stick to such as safety issues – holding hands when out or on the road, etc. These cannot be compromised.

PROGRESS CHECK

What implications for safe practice does autism pose for a childcare worker?

KEY POINT

Families can become exhausted with being constantly 'on duty' and will need support and understanding in management issues. Never forget they know their child best. Support-groups with families of other children with autism are often very helpful.

ONGOING MANAGEMENT

The child with autism in school

It is important to have a sound knowledge of a child's strengths and difficulties to enable you to plan for her schooling. Identifying and listing her special needs and developing action plans for monitoring progress would be helpful.

- Aim to develop her independence and social skills. This may mean watching her developing relationships and intervening if necessary.
- Include her in all activities, but be aware that some team games will be demanding and she may need initially to be involved in one-to-one activities with a specially chosen child. This may help her learn about others' needs and develop her sharing skills.
- Take especial care with your language – both generally and to the class. Avoid sarcasm, innuendo and unclear messages. Always check you have been understood and listened to and be prepared to repeat instructions. Create an environment where a child feels comfortable about asking when she is unsure.
- Always check she is aware that she is part of a group when instructions or requests are made. You may need to identify her by name.
- Develop your story-telling skills and use visual aids and gestures to hold attention. Try to have small quiet groups initially.
- Choose tasks that she can succeed in at the beginning and always break down anything complex you are asking of her into small units. Demonstrate and reinforce, show her again how you wish something to be undertaken such as in writing, pasting or cutting.

Is the child part of the group?

- She may need extra time to complete an activity – she will become anxious if hurried.
- Ensure she knows the school routine and is warned in advance of changes, as things such as fire drills or special visits will make her anxious.
- Check she is not teased or bullied. She may be vulnerable and isolated in the playground. She may laugh at a child who falls or is distressed – remember this is part of her condition and she will need to try to learn acceptable responses. Try to explain to other children the reasons for this.
- Maintain strong liaison with parents and encourage them to help her put into practice at home the skills she is learning in school.

Activity

Plan a talk at a parents' and carers' evening about the advantages of integrating children with special needs into a mainstream nursery and reception class.

Emphasise the benefits there are to the other children in the class in such a situation.

GENERAL IMPLICATIONS

A child with autism will continue to need considerable support throughout her schooling. Remember the condition can be managed and the effects minimised but not cured – autism is for life.

ADDITIONAL DEVELOPMENTS

Some other approaches to the management of autism include other therapies.

Behaviour modification
Punish bad behaviour and reward good. Success is greater if the emphasis is on the reward rather than the punishment.

Holding
This is practised more commonly in the United States. The idea is that autism is primarily a result of the failure of a mother to make an initial, successful bond, for a variety of reasons, with her child, following birth. When the child is distressed she is held close and this is maintained even if the child struggles and resists. In some centres a child is forced into distress by engaging in eye contact or interrupting a ritual so that the 'holding' can take place. This contact can last up to one hour at a time. The aim of this therapy is to try to reduce a child's feelings of isolation.

Some professionals do not advocate this therapy as they feel it reinforces the idea that a parent is somehow to blame for the child's autism.

The treatment has not currently been fully evaluated.

Music therapy
Music is used extensively to break down isolation and reduce disruptive behaviour.

Sometimes parts of the above therapies are used as part of an eclectic approach – making management specific for each individual child and her needs.

CASE STUDY

Ann was born prematurely, the third child in the family. Her mother became anxious about her progress as she was late in vocalising and seemed to forget to use even the odd word she had learnt, by two years. The suggestion of deafness was raised but dismissed following testing. Her mother was told that Ann was a late developer. When Ann became distressed she actively fought against attempts to cuddle or comfort her.

In an attempt to stimulate her daughter's language and social development Ann's mother took her to a parent/carer and toddler group. Ann showed limited interest in the other children, played alone and did not become involved or demonstrate interest in the group activities of stories, songs and action games. When attempts were made to involve her she had temper tantrums and became distressed. She seemed to prefer to spend her time organising the home corner and lining up the cups and saucers. Ann's mother persisted in attending the group but her daughter seemed to make no progress.

Eventually Ann was referred to a local child guidance clinic and at four years of age, after a full assessment, autism was diagnosed.

Ann now attends a mainstream nursery class and has additional support from a nursery nurse. Her progress remains slow and she has begun to develop severe ritualistic behaviour especially over dressing for nursery. However she is beginning to demonstrate some affection to her parents and siblings.

1 What other signs might have indicated Ann's autism earlier?
2 How can you help Ann begin to control her ritualistic behaviour?

RESOURCES

The National Autistic Society
276 Willesden Lane
London NW2 5RB

Speech and communication impairment

Language and communication are complex and complicated areas of child development and delay in progress and the development of these skills can happen for a variety of reasons. It must be remembered that communication also includes a child's ability to play effectively and make relationships, not just the skill to form and choose words.

It is thought that one in ten of all school-age children in the UK have a degree of speech and language difficulty at some time, with up to one in 1,000 with a specific longer-term difficulty needing specialist help. Remember that learning to speak follows a pattern and some children find the whole process much easier than others – there is a wide range in normal development.

Language impairment can be a condition in its own right or as part of another condition or associated illness. Sometimes the condition is known as aphasia (lack of speech) or dysphasia (difficulty with speech.)

WHAT HAPPENS

Any interruption or difficulty in one of the three areas below can cause a child problems with communication. To develop language a child needs to:

- listen
- understand
- speak.

For communication a child needs:

- ears to hear messages
- an intact nervous system to relay messages to the brain
- an undamaged brain to understand the message, memorise and organise a reply
- a voice to respond
- hands to help support messages with gesture and writing
- tongue and lips to formulate sounds.

Delay or difficulty in developing language or communication

Primary reasons

- Articulation problems – a child just finds it hard to learn to control her mouth, tongue and lips – are sometimes due to prematurity, but often the cause is unknown.
- Lack of stimulation.
- Shyness.
- Emotional or psychological problems e.g. of the child who has been abused, has elective mutism or had trauma in her childhood.
- Learning difficulties.
- Hearing problems especially glue ear, frequent coughs and colds.
- Delayed or difficult motor development e.g. dyspraxia or cerebral palsy.
- Other associated conditions e.g. autism.
- Babies born with problems associated with the tongue, mouth or palate.

Secondary reasons

Sometimes specific problems with articulation and control can occur later, after early speech has begun. Examples include:

- 'th' pronounced as 'f'
- 's' giving off a whistling sound
- 'r' pronounced as 'w'
- 'k' pronounced as 't'
- 'g' pronounced as 'd'.

KEY POINT

Speech impairment can be either: a) receptive: a child has difficulty in understanding or receiving what is said to her or b) expressive: a child has difficulty with talking and interacting with her peers.

DIAGNOSIS

Various areas must be considered, often to exclude reasons for a child having difficulty in learning to communicate, rather than to provide simple answers.

A full hearing assessment and birth history will be taken. Obvious mechanical difficulties will be excluded e.g. repair of cleft palate, treatment for adenoids or glue ear, etc. The child will be assessed against the developmental norms for speech for her age.

Terms used in assessing speech impairment

- Fluency: the ability to produce a smooth, uninterrupted flow of speech.
- Dysfluency: speech that is not fluent.
- Stammer/stutter: speech which is interrupted by repetitions, words that are pro-longed and non-fluent speech.
- Prolongations: a vowel or consonant that is 'stretched out' to sound longer than it normally would e.g. 'booook'.
- Blocks: difficulty in making any sound, especially at the beginning of a word. Muscle tension builds up in the face and neck before the sound is finally pushed out.
- Avoidance behaviour: a child feels unable to say words beginning with particular sounds and tries to find alternatives. This can result in an inappropriate use of words or even wrong answers.

Signs to watch for and seek advice on

Birth to 3 months
Mother is not communicating with the child, is seriously ill, depressed or deaf. Severe feeding problems are present with the child.

3 to 6 months
Child is silent most of the time, even when alone. Eye contact not developing. Little or no response to noise.

6 to 9 months
Does not respond to play – vocal and non-vocal. Has not babbled or has stopped babbling. Shows lack of rhythm and intonation when babbling. No consistent response to noise.

9 to 12 months
Not trying to communicate by vocalising or pointing. Not responding to single words and simple commands. Not using a wide range of different sounds and into-nation.

12 to 15 months
Unable to give toy to adult on request, even with gesture. Not trying to copy adult speech. Shows no interest in verbal communication.

15 to 18 months
Not understanding simple instructions. Not understanding new words. Not getting objects by using voice and gesture.

18 to 21 months
Not understanding simple questions and instructions e.g. 'show me your nose'. Not using words to show meaning. Not attempting to copy words.

21 to 24 months
Cannot identify objects and pictures of everyday items. Only grunting and pointing, not using recognisable single words. No variety of different speech sounds shown.

2 years to 2 years and 6 months
Unable to carry out two-step commands e.g.' give dolly a cuddle'. Not linking words e.g. 'mummy drink'. Speech difficult to understand.

2 years and 6 months to 3 years
Not understanding verbs and simple adjectives e.g. little, big, etc. Not asking questions or using a variety of sentences. Speech unintelligible to prime carer. Symbolic play is not developing.

3 to 4 years
Speech unintelligible. Poor vocabulary and sentence formation. Difficulty with both answering and asking questions. Lack of fluency in speech.

4 to 5 years
Unable to relate short sequence of events. Difficulty in understanding complex language. Speech remains unintelligible and with poor fluency. Problems in relating to other children.

PROGRESS CHECK

1 When would you usually expect a child to form simple two-word sentences?
2 When might you expect to understand most of a child's speech?

While it is often helpful to parents to have a well-identified reason as to why their child appears to have difficulty in speech, it is not always possible. Some children may seem to have a combination of factors that are contributing to the impairment. Sometimes, too, professionals are not in agreement as to the reasons for the communication difficulties. Parents can feel anxious about their child being labelled as having a special need when there seems to be no convenient title to cover her individual condition.

However, before any decision is reached, early referral to and the involvement of a speech therapist is important. The speech therapist is the specialist who will have long-term involvement with the child. She understands each child is a unique individual who will need her own specific treatment programme. You should liaise and involve the speech therapist as soon as possible. She will teach the child exercises and develop a programme for her. In addition parents need to understand how to support and implement therapy at home as do the staff in the care and education establishment.

CARE

Principles of good practice will help small children develop their speech potential. If you are working with a young child try to include the following opportunities for a child to practise her sounds. This is relevant for all children, but especially helpful for a child with delayed speech.

KEY POINT

Your positive response will make her want to repeat her noises again – all sounds lead to language development.

Maintain close contact and reinforce her attempts to make sounds

Activities and games to encourage babbling (practising speech)
- Bubble-blowing and any games where excitement can encourage vocalising e.g. 'pat-a-cake'.
- Tongue exercises – licking of chocolate or ice cream from around the lips helps develop the tongue and lips muscles. Let your child copy you and use a mirror so she can see what she is doing. Remember talking and eating use similar muscles so include foods in her diet that encourage chewing, such as carrots and apples.

- Lip shapes – pull faces in front of a mirror at each other, try putting on lipstick and making prints on paper.
- Physical games to encourage vocalising such as tickling, action songs, etc.
- Adapting songs – change familiar songs to include repetition or babbling sounds, e.g. 'John on the bus says b b b' (an adaptation of 'the wheels on the bus'). Be adventurous, now is the time to develop your creativity!
- Make noises to complement situations – always try to make noises to match situations, such as 'ah's with cuddles and 'oh's after mishaps.
- Make noises with toys. Complement games with relevant noises such 'brrm brrm' for cars and make farmyard animal noises for toy animals.
- Reinforce her attempts – always copy and extend her sound attempts such as 'ba' into 'ba ba ba', etc.
- Use games to encourage sounds. Try to use games where she has to vocalise to continue or extend the game e.g. 'more' for extra bubbles, ' higher' for the swing.
- Use everyday situations to encourage her to use her voice to gain items, encourage her to make sounds for more biscuits, another song, etc. Don't do the talking for her.

Games to practise lip movements

Always respond when she attempts to communicate with you, verbally or non-verbally. Use short sentences and speak a little slower and louder. Try and use tune in your voice with the child close to you.

When the child makes a sound repeat it back to her to reinforce her learning. It can help too if you emphasise words and sentences when she attempts to have her needs met by non-verbal gestures. For example if she pulls you to her coat say ' Do you want your coat?' Hold and show her the coat and ask 'What do you want your coat for? Do you want your coat to wear for a walk?' Continue with 'What a lovely red coat you have. Your coat will keep you warm,' and so on.

GOOD PRACTICE

- Learning language should be part of a fun routine that would benefit every young child.
- If a child is having difficulty do not pressure her and make her distressed. Keep your plans short and fun.
- Repeat successful activities and leave less popular ones for a later date.

ONGOING MANAGEMENT

Remember that many children have delayed or less fluent speech, that often it is only temporary and that speech development is not a competition.

Organise your routine so that every day there is time and quiet space to enjoy books with the child. Encourage her to point and then ask questions when she is able. Make sure this is a fun time.

Never leave television or radio on as 'wallpaper' as it will distract the child and smother her developing attempts at words. In school and nursery try to keep noise levels down.

Always respond to the child's attempts at communication but do not insist she tries to speak clearly, just repeat the correct words or sounds back. Use every opportunity to include speech and communication in all activities from bathing and dressing and practical activities to watching television together.

The child may become frustrated if her attempts are not fully understood, so concentrate to understand when she is talking to you.

Management tips for the child in school
- Maintain good liaison with parents, and speech therapists.
- Try to limit questions directed specifically to the child.
- Give her full attention when she is speaking.
- Encourage, but do not force participation in a group situation.
- Do not complete sentences for her – encourage other children not to either.
- Use short sentences with her.
- Never ask a child to 'stop and start again'.

- Try not to correct grammar or pronunciation – repeat the correct form back to her.
- Be calm – this will convey a relaxed feeling to the child.
- Use open-ended questions.

KEY POINT

The child's self-esteem may be low so support all areas of her development to promote her confidence.

GOOD PRACTICE

- You are a role model so speak clearly and use language wisely.
- If the child's first language is not English, consider that she is possibly having to master two skills at one time.

GENERAL IMPLICATIONS

Often childcare workers do not feel confident in helping a child who is dysfluent. Sometimes stammering occurs because a child is very eager and is learning new words quickly – this often settles.

If it persists it may cause embarrassment, possibly resulting in teasing and bullying.

Consider if you are embarrassed by a child who stammers – check that you are not avoiding asking her to participate.

PROGRESS CHECK

1 How can you help a child at infant school whose speech is not clear and is causing her frustration and affecting her social relationships?
2 What activities could you plan to offer her equality of opportunity?

CASE STUDY

Habiba was four when she started school, coming from a part of the city which had high concentrations of families from the Bangladesh community. She had never attended any pre-school playgroup or nursery.

Habiba was strangely silent from her admission. She played alone in a rather aimless fashion rarely completing the tasks requested but she did not appear distressed. Her mother spoke no English and all communication between her family and the school was carried out with interpretation from her outgoing eight-year-old brother.

The staff were not unduly anxious about Habiba, feeling that her limited communication was probably caused by her separation from her family and limited access to English before she started school. They thought she would soon catch up with her peers, as did other children with similar experiences from comparable ethnic backgrounds.

After a term however, Habiba was making only incomprehensible sounds and a speech therapy assessment was sought. The local speech therapist, herself Bangladeshi, found Habiba's understanding and perceptual levels were considerably below what would be expected of a child of her age. She was referred further for educational psychology and hearing assessments.

Following this it was decided that she had learning difficulties. An action programme was developed including speech therapy support.

1 What factors contributed to the delay in discovering Habiba's particular needs?
2 What simple, routine language development activities might you provide as part of her action plan?

RESOURCES

Afasic
347 Central Markets
Smithfield
London EC1A 9NH

British Stammering Association
15 Old Ford Road
London E2 9PJ

Emotional and behavioural difficulties

Children can demonstrate difficult and unhappy behaviour for a wide variety of reasons. Some causes are easily identified but others are more complex. All children will have periods when they are difficult and disruptive – this is part of normal development. The two-year-old is expected to have temper tantrums when thwarted, but by five years a child should have developed other skills to cope with frustration. It is essential good practice that childcare workers have a sound knowledge of the range of normal behaviour. It is important to remember that children coming from similar backgrounds or even within one family may cope with difficult situations with a wide variety of response – not all children will develop emotional or behavioural difficulties even when under considerable stress. Children with behavioural and emotional problems will have the same ability range as other children.

Generally, children whose persistently difficult behaviour causes severe disruption, affects their ability to learn and to develop, and make and maintain relationships, must be considered to have special needs.

This behaviour can result from a wide variety of different causes.

Common causes of emotional and behavioural difficulties

Some of the more common causes of emotional and behavioural difficulties include:

- attention deficit hyperactivity disorder – ADHD – which was previously known as hyperactivity
- physical or sensory impairment
- autism
- learning difficulties
- high abilities
- childhood depression
- emotional deprivation including: separation and frequent changes of prime carers; and difficulties with parenting, especially in the early years, such as chaotic parenting with limited structure or routine, lack of physical care and affection, limited or inconsistent rule-setting and personality conflict between parent and child
- child abuse.

WHAT HAPPENS

Types of behaviour

Whatever the fundamental, underlying cause of a child's distress, the types of behaviour displayed are often similar and can include the following.

- Withdrawal or passivity.
- Aggression – biting, scratching, pushing, hitting , bullying etc.
- Inappropriate social behaviour such as indiscriminate signs of affection or uninhibited behaviour.

Passivity can indicate distress

- Verbal aggression in the older child and defiance.
- Sleep disturbance – frequently a child seems to need little sleep, or her sleep pattern is very disrupted.
- Bedwetting (enuresis).
- Soiling (encopresis).
- Breath-holding and temper tantrums beyond those expected for the developmental age.
- Head-banging and rocking.
- Short attention span, difficulty with concentration, never involved in any structured or free activity for any lengths of time in all care settings.
- Extreme restlessness.
- Phobias or irrational fears.
- Difficulty in trusting and forming relationships with adults and children.

Behaviour can be subdivided into externalisation and internalisation.

Externalisation
Here the behaviour is directed outwards to the world in general and there is a disturbance of conduct.

Internalisation
Here the behaviour is largely directed internally.

PROGRESS CHECK

Which of the listed types of behaviour would you consider externalised and which internalised?

DIAGNOSIS

A child can present with behavioural or emotional distress causing concern early in life. The signs will be different depending on the age.

Remember, a child who has limited language will show her distress through her behaviour – hitting her doll, demanding affection from strangers, sleep disturbance, bedwetting, persistent biting, etc.

Young children will usually see their family doctor or health visitor in the first step towards assessment. Referral can be through a range of professionals depending on the age of the child but most commonly will be the paediatric, psychiatric and child psychology teams and the child guidance clinic. A multidisciplinary approach is followed.

Although some types of behaviour will be common to all conditions additional signs can help the team provide a more specific diagnosis. This is often eagerly requested by parents.

Additional indicators that can occur with specific conditions

ADHD

This condition (see pages 277 and 285) is thought to be the result of a dysfunction of the brain's filtering system, although there are no specific tests available to confirm this at present. Indicators are:

■ poor concentration, easily distracted, overactive – often requiring minimal sleep, impulsive, low self-esteem, poor coordination, disorganised, rigid in response to problem solving and mood swings.

High ability

KEY POINT

Not all children with high ability will present with behavioural difficulties. Many settle well into schools and playgroups, developing good relationships with their talents channelled constructively. A child with high ability may walk and talk early with a wide vocabulary and great attention to detail. This desire for accuracy may lead to tantrums and frustration.

However, some children whose needs are not recognised appear as:

■ verbally cheeky, constantly questioning, appearing to lack concentration as she finishes tasks quickly, disruptive, possibly becoming the class comic or clown, often having limitless physical energy and needing little sleep.

Childhood depression

This is relatively recently recognised as occurring in quite young children. Specific life events such as divorce and separation of prime carers, death and bereavement, or reaction to a parent who is depressed or seriously ill may trigger excessive responses of:

■ guilt and fear, denial, aggression, terrors at parting from carers, sleep disturbance, enuresis, concentration difficulties and labile emotions.

KEY POINT

Mourning following bereavement and loss must be considered part of the usual process of healing. Although distressing, it should be temporary if the child is supported. It should only be considered as depression if this process is extended.

Emotional deprivation

Children who fail to have their growing needs met will show this physically and in behaviour. Specific signs include:

- failure to thrive, delay in meeting all developmental milestones, enuresis and encopresis, inappropriate social responses, volatile emotions, limited differentiation between carers and unfamiliar adults, aggression in play with toys and peers, constant need for approval and attention and difficulties in making and maintaining relationships.

Child abuse

A child who is suffering sexual abuse is the most likely to display overtly distressed behaviour. Specific signs include:
- sexual behaviour displaying inconsistent knowledge for age, sexual advances to adults, sexual play with her dolls and toys, aggression, fears or phobias, biting, food refusal, constipation or encopresis and bedwetting.

However a child suffering physical abuse may also show signs of:
- aggression, fear and delay in reaching her developmental milestones and 'acting out' her hurt in play.

Other specific behavioural signs in autism, sensory deprivation and learning difficulties are covered on pages 247, 251 and 262.

CARE

Parents and carers often blame themselves and feel blamed by a variety of professionals for failure to manage their children. Living with a child with behavioural and emotional difficulties is exhausting, demanding and isolating for both child and family. The effects on peers, other siblings and the extended family can be enormous. Families will need as much care and attention as the child herself.

Whatever the underlying reason for a child having difficulty in managing her behaviour it is universally agreed that early recognition and intervention will help to limit damage to social relationship and learning and lessen long-term implications.

Any child with challenging behaviour will have low self-esteem. The child has difficulty controlling and directing her behaviour and is constantly receiving negative messages about it and herself and she may well have guilt feelings. She may be using her behaviour, consciously or unconsciously in a way to draw attention to her unmet needs. She will be frightened if her world is out of her control and the adults surrounding her also seem unable to organise it for her.

GOOD PRACTICE
- Always consider your own attitude to working with children who have behavioural and emotional difficulties, and to their parents and carers.
- Does your body language give off negative or judgemental messages?

KEY POINT

A child with behavioural difficulties needs structure and consistency in management and a routine developed to meet her individual and developmental needs.

Provide help

There are many ways in which you can aim to help with behavioural difficulties.

- Learning about the specific difficulty that may be provoking the behaviour.
- Developing positive working relationships with parents – joint and consistent approaches with home and educational establishments are most likely to be successful. Remember the parent is in a unique position with very specific knowledge of the child.
- Understanding the aims and helping to implement any procedures that may have been developed as a programme for any specific child. Understanding the roles of the professionals involved in advice and care.
- Providing all opportunities to enhance a child's self-esteem.
- Being aware of the effects of difficult behaviour upon other children – peers and siblings.
- Always being constructive, challenging the unacceptable behaviour, not labelling the child.
- Learning and implementing policies developed for the management of unacceptable behaviour and bullying.
- Learning and implementing policies developed for the management of problems caused by child abuse.
- Ensuring learning is structured at a level suitable for the individual child and providing opportunities for stimulation and success.
- Constantly reviewing and evaluating your own effectiveness in management issues.
- Keeping accurate current records of the child. Observations of times and events of incidents of unacceptable behaviour, together with extended observations will be particularly useful (see page 282).

GOOD PRACTICE

- Be objective in your assessment, use factual words and avoid subjective terms such as 'naughty', 'rude', etc.
- If there is a suspicion of abuse remember observations are an important, objective part of monitoring a child at risk.

Practical care

Changing behaviour will take time and sometimes only small modifications may be achieved. A child will not alter overnight. Issues in very young children such as delayed toilet-training, encopresis, ongoing and persistent temper tantrums and problems over food refusal are best discussed with the local health visitor and at the referral clinic so all involved in the child's care are not causing her further confusion with different demands.

A child's poor sleeping patterns can affect a whole family – however a child who genuinely needs little sleep should not be made to feel guilty. Families can be helped in such a situation by following a 'maximum rest' for the whole family approach. This can be taught by a member of the multidisciplinary team.

From studies of the child a behaviour management plan will be devised.

Specific observations can be an important tool in the objective assessment of a child's behaviour, especially when he/she first joins a group.

Recording specific incidents of unacceptable behaviour can help staff identify the following.

a) If incidents have a clearly identified pattern – time of day, part of week, following certain activities/routines, when a child is tired, etc.

b) If incidents follow an identified trigger – a specific activity, working with particular groups of children or a child.

c) Progress or regression.

Records of specific events can provide information for other team members and for parents, and they can help in the development of a care plan to include rewards for periods when incidents do not happen or are lessening in frequency.

Example of an observation record of unacceptable events/behaviour
Event sample and frequency count

Concern: Heritage language:

Day of week	No.	Duration	Provoked/ Unprovoked	Comments on seriousness

Other types of observations may also be helpful.

Longitudinal studies record both home *and* school behaviour over several weeks, in a number of significant areas.

Time samples look at the quality of a child's day, giving staff information to make positive changes or alterations to a care programme.

Sociograms can assess a young child's potential isolation within a group.

GOOD PRACTICE

Observations of children are an integral part of the work of a nursery nurse. They may have a special use in helping to provide a picture of a child who is distressed and showing challenging behaviour.

Goals set for changing the child's behaviour must be realistic and achievable. Select specific areas for improvement on which she can concentrate and try not to overwhelm her with everything at once as this will reinforce her feelings of failure, her behaviour will worsen and a vicious circle commence.

Ensure that each day the child is receiving praise for her efforts. Try to concentrate on the positives in her behaviour with smiles, eye contact, gestures and open body language to reinforce your positive approach.

The child may constantly demand attention and probably really needs this, even though it can place additional strain within a group. Get her started on a piece of work or an activity and check she understands what is required. Then arrange for her to work or play alongside you. Ensure you observe her attention levels by eye contact or speaking her name.

Arrange for the child to play or work alongside you

Break formal activities down into small chunks, using a variety of activities and techniques, and space them carefully throughout the day. Learn to distinguish between things the child can do and things she won't.

PROGRESS CHECK

1 How many ways can you indicate you are pleased with a child's efforts?
2 Refer to the 'circle of negative image' diagram on page 284. How could you
   a) break the circle or b) reverse the direction of the circle?

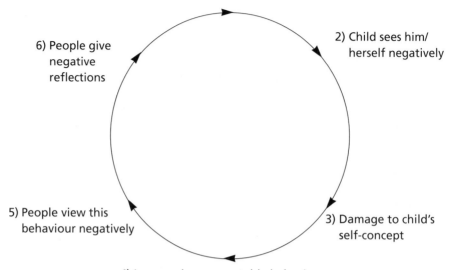

1) Child receives negative reflections

2) Child sees him/herself negatively

3) Damage to child's self-concept

4) Increase in unacceptable behaviour

5) People view this behaviour negatively

6) People give negative reflections

The circle of negative image

KEY POINT

Any vibrant classroom or play setting can be noisy and exciting. Are you sure that you are not expecting a child with limited concentration to compete with too much excitement? Make sure the child's table or desk is not by a door or facing a window.

How a child feels about herself is largely dependent on the way she is valued in the early years. Part of managing a child with behavioural difficulties is helping her to develop social relationships which will promote her self-esteem and feelings of self-worth and teach her skills. A child who is fidgety, impulsive, distracting and sometimes aggressive within a group is often a child with few friends. Consider how you can involve a child who appears on the outskirts of a group.

Activity
One of the uses of creative activities is to provide a release of tension. Arrange a week's programme within the usual classroom plan, where you can provide easily organised activities for a child who needs to use them for this reason.

ONGOING MANAGEMENT

Although the general principles of helping any child develop control and constructive relationships are similar, there are some additional specific measures for identified conditions.

ADHD

Controversy over management of this specific condition continues. Some children have been treated with drug therapy – usually Ritalin – to improve attention and reduce impulsiveness. Many parents and carers have been pleased with the success of this treatment.

However there is another strongly held opinion that medication to control behaviour is not appropriate and that multidisciplinary management strategies are more successful.

Food additives, too, have been blamed for hyperactivity and research suggests that in a few children removing these from a diet will help a child's control. However they are not the cause of the behaviour.

High ability

The identification of children with high ability allows for planning to meet their specific needs and this is a key issue. When this happens, unacceptable behaviour is less likely to occur. Meeting and valuing these special needs, within mainstream schooling, is thought to be most beneficial. Allowing opportunities to stretch an individual child within the curriculum and developing a full programme of extra-curricular activities is valuable. Children of all ages benefit from contact with their peers. Mixing children of high ability with an older age-range is not always helpful as, although these children may be exceptionally able, they are not necessarily socially skilled.

Childhood depression

Intractable depression will need skilled medical help. A child going through a bereavement needs encouragement to discuss her feelings in a one-to-one trusting situation. Her fears and anxieties need acknowledgement. The use of creative activities and imaginative play will be valuable in helping her express her feelings. Remember she is already upset and if she cries you have not made things worse, but perhaps allowed her to release some of her painful feelings. Choose words and language carefully: saying 'cheer up' usually only makes the speaker feel better, not the child.

Child abuse

If the abuse is known and formal procedures are already in motion for assessing the safety of the child then the role of the childcare worker is to record worrying signs, report them if they arise and support the child. Never force a child to disclose information to you, but be available if she wishes to talk. Always maintain complete confidentiality, but tell a child if you are going to relay this information to other workers – never make promises you cannot keep.

Overt sexual advances that sometimes occur when a child has been abused need to be handled firmly but with a matter-of-fact approach. You must indicate that, although such behaviour is not acceptable, the child is not dirty or disgusting. Be careful in your own responses.

Again, allow maximum opportunities for the child to relieve painful feelings through creative and imaginative play.

A child may need encouragement to discuss her feelings

GENERAL IMPLICATIONS

Changing behaviour is demanding and exhausting for all concerned. Perhaps with more than any other condition, a child with severe behaviour problems can dominate her total environment in school and at home. Developing consistent coping strategies that all concerned feel confident in managing, continue to be the underpinning principles of management.

CASE STUDY

Jane's mother had been pressing the school to take her highly active four-year-old daughter into their nursery class as soon as possible, as she was causing considerable family stress.

Jane slept little, often requiring only two hours a night – this caused worries, especially about safety. She had been discovered recently trying to cook at 3am, while the family slept. Not being able to light the gas she had left the taps turned on.

She did not appear to understand the implications of her actions and as a result was constantly in trouble and being told off. She was easily frustrated and with fleeting levels of concentration, starting one activity and moving on if a difficulty arose. She had regular temper tantrums and showed aggressive behaviour towards her eighteen-month-old sister, hitting and biting her. Her family did everything they could to placate her in an attempt to avoid conflict but were beginning to despair.

A home visit by the teacher and nursery nurse was arranged to discuss Jane's needs.

1 What advice might help Jane's family prepare her for school?
2 What preparation will the school staff need to make to ensure both Jane and the group's needs are met as fully as possible?

RESOURCES

The ADD/ADHD Family Support Group UK
1a The High Street
Dilton Marsh
Westbury
Wiltshire BA13 4DL

Compassionate Friends
53 North Street
Bristol B S3 1EN

NAGC
National Centre for Children with High Abilities & Talents
Elder House
Milton Keynes MK9 1LR

NSPCC
42 Curtain Rd
London EC2A 3NH

KEY TERMS

You need to know what these words and phrases mean. Go back through the chapter and make sure that you understand:

articulation
Asperger's syndrome
attention deficit
autism
avoidance
behaviour modification
blocks
child abuse
childhood depression
children with high abilities
dysfluency
dyslexia
dyspraxia
echolalia
emotional and behavioural
   difficulties
encopresis

enuresis
externalised and internalised
   behaviours
finger clicking
holding therapy
hyperactivity disorder
perception
processing and transmitting of
   sensory stimuli
prolongations
receptive and expressive language
ritualistic behaviour
routine dependant
speech and communication
   impairment
stammer/stutter
tongue exercises

9 COMPLEX CONDITIONS

> **This chapter covers:**
> - **Down's syndrome**
> - **Fragile X syndrome**
> - **Hearing impairment**
> - **Visual impairment**
> - **Spina bifida and hydrocephalus**
> - **Cerebral palsy**
> - **Child abuse**

The conditions covered in this chapter are major and complex, frequently influencing several developmental areas. Nursery nurses are likely to meet children with these conditions in many care settings.

Down's syndrome

This particular syndrome was first described in 1866. It is a genetic condition that happens because of the presence of an extra chromosome. Children with Down's syndrome will have some specific physical characteristics but there will be more differences than similarities among children with Down's syndrome because each child inherits characteristics from his own particular family background.

The child with Down's syndrome will have a learning disability and may also have associated physical difficulties such as heart problems, thyroid diseases, extra coughs and colds and hearing or visual impairment.

The number of babies born with Down's syndrome is about one in every 700 births – about 1,000 babies each year in the UK. It occurs in all social, economic, cultural, religious and racial backgrounds. It is not a disease and children do not *suffer* from Down's syndrome.

WHAT HAPPENS

There are three different types of Down's syndrome but the effects on the child are similar.

Standard trisomy
Ninety-five per cent of children with Down's syndrome have this type which is always an accident of nature. Usually a child has 46 chromosomes in 23 pairs which carry the child's inherited characteristics. Half of these chromosomes come from

the mother and half from the father. A child with Down's syndrome has an extra chromosome from either the mother or the father, making 47 in total. The extra chromosome is produced either during the making of the egg or sperm or during the initial cell division at conception.

Translocation

This is a rare *inherited* condition occurring in about 2 per cent of children with Down's Syndrome. Parents pass on an abnormal chromosome 21, which contains extra material, as well as the normal chromosome 21 so the child has the usual total of 46 chromosomes in all.

Mosaic Down's syndrome

This is also extremely rare, occurring in 2 to 5 per cent of children with Down's syndrome. Here some of the child's cells will have the usual 46 chromosomes and some abnormal cells will have 47. The effects of this condition are less severe, with fewer characteristic facial features and disproportionately less learning disability.

Indications at birth that a baby may have Down's syndrome

- The baby is very floppy with poor muscle tone; the joints can be overextended and are highly flexible.
- The mouth is small and often kept open with the tongue protruding; and the palate is high and arched.
- The face and head appear flat; the nasal bridge, too, is flattened; and the hair line is low with extra folds of skin.
- The eyes slant slightly upwards and outwards, with a fold of skin running vertically between the two lids at the inner corner of the eye.
- The ears are small and low set.
- The hands are broad with short fingers and the little fingers curve inwards. There may be only one crease across the palm.
- The feet are short and broad with a deep cleft between the first and second toe extending as a long crease on the side of the foot.

KEY POINT

Shared physical characteristics are not an indication of future ability or capacity to learn.

Possible additional health difficulties

The chromosomal abnormalities cause disruption to the growth of the developing baby and additional health problems may occur.

- Hearing may be affected due to the child's vulnerability to catch frequent coughs and colds, causing glue ear.
- Vision: there is often a squint or other associated difficulties.
- Physical development: the child will be smaller than his peers.
- Due to his floppiness and general poor muscle tone initially, delay may occur in developing gross motor skills. He will have a tendency to gain weight.

- The immune system may be underdeveloped leaving him more vulnerable to illnesses especially in his early years.
- Heart problems may occur. Around 40 per cent of children with Down's syndrome have a heart problem, of which half will be serious and require surgery.

KEY POINT

Not all children with Down's syndrome will have all these health problems and even if some are present they will vary in severity.

DIAGNOSIS

The risk of having a child with Down's syndrome increases with maternal age (see below).

Maternal age	Risk
15–19 years	1 in 1,850
25 years	1 in 1,400
30 years	1 in 800
35 years	1 in 380
38 years	1 in 190
40 years	1 in 110
45 years	1 in 30

- The reason why the rate increases with maternal age is unknown.
- The risk of a subsequent baby having Down's syndrome is increased.
- Genetic counselling is often advised.
- Tests – amniocentesis or chorionic villus sampling – during pregnancy can confirm whether a baby has the condition.

When a baby is born with this condition a mother may recognise he is physically different from other babies, although this does not always happen. A blood test will confirm that a baby has the condition.

While waiting for this information parents will require understanding and support. The process of giving birth is emotionally and physically demanding and any additional anxieties must cause much shock and distress. How the news of the diagnosis is given can often affect the new and developing relationship between mother and child. Both parents should be present and the positive aspects of what a child can do rather than cannot do need to be discussed. Informative and constructive literature needs to be made available for parents to read at their leisure. The voluntary bodies often provide support and 'enablers' at this time of diagnosis.

KEY POINTS

- There is no right or wrong way for a family to react. Families will have differing responses to the news.
- Telling other family members and friends may be stressful.

PROGRESS CHECK

How would you reply to someone who asked if Down's syndrome was inherited?

CARE

The young child

KEY POINTS

- All research tells us that early stimulation and encouragement is vital in helping a child with Down's syndrome to develop his full potential.
- A baby with Down's syndrome has all the needs of any new baby, such as love and security, time to develop relationships and opportunities to learn. He just needs a little extra attention in certain areas.

Physical care and prevention of infection

The child's skin may be dry and fragile so use gentle emollient skin care products in your daily hygiene routines. Maintain a hygienic environment (see pages 181 and 200, chapter 6). While he is very young keep him away from obviously infectious areas such as overcrowded and overheated situations in order to try to limit the number of upper respiratory chest infections he may get. This is important if the child has associated serious heart complications. Routine immunisations will be necessary.

As the child is floppy he will need additional physical support, so hold him firmly with a good grasp. Encourage him to play on the floor on a firm surface to develop his muscles and strength.

Promote his self-help skills, such as washing, brushing his teeth and dressing, as he grows, even if it takes longer.

Toilet-training management means following a consistent approach when he demonstrates his readiness to learn. Watch for non-verbal signs such as taking off a wet nappy or pulling at a soiled one as he may not yet be able to use words to indicate sensations. The principles of how control is learnt will not differ from the learning of other children.

Stimulation and development

He will need all the usual stimulation of any baby, with handling, talking, singing and, in the early days, cot and pram toys to encourage his development. The mother will learn to interpret his needs. Choose ongoing toys carefully to help him develop skills, remembering his hands and fingers may be small and with less strength. Try to choose toys and activities that stimulate all his senses. Remember to allow a little longer for skills to develop – try not to hurry or interrupt him when he is involved. Break down any activity into small units and show him often how something works. Allow him freedom to explore his surroundings and everyday world.

Break down activities into small units and show the child often

KEY POINT

The baby's first responsive smile will be later than other babies – always reward his attempts at communication with smiles, cuddles, etc.

Activity

Create a sensory area. Make sure you are including visual, auditory and tactile experiences. Design this to meet the needs and interests of all children of pre-school age, regardless of ability.

Developing speech and language

A child with Down's syndrome will have smaller nasal passages and sinuses and the roof of the mouth is small and high which reduces the mouth cavity. The tongue is often thicker which leads to him having difficulty keeping it inside his mouth. All this can lead to breathing and articulation difficulties

Always remain in good visual contact when you are talking to the child and hold him close so he can watch your face and mouth. Be patient when he begins to develop speech.

Some children with Down's syndrome are helped by the use of Makaton (see page 295) which is a structured signing system used to complement speech development.

Makaton is used to help speech development

Early language support is important. See pages 272 to 273, chapter 8, for advice on encouraging speech development and pages 313 to 315, this chapter, for promoting oral speech and communicating in hearing impairment.

KEY POINT

A child with Down's syndrome can be taught, with encouragement, to keep his tongue inside his mouth . This helps appearance – important for self-esteem – and reduces mouth breathing and its associated problems.

A child with Down's syndrome will achieve and continue to develop throughout his life, but his rate of progress will be slower than for ordinary children (see below). The pattern and stages of development are the same as for other children

KEY POINT

Each child is individual and may achieve more quickly in certain developmental areas than others.

EXAMPLES OF MAKATON SIGNS

• Always use with speech and complement with facial gestures and body language
• Remember it is a staged programme with levels 1 to 8 increasing in complexity
• Some specific signs will be especially important to certain children.

Stage one

MUMMY MOTHER
tap twice

BROTHER
rub knuckles

**CUP
DRINK
TO DRINK**

DINNER
move hands alternately to mouth

CHAIR

TEA
drinking from
cup, holding saucer

Stage two

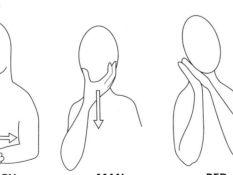

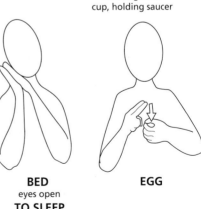

**BABY
DOLL**
same sign but
without movement

MAN
stroke
beard

BED
eyes open
TO SLEEP
eyes closed

EGG

GOOD PRACTICE

Update your skills – learn Makaton. Courses are often available at evening classes.

Examples of Makaton signs

Developmental stage	The ordinary baby	The baby with Down's syndrome
Sits unsupported	5–9 months	7 + months
Walks	9–18 months	1–4 years
First words	10–23 months	1–3 years
Toilet-training achieved	1–3 years	2–7 years

Babies' stages of development

Feeding

Breastfeeding a baby with Down's syndrome can be helped by the advice and support of a lactation sister and health visitor. This may be required as the baby's small mouth, weaker muscle tone and rooting reflex, accompanied by a possibly protruding tongue, may make latching on difficult. The result can be understimulation of the breast and reduced milk production. If so the baby may tire before he has received enough milk. Perseverance and maternal motivation usually overcome such initial difficulties.

If the baby is artificially fed ensure that the teats are both soft and large enough to allow an easy flow of milk.

GOOD PRACTICE

- Always hold the baby closely during feeds and consider it a special time for one-to-one interaction
- If the baby has an associated heart problem his tiredness may be increased during feeding, so do not hurry him and check the teat is not too small.

Weaning

Always supervise well, as the baby's cough reflex may be lessened, increasing the chances of choking.

Tongue thrusting may persist so do not assume a food is disliked just because it appears rejected. Remember that coping with a spoon may just require patience and persistence.

Do not continue with puréed foods for longer than necessary as the baby will need the practise of coping with lumps and the need to develop chewing as any other baby. Introduce foods carefully and slowly one at a time.

Use trial and error to find a comfortable spoon for this new skill. As he develops the baby may find using cutlery difficult, and although finger feeding is acceptable when a toddler, encourage the use of cutlery in preparation for nursery or school.

Aim for a diet not excessively high in calories, in view of the tendency to gain weight easily. It is much simpler to avoid putting too much on, rather than attempting to reduce calorie intake later. Developing healthy food habits when the baby is young will be helpful.

Lauren enjoys her doll

Social and emotional development

It is detrimental to any child not to have acceptable social behaviour, so it is also essential for a child with Down's syndrome. He needs to learn to be part of a wider group, share and take turns and understand the difference between right and wrong. He may become cross and frustrated and have periods of regression, but such skills are essential to his becoming a valued member of a wider society and making friends.

He needs to develop an awareness of when displays of affection are acceptable, and when they are not and learn who to respond to and trust.

GOOD PRACTICE

- Always praise and acknowledge good behaviour – do not constantly criticise failings.
- Be realistic in your expectations. The pattern of development will be the same as an ordinary child but he will take longer to reach his milestones.
- Always explain simply and clearly what you expect.
- Remain consistent in your approach.
- Remember that you are an important role model.

KEY POINT

Children with Down's syndrome are all different. They will have preferences and likes and dislikes, some will be easygoing, some will be forceful, some compliant and some disobedient – but all will be different.

Safety issues
- Double check your environment is safe. Remember the child's control and power may be affected with weaker muscles making him vulnerable to falls. Make sure you always use straps in highchairs, pushchairs, car seats, etc.
- Use non-slip mats in baths, clear toys and debris from floors, keep stairs clear.
- Always check the temperature of food when he is a baby and as a toddler – he may be less sensitive to extremes of temperature.
- Never leave him alone when he is learning to manage solid foods.
- Teach him how to use equipment and undertake any activity safely. Repeat instructions regularly, but best of all show him.
- He may forget safety instructions so do not rely on him always to remember them. When he is excited, hungry, tired or a routine is changed he is even more likely to forget.

A Portage scheme is often used for children with Down's syndrome prior to their entry to care and educational establishments (see page 152).

ONGOING MANAGEMENT

The aim for a child with Down's syndrome is for him to reach his potential without being pushed beyond his capacity. So as a childcare worker it is essential that you motivate and encourage him to regard learning as fun and pleasurable.

Playgroups and opportunities to mix with groups of children are important.

When joining a group of children sometimes a child with Down's syndrome is over-protected by the rest of the children, keen to be caring. This usually resolves if handled sensitively and he is encouraged to interact and behave normally within the group. Do not make excuses if he displays unacceptable behaviour – this may reinforce it and make it difficult for him to know what is expected of him.

Always keep watch in a playground for any bullying or teasing.

Factors to consider for the child in a learning environment
- Check you are not asking the child for two things at once e.g. draw a picture and then go and place it on the wall – especially in the beginning.
- Break down every task into the smallest unit.
- Check the child understands what you want – he may say 'yes', but this does not always mean 'yes'. He may repeat your instructions or question back, again this does not necessarily imply understanding. Demonstrations accompanied by simple instructions are often most effective. Check understanding at each stage of a task.
- Do not assume the child understands basic terms such as 'over and under', 'top and bottom', etc.

- Do not hurry or rush the child, always allow him sufficient time.
- With small hands the child may find pens, pencils and scissors difficult at first. What adaptations might help?
- If you are teaching a new task or developing the child's concentration levels, check the room or area is quiet and not offering competing stimulation.
- Baby or toddler gym clubs, ballet classes and swimming will all be helpful in encouraging gross motor control and development.
- The child needs much encouragement and positive feedback for his efforts.

Carefully supervised gym sessions can promote physical development

Riding is enjoyable for all children

Medical difficulties

Heart lesions

There is a range of severity of the lesions. Often surgery is required early in life and liaison with the medical team will be necessary. Hospitalisation means a child will have to undergo the additional trauma of a change in routine, possibly distressing procedures and increased parental anxiety. Inevitably a change in routine may mean a temporary interruption in his general progress. However, successful surgical intervention means he will be able to participate fully in all activities, without breathlessness and tiredness.

Some cardiac difficulties are such that surgery is not possible.

Respiratory infections

Coughs, colds and chest infections will be more common. Parents and carers need reassurance that it is important to seek prompt treatment for such infections – they are not being over-protective. The effects of persistent infections on general health and especially hearing and associated heart difficulties may be considerable if not treated.

Auditory problems

Most hearing problems result from a conductive loss, as a result of persistent middle ear infections. Treatment before speech development is affected is important. Remember, too, that such infections can occur at any time and an awareness of any child who is failing to respond to sounds should always be investigated – hearing should be checked after colds. (See the discussion on managing hearing impairment on page 317.)

Visual problems

A variety of different visual problems may occur but the most common are squints and short-sightedness. A child needing glasses will need special attention from the optician to ensure they fit well – if not they may fall off the nose more easily due to the child's flat nasal bridge.

If a child in your care is wearing spectacles check they are:

- comfortable
- clean and unbroken
- worn when they should be.

Other difficulties

A range of congenital conditions can occur in a child with Down's syndrome and is more likely than in an ordinary baby. Routine health promotion means that any problems identified can be remedied early. No child should endure an illness that can be prevented or successfully treated.

KEY POINT

Many children with Down's syndrome have no associated health problems and others will be affected in only a minor way.

PROGRESS CHECK

1 What percentage of babies born with Down's syndrome are likely to have associated cardiac problems?
2 Why are respiratory infections more common?

GENERAL IMPLICATIONS

Society continues to have a stereotyped view of children with Down's syndrome: they are considered physically similar, often even with haircuts alike, pliant and good-natured and with limited potential. With the advance of integration this view is at last being challenged.

It is important that you, as a professional, care for every child as an individual, balancing all his needs, and valuing and understanding his differences. Check that you do not reinforce stereotypes.

As children with Down's syndrome grow into adulthood, they are, increasingly, leading full and independent lives and making positive contributions to society. Sometimes this is from within a sheltered community. Long-term institutional care is no longer acceptable.

ADDITIONAL DEVELOPMENTS

In some countries, especially America and increasingly in Germany, Australia, Israel and Canada, cosmetic surgery is being offered to make the physical appearance of a child with Down's syndrome similar to that of his peers. This includes reducing tongue size and altering eye and nose contours. Some people argue this is justified in that changing outward appearance alters people's expectations of children with Down's syndrome. Others, especially in the UK, reply that we should change society's attitudes and not the child with Down's syndrome.

CASE STUDY

Chloe was a keenly awaited first baby, born by Caesarean section, to older parents. Her Down's syndrome was obvious at birth and although she was immediately loved and cherished by her mother, her father found her condition distressing and did not visit his wife or daughter during the week they were in hospital.

On discharge home Chloe had difficulties feeding. She had a poor suck and her mother was unable to continue breastfeeding, much to her disappointment. Chloe's mother was tired following both the birth and the additional emotions surrounding the event, but she felt unable to leave Chloe with her husband as he was still refusing to hold or even look at his daughter.

Despite visits from the health visitor and support from the voluntary association the situation did not improve and the parents' relationship was in danger of breaking up.

Chloe progressed, but a heart defect was identified during routine health examination and she was admitted for repair of the lesion at eight months old. On this occasion her father did go to hospital to see both his wife and daughter and he began to make the first attempts to acknowledge and learn about Chloe as his daughter.

When Chloe was eighteen months old a Portage worker began to visit the home and encouraged both parents to work together with their daughter. Chloe's father later said that having something he could actually do greatly improved how he felt about Chloe – they began learning together. He felt more an integral part of the family with something specific to contribute. The family stayed together as a unit and Chloe blossomed, eventually attending her local primary school. Both her parents are now campaigners for equal access to education for children with Down's syndrome.

1 Why do you think society seems to fail to understand that the father may need support adjusting to the birth of a baby with special needs, in addition to the mother?
2 Why do you consider men sometimes feel threatened by the birth of a baby with obvious special needs?

RESOURCES

The Down's Syndrome Association
155 Mitcham Road
London SW17 9PG

Fragile X syndrome

Fragile X is a relatively recently recognised condition of genetic origin. It is the most common inherited cause of learning disabilities affecting one in 1,000 births – more boys than girls are affected. Primarily the effects are on a child's learning abilities, but there are also some physical characteristics as well.

The specific chromosomal fragility was discovered in 1969. Sophisticated testing mechanisms were developed to confirm the occurrence of this condition, but the associated developmental problems and behavioural difficulties were not fully associated with the chromosomal abnormality until 1977.

WHAT HAPPENS

The condition is passed on by the X chromosome which is one of the pair that decides a child's sex. A boy has an X and a Y and a girl has two Xs. If a girl has a 'fragile' X chromosome she also will have an undamaged one which can sometimes overcome the effects of the fragile chromosome. A fragile or damaged X chromosome appears different under a microscope, with an abnormality at the tip and appearing partially separated.

The condition can be passed by unaffected male and female carriers.

Developmental difficulties

Speech and language
Speech and language difficulties are usually present in all children with the condition. Language delay may be the first worrying sign of the condition. The following are difficulties that may occur.
■ Word and phrase repetition, accompanied by up and down swings of pitch.

- Echolalia – repetition of last phrase or word.
- Palilalia – repetition or words or phrases a child has spoken himself.
- Dysrhythmia – poor control of rhythm and inappropriate use of pauses.
- Comprehension difficulties of the spoken word.

Behaviour and attention

KEY POINT

Often some of the listed characteristics are present. The severity may lessen as the child grows.

- Tantrums continuing after the expected developmental stage.
- Excessive response to stimulation especially by inappropriate behaviour.
- Overactivity/hyperactivity: limited sleep requirements, always on the go and difficulty in sitting still.
- Impulsive: difficulty in waiting and a need for immediate gratification.
- Concentration problems.
- Anxiety: avoiding eye contact, gaze avoidance.
- Short-term memory difficulties but long-term memory is much better.
- Mimicry, especially specific words.
- Ritualistic: having a strong need for routine and is distressed by changes.
- Repetitive behaviour: finger-flicking, hand-flapping and hand-biting can occur.

KEY POINT

The older undiagnosed child may not be noticed as 'badly behaved' – just lacking in concentration or appearing uncooperative at times.

Physical characteristics and health implications

These physical characteristics may not be present in all children and the specific facial appearance may not be noticeable until the child is older.
- Laxity of joints and muscles: late sitting, walking, etc.
- Recurrent middle-ear infections.
- A long narrow face with prominent jaw bone.
- 20 per cent of children will develop epilepsy.
- Adult males have large testes.

DIAGNOSIS

A child may cause anxiety to his parents, perhaps by delay in responsive smiling, sleep disruption, lateness in sitting or walking, delay in language development or behavioural problems.

Confirmation of the condition is by blood test. The severity of the effect of the condition is variable and not easily predicted.

KEY POINT

The term 'fragile' in the condition does not mean a child is sickly or ill.

CARE

As with a child with Down's syndrome, early development and implementation of a multidisciplinary management plan can lessen the long-term effects of the condition, allowing for the development of the child's full potential and promotion of his self-esteem.

Support from a wide variety of specialists will be required with emphasis on early speech therapy. The earlier a parent can understand and respond to the child's speech the better. (See pages 272 to 273 on helping speech development, chapter 8 and pages 313 to 315 on promoting oral speech.)

GOOD PRACTICE

- As a childcare worker working with a child with learning disability, check you know the norms of development so you can plan for the child's progress. Remember his development will follow a similar pattern to any other child's, but he may take longer to achieve his milestones.
- A child with fragile X can be 'routine dependent' so a flexible and realistic care plan should be developed.

Health problems are unlikely to be any different from any other child's. However, strain on families where a child needs little sleep can be great, so liaison with the health visitor will be necessary.

Remember the child may use mimicry in his behaviour, so turn it to constructive use by ensuring you always present as a positive role model – especially important in safety practices.

The child needs to learn to be part of a group whether at home, or in a care and education establishment. This will be by helping him to moderate his behaviour with verbal reinforcement, praise and example. Understanding his difficulties should not affect your efforts to help him change. Always make sure you are realistic in your demands of him. Remember his cognitive stage of development, for example do not expect him to take turns, before he has learnt to share.

Help him develop concentration by breaking down games and activities into small achievable units.

He may benefit from Makaton and Portage schemes carried out in the home by peripatetic workers.

PROGRESS CHECK

Which area of development is the most likely to show signs of delay in a child with fragile X syndrome?

ONGOING MANAGEMENT

When he is involved in more formal pre-school or school settings you can help the child by using the following approaches.

- Providing a distraction-free area and keeping noise levels low to allow the child to concentrate on the task in hand.
- Keeping a calm environment which the child will find reassuring.
- Keeping the child close when he is working. Have him alongside rather than facing you, as he may find eye contact threatening.
- Giving the child short sessions if you are expecting concentration. Ten to fifteen minutes at one time and a little and often is most valuable.

Frequent short sessions are best for maximum concentration

- Alternating quiet and energetic activities.
- Giving the child 'time out'.
- Keeping your expectations clear and consistent – be realistic in your demands.
- Telling the child what behaviour is unacceptable and rewarding positive behaviour.
- Being prepared to repeat instructions and checking the child understands.
- Developing your skills in storytelling and reading. It is found that the child will find a visual-based approach easier.
- Checking the child's hearing has been re-tested following any colds.
- Building the child's self-esteem with praise and encouragement for effort.
- Working to the child's strengths.

- All staff involved in the child's care should follow similar management approaches.
- Maintain good home liaison. A child needs the security of routines and will become distressed by changes whether at home or in a playgroup or school. A key worker will be important.

Activity

Make a story prop which would help hold the attention of a four-year-old with fragile X syndrome during storytime.

Special areas of difficulty

It is thought that reasoning and sequential thinking are areas that can prove difficult for a child with fragile X. He tends to get waylaid and become sidetracked with irrelevancies. Number work can be demanding for him. Provide structured well-presented activities to gain his attention. Avoid using generalities as he will be confused.

The use of computers, which are non-threatening, consistent and allow for constant task repetition, is often valuable.

GENERAL IMPLICATIONS

Effective communication and sharing of knowledge of the child and the condition is important. Remember he will look similar to his peers and the realisation that he has special needs may sometimes occur after his self-esteem and confidence have been affected.

ADDITIONAL DEVELOPMENTS

Genetic counselling may be offered to families who have a child with fragile X syndrome. Improving public awareness of the condition and its effects, is happening mainly due to the efforts of the voluntary body concerned.

CASE STUDY

Jason is the middle of three children and his mother sensed from his birth that something was wrong – he seemed slower in all areas than his siblings. He was late in achieving bladder and bowel control and it was only when he began attending playgroup that his special difficulties became even more apparent.

He was easily frustrated, his language was considerably behind his peers and his limited concentration meant he often disrupted stories, songs and games. His rigidity in the way he wanted help with putting his coat on and taking it off sometimes dominated a session.

All adults involved with Jason agreed he needed assessment. Advice on how to meet his needs was urgently requested.

1 What therapy would help Jason?
2 How much do you consider the public know about fragile X and why is it important to increase knowledge of this condition?

RESOURCES

Fragile X Society
53 Winchelsea Lane
Hastings
East Sussex TN35 41G

Hearing impairment

Up to 65,000 children in Britain have a degree of hearing impairment. About one in 1,000 of these children are born profoundly deaf. For other children the severity of impairment will range from mild to moderate and can be either permanent or fluctuating. At any one time up to one in four children under seven will have some form of hearing impairment.

Nine out of ten children who are deaf will have hearing parents.

KEY POINT

The major effects of hearing impairment are on the development of language, communication and understanding of the spoken word.

This development of language, communication and understanding of the spoken word has a direct impact on a child's access to the wider world and education in particular, which is designed for the hearing child and the use of English language.

Behaviour and social and emotional development, too, are often affected by a failure to discover the impairment early.

WHAT HAPPENS

Types of hearing impairment

Sensorineural hearing impairment
In this impairment, damage to the nervous system and the hearing apparatus occurs. This can be one-sided (unilateral) or affect both ears (bilateral). It is usually permanent.

The cause of the impairment may be one of the following.
■ Genetic/unknown/family history of deafness.

- Maternal rubella (German measles) during pregnancy.
- Certain drugs, especially during pregnancy.
- Severe jaundice at birth.
- Prematurity.
- Lack of oxygen at birth.
- Brain damage at birth/brain injury later in life.
- Some chromosomal disorders.
- Some infections especially:
  - measles
  - meningitis
  - mumps
  - viral infections.

KEY POINT

Some of the causes of sensorineural hearing impairment are congenital – the child is born with the condition. Others are acquired after birth.

Conductive hearing impairment

In this impairment the sound waves are unable to pass through the eardrum, or the eardrum is prevented from vibrating through the middle ear (see page 309).

The cause of the impairment may be one of the following.

- Blockage of the outer ear, external canal or middle ear by wax or foreign bodies such as beads, peanuts, etc.
- Swollen adenoids at the back of the nose, often following recurrent coughs and colds.
- Middle-ear infections – otitis media. Infections enter via the Eustachian tube.
- Otitis media with effusion – OME or 'glue ear'. After an infection of the middle ear or because of an allergy, fluid remains in the middle ear and becomes thick. As a result the sound waves are stopped from travelling along the ear and the drum from vibrating.

KEY POINTS

- Conductive hearing impairment is usually temporary and often fluctuating – the degree of loss will vary from day to day. As a result a child with a conductive impairment is often unacknowledged.
- A child typically says 'what' and 'pardon' a lot, may speak loudly and appear to ignore other adults and children.

Mixed impairment

Here a child may have a combination of sensory and conductive deafness.

Hearing assessment

Hearing assessment also measures frequencies. Sound varies in loudness and pitch and is divided, for assessment purposes, into high, middle or low frequency, or pitch. The frequency of sound is measured in kilohertz and one kilohertz is 1,000 hertz. Low frequency is up to 500 hertz; middle frequency is from 500 hertz to 1 kilohertz; and high frequency is above 1 kilohertz.

The lower and middle frequencies tend to convey the louder and vowel sounds in speech; and the high frequency the consonant sounds and is responsible for the intelligibility of speech.

A child with high-frequency impairment will respond to sound, as she hears low and middle frequencies in speech, but she will have great problems in learning and understanding speech. She will be hearing indistinct speech.

HOW SOUND WAVES TRAVEL IN THE EAR

Sound waves are collected by the outer ear (**1**) and directed into the ear canal (**2**) where they meet the eardrum which is a tightly stretched membrane (**3**). When the sound strikes this drum it starts vibrating. The vibrations pass into the middle ear (**5**) by three tiny bones linked together (**4**). The first is attached to the eardrum and the last embedded into a second membrane called the oval window (**10**). Behind this second membrane is the cochlea (**6**). This is filled with fluid and contains the hearing nerves (**9**). When the vibration is passed to the fluid it stimulates the nerves which pass the sound signals to the hearing area of the brain.

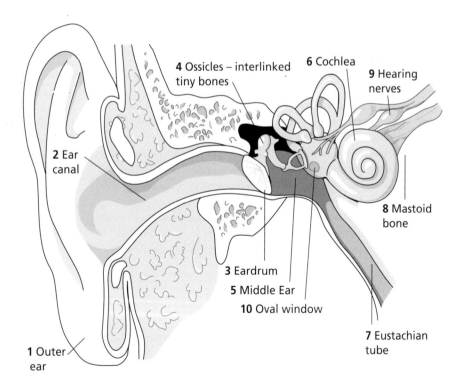

4 Ossicles – interlinked tiny bones

6 Cochlea

9 Hearing nerves

2 Ear canal

8 Mastoid bone

3 Eardrum

5 Middle Ear

10 Oval window

7 Eustachian tube

1 Outer ear

DIAGNOSIS

Parents, following the birth of their new baby, are often given checklists and leaflets to help them identify worrying and significant signs, in the early months.

Early signs that might indicate a child is not hearing

Infant–6 months
- Does not blink or startle at loud noise.
- Does not notice household noises such as vacuum cleaner, telephone, either by 'stilling' or appearing to listen when they start.
- May not smile responsively by 6 weeks.

KEY POINT

A baby profoundly deaf from birth may coo and gurgle initially as a hearing baby.

6–12 months
- Does not turn to mother's voice across the room.
- Does not babble in conversation – vocalizing begins to decrease.
- Does not respond to own name.

Pre-school and infant school
- May have little or no vocalization.
- Sounds indistinct/limited speech.
- May have monotone quality of speech.
- Active and inattentive.
- Repeated respiratory or ear infections, sounds 'adenoidal'.
- Temper tantrums persist or behaviour problems occur, may seem to daydream.
- Sits close to television with sound loud.
- Does not respond to instructions or answer when called.
- Asks for questions to be repeated or copies other children.
- Difficulty in listening to stories in a group, may be disruptive.
- May watch adult's face intently.
- May complain of earache or have a discharge from the ear.
- May begin to lose confidence, not wish to go to school.

Not all signs will apply to all types of hearing impairment.

KEY POINTS

- A child who is born deaf will have the usual capacity to develop language and communication, but is prevented from doing so by not having access to the speech of others. She cannot hear all the necessary sounds.
- Helping the child access speech, from a variety of methods such as lip reading and signing gives her the opportunity to learn and develop as her hearing peers, from all aspects of her environment. As with all children the early years are important in the development of communication skills, so early detection is vital.

PROGRESS CHECK

1 When does a profoundly deaf baby show the first difference in the sounds she makes in comparison with a baby of similar age?
2 In what common childhood infections is it advised a child should have her hearing checked when she recovers?
3 Why is early detection of a hearing impairment so important?

Formal testing

Brainstem audiometry

This is undertaken within the first week of life in some centres. Babies thought to be 'at risk' (see causes of sensorineural impairment) are often routinely tested in this way.

Electrodes are attached to the sleeping baby's head to detect electrical activity. Sounds, at a level to stimulate normal hearing, are then fed into her ear to stimulate the nerves involved in hearing and the brain's response is monitored.

The frequency levels cannot be assessed nor can a mild to moderate loss, however a baby with a profound hearing loss will be identified.

Distraction tests

All babies are, at present, assessed at around eight months of age, either in the family home or child health clinic, usually by the health visitor.

The baby's attention is gained by a tester playing with a toy in front of her. A second tester then plays sounds of different volumes and frequencies to the child whose response is noted. If the child 'fails' this test it is then repeated within a month.

Possible causes for a baby failing to respond include:

■ poor technique of the tester
■ tester with poor hearing herself
■ additional noise in the testing area
■ a tired or unwell baby
■ current cough or cold.

Cooperative and performance tests

From about eighteen months of age children can be involved in testing that requires a response to a specific instruction. These include requests in play situations using measured speech volumes, for example 'put the dolly in the pram'.

A slightly older child can have frequency levels tested by being asked to wait for certain sounds before finishing a task such as building a tower of bricks in stages.

Pure tone audiometry

This measures a child's ability to hear pure tones produced by a machine known as an audiometer. The intensity and frequency of the tones are adjustable and the child wears headphones and indicates when a sound is heard.

The child must be of an age to understand what is requested and be able to cooperate.

The sweep test

This is a system designed to test large numbers of children, often on school entry. Pure tone audiometry is used and various ranges of frequencies are tested, at fixed levels of intensity. Each ear is tested individually and the child asked to indicate when a sound is heard.

Despite the attempts to screen all children for hearing impairment many still remain incorrectly diagnosed. Referral to a specialist in audiometry should be undertaken in the following.

- A child who has significantly impaired language development.
- A child with a history of chronic or repeated middle-ear disease, or upper airway obstruction such as adenoids.
- A child with developmental or behavioural problems.
- Any child who does not appear to respond at routine hearing testing such as sweep or distraction testing.

CARE

Conductive hearing impairment, where the effects are fluctuating, can easily be overlooked. Remember at times a child will hear fairly well. She does not live in a quiet world, she will respond to some sounds. However, her sounds are muffled and cause her confusion. To an uninformed observer she may appear lacking in concentration or attention.

KEY POINT

A child may give the impression, by not turning readily to sound, that she is difficult or naughty.

Types of hearing impairment

Otitis media
Treatment is usually with antibiotic medicine to treat the infection.

KEY POINT

Research tells us that passive smoking greatly increases the chances of otitis media.

Otitis media with effusion – OME – 'glue ear'
If the otitis media persists it may lead to glue ear. Sometimes grommets – tiny plastic tubes – are inserted into the eardrum. These allow the air to circulate within the middle ear and the thick fluid to disperse, the cycle of infection is broken and hearing improves.

Sometimes the child is left to grow out of the condition – the Eustachian tube will change shape making it less likely as a focus for ascending infections. During this period of growth, developing from what a child *can* hear is important.

Ear wax and foreign bodies
When this reason for a child's difficulty in hearing is found the solution is simple and usually easily managed by the family doctor.

GOOD PRACTICE

Never poke around in a child's inner ear as you may push any object further in and cause additional damage. Never use cotton buds to clean a child's ears.

Communicating with a child with hearing impairment
There are different views on the most effective way of developing communication with a child with a hearing impairment. The three main approaches being used at present are:
- the auditory–oral approach
- total communication (sometimes called a flexible approach)
- bilingualism.

The auditory–oral approach
The central principle in this approach is the development of a child's spoken language and understanding of speech by the maximum use of a child's residual hearing. Hearing aids (see page 318) are used extensively, signing is not. The key to success is felt to be early diagnosis, and the consistent use of aids.

A child is taught to listen to help her brain make sense of the meaning of spoken language which surrounds her, however indistinct. A child is flooded with language in her early years in a variety of environments – playgroups, nursery and school. This approach is reinforced by lip reading – helping a child recognise word and sound patterns from lips and sometimes also by cued speech (see page 315).

Whether all deaf children will be able to communicate through speech is controversial. However, recent research indicates the majority of even profoundly deaf children who have been given a true auditory–oral approach can achieve fluent and comfortable communication through speech and with good standards of fluency.

The gaining of such skills in a child with a severe impairment, will take considerable time and commitment.

GOOD PRACTICE

- Remember communication is two-way. You must develop active listening skills yourself and show attention and response.
- A child will understand more than she will be able to communicate with you.
- Do not teach a child to talk – surround her with language that interests her and stimulates he and make communication fun.

Promoting oral speech
- Play and spend time with the child just like any other – she needs to hear your voice.

- Always respond to her sounds with a positive response such as a cuddle or clap.
- Talk meaningfully to her, talk her through routines and describe her clothes, meals, etc.
- Make sure you have her full attention using eye contact, touching, or pointing as necessary.
- Keep at face level to her, sit in front and keep close.

Have full attention and sit in front so the child can see your face and lips

- Have the light in front of you and not behind.
- Keep background noise low.
- In the home, turn off the radio and television. Do not have permanent background music.
- Do not shout in order to make a child hear you as you will frighten her and may make her fearful – she will feel you are angry with her.
- Maintain normal speech rhythms, do not exaggerate your mouth patterns, but speak slower.
- Accompany words with visual clues, especially for a young child – show her a teddy when you are naming one, remember she will use gestures before she uses words.
- In the older child, sentences are easier to understand than single words – extra words give a child context clues.
- Be careful with the words you choose and use, if they are unfamiliar this will be especially difficult for a deaf child.
- Check the child is understanding you as you talk.

- Use gestures and other visual clues to help her and always use expression to show pleasure, joy, questions, etc.
- Use your hands to help complement the meaning of words.
- Do not cover your face when talking – remember the shape of your mouth will change when you are eating and this will confuse her lip reading attempts.
- Remember moustaches and beards that partially cover the face can hide the lips.
- Large earrings are a distraction to a child who is trying to lip read.
- Never talk over her to a hearing child or adult – always include her in conversations.
- Allow pauses between changes in topics to allow her time to adjust.
- If an older child is frustrated try writing things down – increase mime and demonstration with the younger child.
- Try not to correct her efforts at speech, you may undermine her confidence.
- Give her plenty of time to attempt speech.

KEY POINTS

- Lip reading requires considerable concentration that may be difficult for a young child.
- Always keep sessions short and check she is understanding as, inevitably, some lip reading is guesswork.
- Remember she may tire easily.
- Always give praise and encouragement for her efforts.

Total communication

This approach follows a combination of systems, involving the development of speech, as above, complemented by an adapted signing system.

In total communication (TC) the signs are arranged so that they are in English word order. TC aims to use a deaf child's hearing and supplement her imperfectly heard speech with visual signs. Remember visual signs are accessible to all hearing impaired children with usual sight.

It is thought this TC approach is especially helpful in the early years and makes the development of oral language easier, limiting delay.

In TC it is therefore vital that all carers can sign competently, confidently and with a depth of vocabulary and combine this with the spoken word. This will have to be learnt for this system to be successful.

Other techniques

Other techniques sometimes used to supplement residual hearing include the following.
- Cued speech: some words appear to have a similar pattern when lip read e. g 'cat and cut', so a hand is placed near the mouth with a variety of hand shapes to highlight differences.
- Finger spelling: each letter of the alphabet is represented by a different hand position – in Britain with two hands. Words are spelt out.

- <u>Signed English</u>: signs are taken from British Sign Language (BSL) and used with additionally developed signs, which are only used in signed English. It is used with two-handed finger spelling to give an exact manual representation of spoken English. Unlike BSL it is designed to be used at the same time as spoken English.
- <u>Makaton</u>: see page 295.

Bilingualism

Sign language is regarded as a language in its own right and used solely. Here oral language is not developed and signs do not supplement speech. Communication is solely through BSL which is **considered to be the main language of deaf people.** BSL is another independent language such as French or Swahili – it is not just gesture or mime but a combination of these, including using the face and whole body. It is a visual language both in the way it is used and understood. It has the richness, depth of vocabulary and grammatical rules of any spoken language. The signing is three-dimensional and so complex, simple gesture, or a minute change in movement or facial expression can change a meaning. It cannot be used at the same time as speech.

Using BSL solely as a communication method, it is argued, allows a child to develop a full language in the important early years and so access the curriculum easily. This approach is primarily for the profoundly deaf child. Deaf children are considered to have a right to their own signing language, in which they can communicate easily with other deaf children and adults and gain access to their own culture. Pride and self-esteem are raised by helping a child feel part of her own group whose traditions are special, valued and promoted, a distinct deaf identity can develop.

Once sign language is established as a first language it is thought to be a good basis for learning English, in its written form, as a second language.

KEY POINT

- This approach demands *high-quality signing skills* from all involved in a child's care – learning just a few signs will not help a child develop communication at a sufficient depth.
- Parents and hearing siblings usually learn easily alongside a deaf baby.
- The involvement and training of deaf nursery nurses, teachers and other carers as experienced, positive role models is needed to extend this approach.

Which approach?

No system will be the complete answer for every child; the degree and type of impairment a child has will be one of many factors in a final choice.

All approaches have advantages and disadvantages. Parents should make the decision for their young child themselves.

KEY POINT

In any approach the quality and depth of communication, whether in signing or speech, is important in achieving helping a child achieve her potential.

Activity

Prepare a talk for your peers describing the different ways available for developing communication and language for children who are deaf.

Prepare arguments for and against each main approach. You will need to undertake additional research.

ONGOING MANAGEMENT

- Carers must learn the skills and knowledge needed for implementing the chosen choice of communication.
- Good practice started at home must continue in any care and educational establishment. See 'Promoting oral speech', pages 313 to 315.
- You must understand the specific type of impairment a child has and be particularly aware of a child with a fluctuating loss.
- Develop 'listening' activities in the curriculum – helping her discriminate between different non-speech sounds such as animal noises or musical instruments.
- Develop music and sound-making activities and use different types of sounds and vibration.
- Be aware that changes in routine may be confusing to a child who is deaf.
- Understand why behaviour is sometimes demanding – her world may at times be frustrating.
- Use visual aids freely and imaginatively.
- Discuss in advance how you will manage emergency procedures such as fire drills and other safety procedures.
- Be vigilant in looking for non-verbal clues a child may give that she is not understanding, is bored, confused or unhappy.
- Investigate areas of modern technology that will enrich her world:
  - doorbells can be extra loud, or accompanied with flashing lights
  - telephones can have different tones on their rings and lights can be fitted to flash when the telephone rings.
  - loop systems are microphones placed on the speaker of the television. A loop amplifier feeds the signal through a piece of thin cable, running around a skirting board. A magnetic field is created within this loop and a hearing aid can be programmed to pick this up and change it back into sound. A child can then listen to television at a level comfortable to both her and her hearing parents and friends.

HEARING AIDS

Post-aural (behind the ear) hearing aids

Mini ones are available and are suitable for babies and for certain types of hearing impairments.

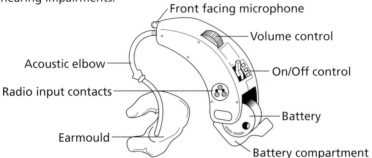

Front facing microphone

Volume control

Acoustic elbow

On/Off control

Radio input contacts

Battery

Earmould

Battery compartment

Body worn hearing aids

Used mostly for profoundly deaf children and especially in very young children. They can produce high levels of volume, with less sound distortion, especially at low frequencies. They are less prone to whistling. They are often worn with an accompanying harness – **check the microphone is not covered.**

Microphone –
do not cover

In the ear hearing aids

These types are becoming more widely used. They are often most suitable for children with a less severe impairment.

Remember

- Hearing aids cannot make a child hear normally, they amplify **all** sounds.
- New developments have produced high powered aids to help profoundly deaf children.
- As soon as possible after they are fitted a child should wear them all day.
- Your attitudes to hearing aids will influence how a child feels about hers.

Hearing aids for children

Supporting a child with a hearing aid

- Always be positive about a hearing aid – encourage the child to value it.
- Check a hearing aid daily (use a stetoclip which allows you to listen at a comfortable level yourself).
- Change batteries regularly.
- Check the condition and comfort of any ear-pieces. Earmoulds need replacing regularly, often every four to six weeks.
- Check leads are not loose, chewed or punctured.
- Switch the aid on and off.
- Check any microphone grilles are not blocked (perhaps covered with rusk or food!).
- Encourage the child to learn to care for and check her hearing aid herself.
- If you think the aid is not working, do not leave the situation. The parents will have access to advice and maintenance support.
- *Remember*, hearing aids amplify sounds, they do not make them 'normal'. In amplifying all sounds they may mask speech.

A radio hearing aid

Some children are given radio hearing aids as well as their own hearing aid. Someone else wears the transmitter and can switch it on and alter the setting of a child's hearing aid if necessary. When the radio aid is switched on the child hears the voice of the person wearing the transmitter as if the person was standing next to her. This is especially useful in playgroups, busy classrooms, outside or in playgrounds or in a class itself where the teacher may be across the room. These also help limit the background noise with which a child may have to cope.

GENERAL IMPLICATIONS

Deafness is a condition from which children have additional needs. How to identify and meet these needs most effectively, is not universally agreed within the deaf community.

A carer and child using radio aids

One school of thought feels that this may be by a variety of combinations including the use of BSL language or other signing systems and a combination of spoken and written English supported by the use of aids and should be flexible depending on the resources and skills available.

A second school feels that only through the medium of spoken communication can a child truly have the freedom to access the wide social community.

The bilingual school feels children who use their own sign language are freed from disability and able to develop a proud self-identity, without the inbuilt disadvantage of producing speech. They argue that the hearing society should not impose their norms on the deaf community.

ADDITIONAL DEVELOPMENTS

For children who are following a flexible approach to hearing impairment increasingly sophisticated hearing aids are being developed, both smaller and more powerful.

The development of cochlea implants to treat sensorineural deafness is being successfully undertaken in several major centres. Following surgery children will need intensive oral teaching and support.

CASE STUDY

Jenny's teacher noted that at five Jenny was constantly saying 'What?' Often Jenny ignored instructions and she shouted loudly when involved in group work. Her voice could always be heard across the classroom. She began to get a reputation as noisy and difficult.

When this was brought to her mother's attention she said it was what the family described as Jenny's 'domestic deafness' – ignoring what she did not want to hear, but always making sure she was heard when she wanted something.

The teacher felt it was more than this and a hearing test was arranged through the school health service. Jenny was discovered to have quite a marked but fluctuating hearing loss caused, it was thought, by unresolved glue ear. She was treated with antibiotics and the school developed a management plan. This included encouraging Jenny to sit at the front of the class and in the teacher's vision so her lips could be read. At any apparent signs of ignoring instructions, the staff immediately repeated them clearly and plainly.

1 What other measures would help Jenny?
2 What preventive health measures might have avoided the difficulty in the first place?

RESOURCES

British Deaf Association
1–3 Worship Street
London EC2 2AB

The National Deaf Children's Society
45 Hereford Road
London W2 AH

DELTA – Deaf Education through Listening and Talking
PO Box 20
Haverhill
Suffolk CB9 7BD

Vision impairment

Impaired vision or blindness means a child has insufficient or inadequate vision for certain everyday activities. The World Health Organisation (WHO) defines blindness as the inability to count fingers at 6 metres (20 feet) or less.

KEY POINT

Total blindness is rare. Most children can see something even if only the difference between light and darkness.

Sight continues to develop after birth and vision must be stimulated to allow it to reach its full potential. Seeing also requires perception to make sense of the images sent from the eye to the brain and complex language and communication skills to describe what is perceived. As a result it may be many months before a final decision on the full extent of a visual impairment is made. It is thought that 20,000 children in this country have a visual impairment.

About half of all children with impaired vision will have associated additional special needs – hearing or learning disabilities being the most common.

WHAT HAPPENS

**THE EYE AND
HOW IT WORKS**

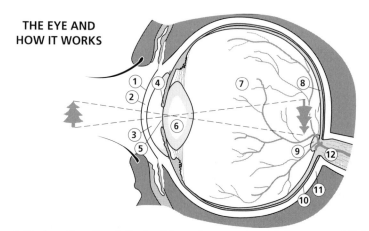

1 Conjunctiva: the delicate thin outer covering of the eye and lining of the eyelids.
2 Cornea: the window of the eye which allows light through to fall on the retina.
3 Aqueous humor: clear jelly-like substance.
4 Iris: the area that gives the eyes their individual colour, in front of the lens and behind the cornea.
5 Pupil: the central hole in the eye that varies in size to allow different amounts of light through.
6 Lens: a capsule containing clear fluid which focuses images upon the retina.
7 Vitreous humor: clear jelly-like substance.
8 Retina: the inner lining of the eye which receives and transmits the images via the optic nerve to the brain.
9 Macula: a small circle of cells on the retina which forms the area of fine sight.
10 Choroid: the layer between the retina and the sclera which contains the blood vessels in the eye.
11 Sclera: the white, tough, protective covering of the eye.
12 Optic nerve: the main nerve of the eye along which messages are sent from the retina to the brain.

The eye

Damage to the development of the eye or the nervous system that sends and translates visual messages to the brain can occur at any time.

Causes of visual impairment

The following are the main causes of visual impairment.

Before birth

- family history of blindness
- rubella or other infections such as syphilis or toxoplasmosis in pregnancy.

Around birth

- prematurity
- infections
- oxygen poisoning.

After birth

- injury
- infections
- severe inflammatory disease.

Types of visual impairment

Types of visual impairment vary and will depend on which part of the eye or nervous system is affected. The following are some of the more usual problems.

- Albinism: too little coloured pigment is present in skin, hair and eyes resulting in too much light being admitted to the eye.
- Astigmatism: the eyeball is unevenly shaped and the light fails to fall on the most effective part of the retina, for focusing. Vision is blurred and distorted.
- Cataracts: part of the lens becomes cloudy and the images the child receives are blurred and unclear and vision is lost.
- Conjunctivitis: inflammation or infection of the conjunctiva.
- Hypermetropia: long sight – only distant vision is clear.
- Keratitis: infection or inflammation of the cornea and conjunctiva – if severely affected a child will only see light and the definition of objects will be limited.
- Microphthalmos: unusually small eyeballs, sometimes unable to function for sight.
- Myopia: short sight – only near vision is clear.
- Nystagmus: involuntary flickering of the eyes.
- Optic atrophy: the optic nerve fails to send sight messages to the brain.
- Strabismus (squint): weak muscles allow the eye to 'wander' – the eyes appear to look in different directions. It affects three in every 100 children. Common in the newborn, it should disappear by three months of age.
- Tunnel vision: only part of an image is seen, vision appears as if looking down a tube.

KEY POINT

Strabismus can cause blindness in the affected eye if untreated.

DIAGNOSIS

Any obvious difficulty will be identified during the routine examinations given to all newborn babies.

Additional signs to watch for will depend on the age of the child. The mother is the best person to notice early difficulties and can be guided on what to look for by the use of an ongoing checklist. This is given to some parents to monitor the sight development of their baby.

What should you watch for?

Babies
- No eye-to-eye contact, especially with the mother.
- The baby does not react to light.
- 'Abnormal' eye movements.
- Eyes not following objects at two months.
- Failure to locate objects at six to twelve months of age.
- A parent expresses worries.

The older child
- Cloudy or bloodshot eyes, unusual eye movements, excessive rubbing or blinking of eyes.
- Clumsiness and poor hand–eye coordination.
- Moving the head rather than the eyes when involved in looking at pictures or stories.
- Holding objects close to the face.
- Loses interest quickly in activities needing the use of near vision.
- Difficulty in matching or naming colours.
- Sometimes walks with head down and is reluctant to join in physical activities.

Vision screening tests
Vision screening tests for all children are undertaken from six weeks of age by the family or clinic doctor. A baby's emerging ability is assessed in:
- following moving objects
- locating small objects
- more refined testing undertaken during the toddler stage by asking a child to:
  - identify miniature toys at distances
  - match shapes and letters of different sizes
  - pick up minute particles e.g.' hundreds and thousands' – a near vision test.

KEY POINTS
- Each health area will have different time schedules for routine screening.
- Specific tests to exclude squint are undertaken if there are worries.
- Referral to a consultant ophthalmology unit, for full assessment, will be made if a child's vision is causing concern.

PROGRESS CHECK

Why is it important to detect any squint early?

KEY POINT

Levels of vision may not be constant and will change from day to day and often within a day. Factors affecting this include:

- lighting
- mood/tension
- tiredness
- illness.

TERMS ABOUT VISION

Accommodation: the eye's ability to see distant or close objects by focusing.

Binocular vision: sight through both eyes at the same time.

Colour blindness: inability to distinguish certain colours from each other.

Field of vision: the area seen without moving the gaze.

Focal point: the area of the retina where the light rays meet.

Light adaptation: the eyes' ability to increase or restrict the amounts of light entering.

Low vision aids: aids to help residual vision – glasses, magnifying lens.

Partial sight: limited vision sufficient for eventual reading and writing.

Refraction: the bending of the light rays to focus on the retina.

Refraction error: a changed eye shape prevents light rays focusing exactly on the retina.

Visual acuity: ability to see the shape of objects.

Visual motor functioning: the use of the eyes to guide movement.

Visual perception: the ability to give meaning and understanding to what has been seen, rather than just looking.

CARE

Part of the initial important bonding process between mother and child is built upon their emerging communication. Eye-to-eye contact is absent in a blind baby and first smiles may be late. Parents will need to learn to respond physically to a baby's smiles, by touch or voice, to encourage him to repeat this action. Apparent lack of response can cause a parent frustration and undermine confidence, even affecting the initial pleasure gained from their child. Early involvement for parents with a support agency or group, who have personal experience of such feelings is often helpful.

KEY POINT

It is thought that sight contributes to 80 per cent of a child's learning.

For compensation, a baby who is blind or visually impaired will need to learn to develop his other four senses – *touch, hearing, smell and taste* – to their maximum as well as using any residual sight. He needs these senses to gather as much information about his surroundings as possible and then learn to make sense of the images he receives or 'sees'.

Your role is to teach him how to fully use these four remaining senses. The following are suggestions on how to do this.

Encouragement

Help the baby use his hands, fingers, feet and mouth – these will eventually tell him about touch, smell, taste and the direction and types of sounds that he hears.

There are many things you can encourage him to do.

- Reach and touch – put toys into his hands.
- Learn about his body and how to move and control it – keep his early clothing free and unrestricted and feet bare.
- Link gesture and touch to actions and words – tell him before you touch him, even when he is a baby – he can't see your hand or know whose hand it is he feels. Always respond to him by word or touch, remember how much sighted people show feelings such as pleasure, by visual gestures.
- Develop his confidence when he is surrounded by unfamiliar noises which may cause him concern by telling him you are there and explaining the unknown to him.
- Teach him to discriminate between types of sounds, noises, smells and taste.
- Develop self-help skills such as washing, cleaning teeth, dressing and undressing as early as possible. Use easy to get on and off clothes with Velcro fastenings. Remove his clothes in the same order coming off so he will learn how to put them on again in the correct order. Choose clothes that will give him positional clues such as buttons at the front, pockets at the sides.
- Help him gain bladder and bowel control. Choose a firm pot that will make him feel secure. Reinforce what you expect him to do with words and by familiar noises – the flushing of the lavatory, the taps running, even a musical potty.
- Exploration and experimentation are important and to do this he needs protection but not smothering. Check fireguards are fixed and secure, electrical sockets covered, loose dangerous ornaments out of reach, always use stair gates and initially a wooden playpen may be helpful (this would allow him to pull to stand). Discuss safety with him, explain words such as 'sharp', 'steep' and 'slippery'.
- Teach him to feed himself. Encourage him to hold his bottle, give him a spoon when weaning. Expect mess and plan for it, but help with experimenting with different types of spoons and suction dishes. Choose bright colours to supplement any vision. Let him use his fingers to feel the position of his food as well as

enjoy the sensation. Introduce one food at a time – do not overwhelm him. It is helpful for him to take cutlery, beakers or mugs from a firm surface and return them to the same surface – otherwise he may drop them into mid-air.

■ Always tell him what you are giving him and expand the range such as sweet, savoury, hot, cold, warm, etc. and as he grows give him choices.

■ Make mealtimes learning, relaxed and fun opportunities.

KEY POINT

The baby needs total experience – to feel his food, hear it being prepared, perhaps in a kitchen away from where he is, smell it and taste it and have you describe it to him.

Stories are important to describe the world

Verbal communication

Every aspect of the child's life will need to be explained and talked through so he can learn the association of words to objects, shapes, and sounds. This will extend his world. The following will encourage him.

■ Describing everyday events, for example how you run the bath, what clothes you are collecting, what bubbles you put in the water, confirm if they or the soap are the source of the perfumes he smells, show him the difference between warm and hot. Tell him you are rubbing him dry, patting his delicate face, massaging his skin with creams, blowing on his tummy to make him giggle, etc.

■ Linking sounds to noises, 'This is a rattle'.

■ Using an exaggerated sound for key words such as 'up' or 'down'.

- Developing conversations as he begins to learn to imitate. Always listen – he may copy whole sentences but have little idea of what it really means. Reinforce with complementary sounds, for example 'Johnny went in the car' – let him touch the car, feel his seat, toot the horn, etc.
- Not anticipating or answering his speech before it is complete.
- Using books and stories freely, showing clear bright pictures or having 'feely' books.
- Using rhymes and action songs.
- Using simple clear language.

GOOD PRACTICE

Never talk over or about the child, always to him. Encourage relatives, peers and friends to direct questions to him.

Initiation

Most learning takes place, by imitation, copying and discovery. Exciting activities and objects are not as readily available to the child as a sighted child and so he may be unaware of their existence. Help him by using everyday routines as learning times. Encourage him by using the familiar.

- In the home and garden use opportunities to open drawers, turn water taps, empty cupboards full of interesting and safe objects such as saucepans, ladles, jugs, sieves, etc. Involve him in make-believe activity such as showing him how to 'vacuum' the carpet, knead dough for baking or wash up.
- Bathtime provides opportunities for water play and relaxation.
- Outdoors, a well-fenced garden is ideal for exploration, digging, getting dirty, smelling flowers and growing plants. On park visits you will be using swings, collecting leaves, feeling wind and rain, learning to pedal a tricycle and developing spatial awareness. Use shopping trips for discriminating about traffic sounds, shopkeepers' voices and so on. Well-supervised visits to the swimming pool are fun, developing motor skills and body awareness.
- Visits to and from friends and relatives provide opportunities to socialise and develop acceptable behaviour, sharing and taking turns. They should begin with a single child, then a small group increasing in numbers in preparation for play-group or nursery.

Toys and activities

Toys and activities chosen need to be *big, bright* and *colourful.*

- *Big:* the larger the object, or the closer to the eye, the easier it is to see.
- *Bright:* the more light there is, the better, so ensure play areas are well lit. Use additional lighting if necessary and use reflective or fluorescent lights. Choose matt light surfaces for reflection and visual comfort, as shiny surfaces can produce unwanted glare
- *Colourful:* eyes work best with contrasts so develop this with colourful toys against contrasting backgrounds and spread a sheet on the floor as a setting for toys.

Keep toys within the child's reach when he is very young, but gradually move them away to encourage him to move. Use noises from the toys as clues for him such as squeaking, rattling, banging, etc.

Toys chosen should have different textures, colours, sizes, shapes, weights, smells and sounds.

Identification

Interpret the child's world, explaining the nature of objects and the meaning of sounds. Keep him informed of routines, events and everyday happenings.

Remember his ears are especially important so leave them uncovered even on cold days outside.

PROGRESS CHECK

What are the three main points to consider when choosing toys for a child who is blind?

Activity

To develop identification of sounds: make a tape recording of some the sounds of the child's day – doors opening and shutting, introductory music to television programmes, the sound of the toaster popping, taps running, the washing machine working, the dog barking, the milkman leaving the bottles, birdsong, and so on.

Talk him through his day, ask him about the sounds and what they tell him. This will help his memory too.

Mobility

Help the child learn about the position of his own body, how it moves, how it changes position and about influences affecting it.

Tell him the names of his body parts and repeat them in rhymes, songs and games.

Support his mobility in line with his developmental progress.

- Place him to kick and move on the floor, on his back and his tummy.
- Use baby chairs so he can be with you in different parts of the house and be near your voice.
- Encourage him to roll and reach, prop him in a sitting position and 'show' him sound toys near.
- Be prepared that he may not crawl, but roll – he cannot see so he will bump his head more readily crawling than rolling.
- Use a wooden playpen not a lobster pot as he will find pulling to stand easier – show him where the rails are.
- Hold his hands firmly when he starts to toddle, at first by standing behind him. Keep his hands no higher than his shoulders – use push-and-pull toys that are well-balanced when he is stable.

- Let him walk alone when he is ready, keep an uncluttered room, and bind sharp corners with foam in the early days of mobility.
- Provide clues to help him know where he is, such as a clock ticking or a window open for the breeze to blow on him. Let him learn by exploring.
- Teach him about stairs and use safety gates so he can develop skills of climbing and descending one at a time.

As the child learns and develops you can provide further progress.

- Make obstacle courses where he goes over, under and around.
- Develop his running, at first with his holding your arm, then help him to run towards you. Tie string between posts or trees for him to use as a guide.
- Pace out distances for him between objects and encourage him to count them.
- Use trampolines with added bars for him to hold.

Safety

Provide an environment where the child can explore within safe but extending boundaries. Initially use the playpen or cot, then a safe part of the room fenced off by solid furniture, then the whole room, gradually extending his world. Remember objects will go to his mouth for him to discover shape, texture and size for much longer than his sighted peers.

The safe practice procedures needed in working routinely with children will usually be sufficient. However you must remain vigilant and careful, always linking the possibility of safety hazards to his emerging development.

KEY POINT

Your role is to ensure the child is neither over-protected nor placed in danger.

GOOD PRACTICE

- Adult involvement is especially important in the early stages for a baby with a visual impairment.
- Reinforce pleasure for the child by touch – he cannot see your facial response.

ONGOING MANAGEMENT

As with any child the opportunities available in a playgroup, nursery and school are important in enriching his quality of life and learning potential.

Preparing for admission

Preparation for admission is the key to success. The following are points to consider.

- Communication between parents and childcare workers.
- Discussion with parents to allay any potential worries.
- Time for staff to update their own knowledge.
- Time for a child's specific visual needs to understood, following liaison with any other involved professionals.

- Minor adjustment to toys may be required. There should be emphasis on sound-makers and bright coloured toys with moving parts.
- Ensuring light sources are adequate – especially in corridors, toilets and stairways.
- Assessment of the environment for safety hazards.
- Preparation of individual children – the importance of naming themselves to him.
- Preparation for introducing a visually impaired or blind child to the group.

Initial admission

A good settling-in procedure with the reassuring presence of his parents, should allow a child to become confident with his new surroundings. Involve and listen to the parents as they will be aware of any specific areas that might pose problems for him.

Initially a safe corner could be sectioned off for him, allowing him the opportunity for exploration within a controlled environment. Individual or small groups of children can join him gradually to allow him to begin to meet his peers. Such a system would allow him to familiarise himself with some of the new toys and equipment available.

Encourage him to stamp the floor or tap a wall to identify the different surfaces he is meeting. Carpets, tiles, wooden floors and tarmac will all sound different and help him identify where he is. Give him other clues too, such as sounds and textured wall areas at hand height and add bright or white tape or paint to the edges of tables and steps.

KEY POINT

Changes in the way a room is set up, chairs left out or clutter accumulating on the floor will all be potentially hazardous for the child.

Meeting and learning with his peers
- Sing songs which use names of the children to help the child identify his friends.
- Choose stories which mention sounds or encourage staff and children to add their own voices and sound effects.
- Encourage activities which children can enjoy equally together such as water and sand play.
- Develop cooperative play such as seesaws and trikes with trailers, but always supervise well.
- Develop listening games such as sound lotto and remembering games such as 'My mother went to market'.
- Sing action songs together.
- Encourage children and staff always to identify themselves by name to him.

It may be helpful to spend time just observing the child and assessing at the beginning, learning what he actually can do.

Codes of behaviour must be applied to all children, including a child with a visual impairment. He needs the security and stability of learning right from

A music session should include everyone

wrong. It would be additionally disabling for him, if your expectations were low and you allowed his impairment to be used as an excuse for unacceptable behaviour.

Braille

Some children will have insufficient sight to read print and may need to learn Braille. This requires the child to discriminate by touch between patterns made by sets of raised dots representing letters or words. Preparation for this means helping him identify shapes and objects by touch. Smaller and smaller objects are presented with increasingly subtle differences. Promoting fine motor development and strong fingers and hands through play will also provide a firm foundation for learning Braille.

A childcare worker too can gain Braille skills through a distance learning course.

PROGRESS CHECK

What area of development needs stimulating to prepare a child to use Braille?

Managing glasses

If a child wears glasses check the following points.
- Know how often and when the glasses should be worn.
- Encourage parents to get a spare pair.
- Check the condition daily to ensure they are unbroken with screws tight and lenses still present!

- Check the comfort. Remember the child will grow out of his frames.
- When the glasses are taken off never put the lens side down.
- Clean glasses regularly and with a non-scratch cleaner.
- Remember the child's prescription will probably need changing and his eyes retesting.
- Are you showing positive images of children with glasses in your displays?

GENERAL IMPLICATIONS

Visual impairment can delay a child's development, so stimulation and opportunities for play are important. Repetition and reinforcement of learning experiences may be needed for longer than for sighted children. Occasionally some aspects of behaviour such as placing objects in the mouth or tapping and shouting for an echo, may be mistaken for a learning disability. Developmental stages may be different and pretend play may show itself in sounds rather than in action.

Specialist support and advice is important in ensuring that all his needs are both understood and met by all involved in his care.

ADDITIONAL DEVELOPMENTS

Complex sensory rooms are available for some children, incorporating areas with music, fans, vibrating mats, feely boards, lasers, strip and bubble tube lights.

The National Library for the Blind has 3,440 children's titles in Braille, including 'Two-ways', a series in which print and Braille are combined so they can be enjoyed by blind and sighted children together.

Increasingly, modern technology, especially sophisticated computer equipment, will be valuable in supporting learning. Closed circuit television has already been developed for use as a powerful microscope.

CASE STUDY

When Jo was having her six-week developmental examination the family doctor noticed that her eyes seemed different and did not appear to be of the same size. Jo's mother, who had no other children, also confirmed that Jo had not yet smiled responsively for her. After further investigation it was discovered that Jo had no sight in one eye and only minimal peripheral vision in the other. She was registered as blind. This was an enormous shock and distress to her young mother, who felt the cause might have been due to the rubella she had contracted during her pregnancy.

1 How could you explain the importance of stimulating Jo's residual vision and other four senses to her mother?
2 What support could you give Jo's mother about providing a safe but stimulating and extending environment for her baby?

RESOURCES

LOOK!
National Federation of Families with Visually Impaired Children
49 Court Oak Road
Harborne
Birmingham B17 9TG

National Library for the Blind
Cromwell Road
Bredbury
Stockport SK6 2SG

Partially Sighted Society
Queen's Road
Bredbury
Stockport SK6 2SG

RNIB Customer Services
PO Box 173
Peterborough PE2 6WS

RNIB Education Information Service & Children's Policy Unit
224 Great Portland Street
London W1N 6AA

Spina bifida and hydrocephalus

Spina bifida is caused by a fault in the spinal column (the backbone) when part of the rear section of one or more of the vertebrae (the thirty-three bones which make up the spine) fails to form properly. It happens when the baby is developing in the womb. The result of this malformation is a gap or split in the column leaving the spinal cord inadequately protected. It can be damaged or ruptured, resulting in:
- paralysis
- loss of sensation
- bladder and bowel control problems.

Spina bifida is the most common developmental problem of the central nervous system, occurring in up to 10 per cent of all births.

The causes of the condition are unknown but are thought to include both genetic and environmental factors.
- It occurs more often in white races.
- It occurs in babies born prematurely.
- It is more likely to re-occur in families who already have a child with the condition.

- Increasingly, diet at the time of conception and in the first twenty-five days of pregnancy, when the neural tube is developing, is considered to be important. Extra dietary folic acid (vitamin B9) is thought to reduce the chance of a problem in tube development.

Babies born with spina bifida can also have the associated condition hydrocephalus. This is often known as 'water on the brain' and occurs because there is an imbalance between the production and drainage of the special fluid (the cerebro-spinal fluid) which bathes the brain and lubricates the spinal cord. Swelling inside the brain develops, causing damage if left untreated.

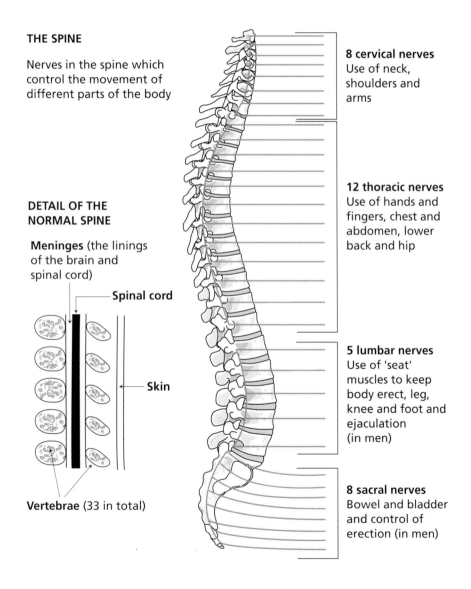

THE SPINE

Nerves in the spine which control the movement of different parts of the body

8 cervical nerves
Use of neck, shoulders and arms

12 thoracic nerves
Use of hands and fingers, chest and abdomen, lower back and hip

DETAIL OF THE NORMAL SPINE

Meninges (the linings of the brain and spinal cord)

Spinal cord

Skin

Vertebrae (33 in total)

5 lumbar nerves
Use of 'seat' muscles to keep body erect, leg, knee and foot and ejaculation (in men)

8 sacral nerves
Bowel and bladder and control of erection (in men)

WHAT HAPPENS IN SPINA BIFIDA

There are three main types of the condition.

Spina bifida occulta
Here only the vertebrae are affected, the condition is mild, common and rarely causes problems. It is thought to occur in one in 10 of the population. Occasionally there is a slight dimple or small hair growth on the lower back. In some children the spinal cord may become caught against the vertebrae and as growth increases, cause minor difficulties with bladder control and mobility.

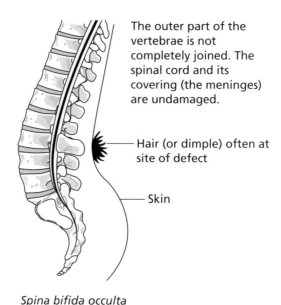

The outer part of the vertebrae is not completely joined. The spinal cord and its covering (the meninges) are undamaged.

Hair (or dimple) often at site of defect

Skin

Spina bifida occulta

Spina bifida cystica
Here a blister-like swelling occurs at the lower back, covered by a thin layer of skin. It can be either meningocele – the least common form – or meningomyelocele, the most common and most serious form.

Meningocele
Meningocele is the least common form of spina bifida cystica.
- The sac will contain tissues which line the spinal cord (the meninges, see pages 335 and 337). These produce the cerebro-spinal fluid which bathes and protects the brain and spinal cord.
- Usually the nerves are undamaged.
- Usually there is little disability.

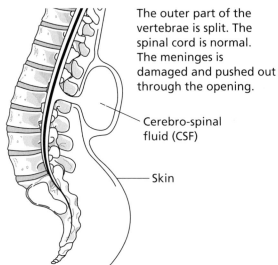

The outer part of the vertebrae is split. The spinal cord is normal. The meninges is damaged and pushed out through the opening.

Cerebro-spinal fluid (CSF)

Skin

Spina bifida cystica: meningocele

Myelomeningocele

Myelomeningocele is the most common and most serious form of spina bifida.

- Both the meninges *and* the cord protrude through the gap, which is covered with a thin membrane.
- The membrane may rupture and leak fluid, making the child vulnerable to infection, especially meningitis.
- The spinal cord will be damaged or not properly developed.
- There is *always paralysis and loss of sensation* below the damaged vertebra.
- A child may also have problems of bowel and bladder control.
- Two thirds of children with this type of spina bifida will also have hydrocephalus.

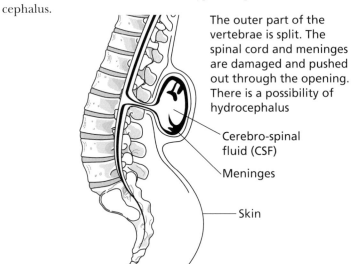

The outer part of the vertebrae is split. The spinal cord and meninges are damaged and pushed out through the opening. There is a possibility of hydrocephalus

Cerebro-spinal fluid (CSF)

Meninges

Skin

Spina bifida cystica: myelomeningocele

KEY POINT

How severely a child is affected will depend on the following two factors.
- The position of the lesion – any part of the spine may be affected and the higher in the spine the malformation, usually, the greater the effect. However occurrence in the lower spine is more common.
- How much damage there is to the spinal cord.

Cranium bifida
The bones of the skull fail to grow properly. The sac which forms sometimes contains tissues and fluid only and occasionally a very small and damaged brain which fails to develop.

The baby will either be stillborn or die shortly after birth.

PROGRESS CHECK

1 Why is a child with myelomeningocele more likely to be severely physically affected by spina bifida than a child with spina bifida occulta or a meningocele?
2 What is hydrocephalus?

DIAGNOSIS

Spina bifida can be detected while the baby is in the womb, but not treated.

After birth the more obvious malformations of the spine in spina bifida cystica are usually noted immediately. The neurological examination routinely given to all newborn babies will detect spina bifida occulata.

CARE

In a child who has a meningomyelocele, surgery is required to close the lesion. This is completed as soon after birth as possible for the following reasons.
- To prevent deterioration and further damage to the spinal cord.
- To prevent the sac from bursting, leaving the child vulnerable to infection, especially meningitis.
- To make handling and general personal care easier for all carers.
- To improve appearance and help promote long-term self-esteem.

On discharge home to the family, after surgery to close and repair a meningomyelocele, a baby needs the following care.
- Security, stimulation, love and his basic needs as a new baby met. Feeding procedures will have to be adapted to avoid pressure on any wound.
- To establish eye contact – he may spend time on his tummy initially.
- Appropriate toys provided, such as mobiles and musical toys.
- Care of any wound with strict implementation of hygiene procedures. Any dressing required would be undertaken by a community nurse.
- Urine and faeces must be kept away from any wound. A baby is frequently cared

for on his tummy, with his buttocks exposed. When healing is complete nappies are used as usual. Sometimes the urine is removed by a catheter (a tube) into the bladder. If this is so, extra fluids will be needed to limit the increased chances of urinary infection.

Immediate and long-term care
In any condition where there is a loss of movement and sensation it is important to be aware of the dangers of pressure sores.

Pressure sores
A baby born with full sensation will automatically move to relieve weight, he will wriggle, squirm and eventually turn and sit. This is a natural way of preventing tissues being deprived of oxygen and sores developing. In a baby with paralysis the carer must undertake this for the baby, otherwise ulceration will occur. If this happens healing will take a considerable time and be difficult.

KEY POINTS

- A baby with paralysis and loss of sensation will feel no pressure or pain and so is especially vulnerable to sores.
- The baby will not indicate distress even if sores are present.
- The baby will be unable to discriminate between hot and cold and may be vulnerable to scalds and burns in the parts of his body that are paralysed.

GOOD PRACTICE

- Always check clothes are not rubbing or chaffing. Initially the baby may sleep on a sheepskin or have extra foam over the mattress for softness.
- Check the condition of the skin is healthy. Keep it dry, clean and moisturised, pay special attention to creases in ankles, knees, tips of nose, cheeks and chin. You may not be able to use a bath initially.
- Move him and change his position frequently.
- Watch for any signs of rubbing or pressure.

Movement
Muscles and limbs that do not move of their own accord must be exercised for the baby, by you. A physiotherapist will arrange passive exercises for you to undertake for him. These involves regularly gently moving the muscles and joints that he cannot move himself.

Position
The baby's body may be pulled into abnormal positions by gravity and the weight of his paralysed limbs. You will be taught how to position him to avoid this. Check that this is maintained. Especially vulnerable areas are the hip and ankle joints.

PROGRESS CHECK

1 What would lead you to think a child was showing signs of the start of pressure sores?
2 What equipment must you check to ensure friction is not caused?
3 Where are the vulnerable areas on his body?

Bladder management

A child who has lost sensation below the waist will have difficulty controlling his bowel and bladder needs. There are several reasons why managing this is important.

- Failure to empty the bladder regularly leaves him vulnerable to infection.
- The smell of urine is demoralising for him and may affect his developing social relationships.
- Effective management will keep his skin healthy and prevent sores.
- Failure to provide him with extra fluids may cause kidney infections.

For effective management one of the following may be necessary.

- A catheter (a tube) is used to empty the bladder regularly during the day, often every three to four hours.
- A catheter is left in the bladder continuously and left to drain into a bag.
- Boys may have a penile sheath which covers the penis and drains into a bag.
- Medication may be prescribed by the family doctor.
- Occasionally various surgical techniques are undertaken.
- Pads and special pants may be used.

Your role is to:

- support the child in whatever system is chosen
- learn about the techniques and help required
- encourage the child in managing this himself as he grows.

Bowel management

A diminished sensation means the child is unaware when he needs to pass stools. Learning control over this aspect of his life prevents:

- embarrassment and loss of self-esteem
- leaking into his clothes
- constipation.

What help is offered?

- the child is taught to sit on the lavatory at a set time each day, usually following a certain meal
- he is taught pushing techniques.

Further help sometimes includes:

- enemas or suppositories to stimulate the bowel
- medication
- bowel washouts
- surgery.

Your role is important.

- Offer him a high-fibre diet with plenty of fluids to prevent constipation.

- Encourage exercise, both to help elimination and prevent him becoming over-weight.
- Learn about and support him in his programme and techniques.

Help the child to become independent

KEY POINT

Most children with spina bifida do develop routines of control over the personal needs aspect of their lives.

GOOD PRACTICE

- Your support in helping a young child manage his personal needs will affect how he regards himself. Be sensitive and careful in your choice of language.
- Always find privacy when helping him meet his needs.

Mobilisation

For a child who has a paraplegia (no movement or sensation below the waist) mobility is primarily achieved through the use of wheelchairs. Children who have more controlled movement may be helped by using crutches and frames.

Both occupational and physiotherapists will be involved in deciding the most effective way of improving mobility.

Make sure that your environment is wheelchair friendly (see page 240, chapter 7).

Focus attention on the parts of his body that the child can control.

ONGOING MANAGEMENT

Planning and preparation before a child starts in a pre-school or school group will be needed. The more independent he is allowed to be the more confident he will become. Good communication and liaison will be essential.

Specific areas that will need consideration are:

- toilet needs
- mobility and access
- specific health needs
- continuation of programmes of care such as physiotherapy and occupational therapy
- any special dietary requirements.

For a child who is using a wheelchair or crutches for mobility all carers need to develop awareness of how much help to offer and when. Often only verbal guidance is needed.

Becoming wheelchair proficient and being able to manage small steps and uneven surfaces with confidence will need teaching. A child from five can manage to push up slopes and control his chair on inclines. Young children in wheelchairs usually are accepted well into group situations, a 'watching' eye needed only to ensure safe play for all.

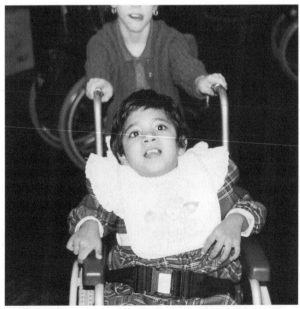

Young children in wheelchairs are well-accepted by their peers

KEY POINT

- Always keep the wheelchair in good condition.
- Keep any used cushions clean and change covers frequently. This is especially important if bowel and bladder control are not complete.

> ### Activity
> Create a raised garden that is easily accessible for a child in a wheelchair.
>
> Involve the children in planning, choosing and planting. Find plants that have different scents and offer a range of tactile experiences.

Hand skills

Some children with spina bifida are less skilful and dextrous manually than their peers of similar age. At the same time they are more dependent on their upper limbs as they need strength and power for controlling wheelchairs and crutches.

Activities to develop fine motor movement should be developed and additional sensory input arranged.

- Play with textured materials.
- Finger painting.
- Sand and water experience.
- Games and activities that encourage the development of two hands such as ball games and Stickle Bricks and Duplo play.
- Games to encourage fine finger movement such as finger puppets and pegboards
- Encouragement in dressing, doing up buttons, zips and laces and using knives and forks.

A child with such a special need may be physically slow, so make sure you allow sufficient time for him to move around a building and prepare for activities, mealtimes, etc. Do not hurry him up or do everything for him, but try setting achievable goals for him to reach.

KEY POINT

Some children with spina bifida follow a conductive education approach to promote mobility (see page 360, this chapter).

Hydrocephalus

This is a condition where there is an imbalance between the production of cerebrospinal fluid and its absorption over the surface of the brain and into the circulatory system.

WHAT HAPPENS

Cerebro-spinal fluid (CSF) is produced constantly inside each of the four spaces (the ventricles) in the brain. If a drainage path is obstructed then fluid accumulates in the ventricles causing them to swell and compress the surrounding brain tissue. In babies and young children the head size increases as the bones are still flexible and not fused.

The are several reasons why this may happen.

Congenital
Hydrocephalus may occur at birth but the reasons are often unknown.

Prematurity
A baby born early is very vulnerable. The brain is still actively developing, the blood vessels are fragile and easily damaged. If these break then clots can occur blocking the flow of CSF and causing hydrocephalus.

Spina bifida
Babies born with spina bifida, especially with myelomeningocele and sometimes meningocele, often will have hydrocephalus. In addition to the lesion in the spinal cord there are also abnormalities in the physical structure of parts of the brain that develop before birth which prevent adequate drainage of CSF. This can result in even further pressure on the brain.

Meningitis
When an infection of the meninges or linings of the brain and spinal cord occurs, the resulting debris and inflammation can block drainage pathways of CSF.

Brain and spinal tumours
Brain and spinal tumours can also cause compression and affect drainage of CSF

Signs of hydrocephalus
- Excessive head growth. All babies, from birth, should have their heads regularly measured and charted on a percentile chart for spurts of growth.
- Delayed closing of the anterior fontanelle in the skull. This is usually fully closed by ten to fourteen months.
- The fontanelle may be tense and bulging.
- The baby is fractious and restless, with a high pitched, shrill cry.
- Vomiting.
- Changes in the size of the pupils in the eye – they may be uneven.
- If untreated coma, seizures and death will occur.

Hydrocephalus produces delayed maturation of the brain and so all a child's senses may be affected to a degree.
- Sight: squint, double vision or nystagmus (rapid involuntary eye movements)
- Sound: initially a child might have a hypersensitivity to noise.
- Touch and taste: problems with shape, texture, temperature and taste.

- Learning difficulties:
  - short attention span
  - poor short-term memory
  - spatial awareness and visual perception problems
  - sequencing difficulties
  - delayed fine motor control.
- Emotional problems: the likelihood of behavioural difficulties is five times increased.

KEY POINT

Not every child will have all these difficulties and the levels of severity will vary widely.

DIAGNOSIS

Diagnosis is confirmed by a special brain scan. Early treatment is important to limit the possibility of brain damage.

CARE

The usual form of immediate treatment is the insertion of a shunting device by a surgical operation.

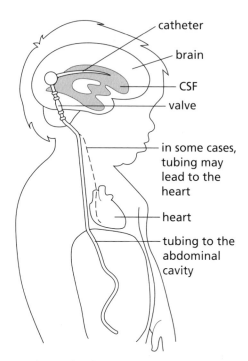

An example of a valve, or 'shunt', in place

This shunt diverts the accumulated CSF from the obstructed pathway and returns it to the bloodstream. It consists of a system of tubes with a valve to control the rate of drainage and prevent back-flow. It is inserted at the upper end into a brain ventricle and the lower end into either the heart or abdomen. The fluid collected is returned into the bloodstream. The shunt is not seen, it is all completely enclosed in the child's body.

KEY POINT

A shunt does not cure hydrocephalus and brain damage that has already occurred, remains. A shunt's function is to prevent further damage happening.

Important signs that there may be something wrong with a shunt
Something wrong with a shunt is usually a blockage or infection. Remember each child is an individual and may present with different symptoms, however, the main signs to watch for are presented below.

Treatment
Treatment for a blockage is by surgery to replace or adjust the damaged shunt.

Treatment for an infection is by surgery to remove the shunt, treating the infection with antibiotics and when clear, inserting a new shunt.

Infants	Toddlers	Children
Enlargement of head	Head enlargement	Headache
Full tense fontanelle	Fever	Vomiting
Dividing skull sutures	Vomiting	Fever
Swelling or redness along tract of shunt	Headache	Irritability/sleepiness
	Irritability	Personality change
Fever	Swelling or redness	Loss of bladder and bowel control
Irritability	Seizures	Staggering
Seizures		Seizures
		Lethargy/loss of interest

Signs that there may be something wrong with a shunt

PROGRESS CHECK

1 You are a nanny with a new baby. What might indicate the baby was developing hydrocephalus?
2 You are a nursery nurse in an infant school, what might tell you a child of four with hydrocephalus has an infection in her shunt?

ONGOING MANAGEMENT

All the initial and ongoing management needed by a child with spina bifida will be required if both conditions are present.

A child with an obvious physical condition can have those physical needs met while her hidden ones are overlooked, for example any learning and emotional difficulties.

KEY POINT

The child will need full stimulation of all her senses – seeing, hearing, smelling, touching, tasting and moving – from her early years.

Check that the child is comfortable at any table for activities and that she can reach easily, manoeuvre her wheelchair and has access to all the equipment available.

The child needs release of tension by physical exercise and this will also help her develop spatial awareness.

Activity

Design a physical exercise programme for a child of five, with limited mobility who is using either crutches or a wheelchair.

In your plan try to develop the child's gross motor skills, stamina, spatial awareness and concentration.

Could your plan include children without limited mobility? How could you adapt it to make the efforts required equal for all?

Remember to consider safety factors, an element of achievement and making it fun!

Other relevant issues of management are covered in the sections on behaviour and emotional management in chapter 8 and vision and hearing stimulation and promoting learning in fragile X and Down's syndrome, this chapter.

GOOD PRACTICE

The visual aids, pictures, books, games and stories that you use should reflect the child's special condition showing wheelchairs, crutches and frames.

They should promote a positive image, with involved and fully participating children having individual likes, dislikes and wishes.

GENERAL IMPLICATIONS

The degrees of disability may vary enormously in a child with spina bifida and hydrocephalus. Many different professionals may be involved in her care and good communication and liaison between them, her parents and yourself will be especially important in helping the child's full development.

Sharing expertise and being able to ask questions will be necessary. No one will know all the answers and your input may be a vital part in preparation for her future.

CASE STUDY

Shona was a first baby born by normal delivery and her mother was discharged home immediately following the birth, as both she and her daughter appeared well.

Shona thrived during the first weeks of her life. At her routine six-week check at the local child health clinic, the doctor measured her head circumference as part of the normal screening procedure. On comparing the results of this measurement with those undertaken after her delivery it was noted there had been a considerable increase in the size of Shona's head which had not been visually obvious.

Shona was referred immediately to a hospital where hydrocephalus was confirmed and a shunt inserted to drain the fluid and relieve pressure on her brain.

1 What ongoing observations will be needed to check the shunt is working effectively?
2 What other areas of Shona's development may possibly be affected by the discovery of her condition and how would you plan to meet these needs?

RESOURCES

The Association for Spina Bifida and Hydrocephalus
ASBAH
42 Park Road
Peterborough PE1 2UQ

Cerebral palsy

Cerebral palsy (CP) is a complex physical condition affecting a child's posture and movement. It is caused by damage or failure of the brain to develop in the specific area which controls movement.

Sometimes the area of the damage involves nearby parts of the brain which can cause hearing impairment and perceptual difficulties. CP can cause a child to have difficulty in controlling her facial expression and in communicating. She may, as a result, be labelled as having learning difficulties where none exist.

CP is not usually inherited and can occur in any family regardless of sex, race or social background. It is thought that one in every 400 children is born with CP – a total of 1,500 babies each year in Britain. It usually occurs at, or immediately after birth, but it can also happen following brain infections such as encephalitis or meningitis.

The range of the effects of the condition is enormous. Some children will appear to have no obvious disability apart from perhaps a mild clumsiness, while others will be severely disabled.

Associated difficulties that may also be present with CP

- Seizures: one in three children will also have epilepsy.
- Hearing impairment.
- Visual impairment – especially squints.
- Speech impairment – either delayed or indistinct speech.
- Perceptual difficulties/learning delay thought to involve up to 50 per cent of all children with CP. Some children, however, will have above average intellectual ability.

KEY POINTS

- There is no cure for the condition. It does not worsen as the child grows, but difficulties may become more apparent. Support and good management can ensure a child leads a full and active life.
- There is no relationship between physical appearance and intellectual ability.

WHAT HAPPENS

Anything that damages the growing brain may cause cerebral palsy. Often the reasons for this are unknown and it can occur before, during or after birth. The following are some of the known reasons for the condition.

Before birth
- Infections: especially rubella, toxoplasmosis and other viral infections.
- Failure of the placenta to develop or function effectively.
- Some drugs.

Around birth
- Prolonged or very difficult labour.
- Prematurity.
- Infections.

After birth
- Head injuries.
- Infections such as meningitis.
- Brain tumours.

KEY POINT

Whatever the reason for the damage to the brain, it does not get worse once it has happened, however, neither does it recover.

There are three main types of cerebral palsy thought to depend on which area or part of the brain has been affected (see page 350).

The three main types of CP are spastic cerebral palsy, athetoid cerebral palsy and ataxic cerebral palsy.

AREAS OF THE BRAIN AFFECTED BY CEREBRAL PALSY

Different areas of the brain are thought to be affected in the three major types of cerebral palsy.

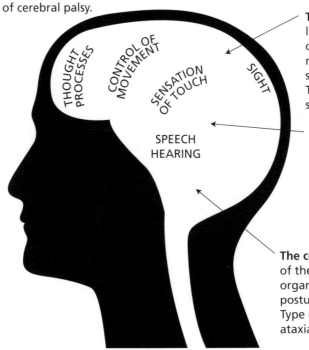

THOUGHT PROCESSES

CONTROL OF MOVEMENT

SENSATION OF TOUCH

SIGHT

SPEECH HEARING

The cortex The outer layer of the brain – concerned with thought movement and sensation.
Type of cerebral palsy: spasticity.

The basal ganglia In the middle of the brain below the cortex – concerned with the organisation of movement.
Type of cerebral palsy: athetosis.

The cerebellum At the base of the brain – concerned with organisation, coordination, posture and balance.
Type of cerebral palsy: ataxia.

Spastic cerebral palsy

This is the most widely known and most common form of CP, affecting 50 to 60 per cent of all children with the condition.

Damage occurs to the cortex or outer brain layer, concerned with thought, movement and sensation. This results in abnormally strong tension in certain groups of muscles (this has been likened to muscle cramps) and sometimes pain. Attempts to move a joint cause muscles to contract and block the movement.

Areas affected are arms and legs.

Arms

Arms are often held pressed against the body with the forearm bent at right angles to the upper arm and the hand bent against the forearm. The fist may be clenched tightly.

Legs

The legs are often less involved than the arms and the effect may be evident only when a child walks. The child may typically walk with legs wide apart and sometimes with arms outstretched.

With moderate involvement, movement may be slow and laboured with poor balance and a jerky motion.

Severe involvement, involving both legs, may result in 'scissoring' where the legs are crossed and the toes pointed.

Permanent contractures and resulting loss of mobility, may develop without muscle training.

KEY POINTS

- The term 'spastic' should never be used as a noun – it is offensive to people with CP. It has been misused as a term of abuse.
- It is however correct to use the term *spasticity* when describing the type of muscle tension in this sort of CP.

Athetoid cerebral palsy

This type of CP is thought to occur in 20 to 25 per cent of children with the condition. It results from damage to the basal ganglia in the brain which results in involuntary, uncoordinated and uncontrolled movements of muscle groups. It is thought to be made worse by emotional stress.

All limbs

All limbs may be involved. Movement is uncontrolled, jerky and irregular, accompanied by twisting movements in the hands, involving the fingers and wrists.

Leg involvement

If the legs are involved then the child may walk in a writhing, lurching and stumbling manner, with noticeable difficulty in coordinating her arm movements.

KEY POINT

When calm and rested a child may walk well and when asleep or at rest may not show writhing hand movements.

Speech

This may be difficult to understand as the child's vocal cords and tongue may be affected. The likelihood of hearing impairment is increased.

KEY POINT

A child with athetosis will be delayed in her early physical development, slow to sit and 'floppy' in her muscle power. A child with spastic cerebral palsy will not show this.

Ataxic cerebral palsy

This type occurs in about 1 to 10 per cent of children with CP. It results from damage to the cerebellum which is concerned with balance.

Movement
The child typically finds difficulty in balancing and coordinating her movements. Often gross and fine control is affected. The child may walk with a high stepping motion.

Vision
Often nystagmus – rapid eye movement – is present.

Combination
In addition to the three identified types of CP around 15 to 40 per cent of all children will have a combination of effects.

In **quadriplegia**, the most severe form of cerebral palsy, all four limbs are affected.
In **hemiplegia** one side of the body is affected.
In **paraplegia** the legs only are affected.

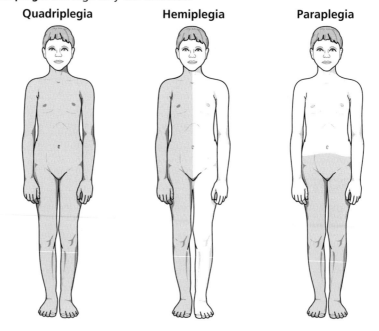

Quadriplegia   Hemiplegia   Paraplegia

Terms used to describe which areas of the body are affected in cerebral palsy

DIAGNOSIS

Early signs
The following are early signs that might suggest a child may have CP.
- Asymmetry (unevenness) in movement or contour. Creases in the groins or

axillae may be different on each side of the body. One hand or limb moves more freely than the other.

- Listlessness or irritability.
- Feeding difficulties – poor sucking or swallowing.
- Excessive or feeble cry.
- Long, thin baby who is slow to gain weight.

Later signs
- Failure to follow normal patterns of motor development.
- Persistence of primitive reflexes.
- Weakness.
- Early hand preference shown (often before twelve to fourteen months).
- Abnormal postures.
- Delayed or impaired speech.

GOOD PRACTICE

- Parents' anxieties about the progress of their child must always be acknowledged and investigated.
- Knowledge of the norms of development are essential for you in identifying a child who might have CP.

PROGRESS CHECK

1 What are the main early developmental differences you might notice between a child with spastic CP and a child with athetoid CP?
2 What differences might you notice when a child is at rest?

A child who is suspected of having CP will have a full developmental history taken and neurological examination by a paediatrician. An accurate assessment of a child's abilities will be made in conjunction with a variety of professionals, and in partnership with parents.

CARE

Early diagnosis allows for the following.
- The development of a programme of care, specific to a child's total individual needs and the identification of her particular strengths.
- Help to limit or prevent limb contractures (fixed abnormal limb positions).
- The development of maximum mobility, preventing restricted movement and faulty posture.
- The identification and planning for any associated needs involving hearing, vision, speech and learning disability.

A parent may be supported by a variety of professionals depending on the specific needs of the individual child.

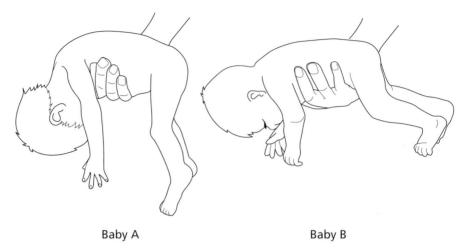

Baby A   Baby B

Both babies are the same age. Which type of cerebral palsy does baby A have?

KEY POINT

The degree a child is affected by CP varies enormously, depending on a) the type of CP b) the location of the affected area of the brain c) the age at which the damage occurred.

Ensuring physical comfort and developing mobility
- Make sure you handle the limbs of a child affected with CP with care and attention and ***never hurry a movement***. Always tell the child you are moving a limb.
- Try to maintain good body alignment to prevent contractures. Splints, casts, braces and wedges may all be used to help the child keep a comfortable position. Remember the stronger 'contracting' muscles are the most likely ones to pull a limb into an abnormal and potentially less useful position such as hips and knees becoming flexed and turned inwards – the classic 'scissoring' position.
- Certain situations, too, may produce tension and stress in the child, leading to increased muscle spasm. Know when this might happen and try to avoid it.
- If a spasm occurs never try and control it by force, but gently rock that part in spasm, as this often helps the muscles relax.
- When lying the child down, place her on her side to limit muscle spasm. As she grows older she may also be safe and comfortable on her stomach.
- Ensure you know how to lift correctly to prevent strain to your own back (see page 241).
- When helping the child to stand, always position yourself in front of her. This encourages her to develop balance. Ensure her feet are firm to the floor with a wide base, check her body is leaning slightly forward and encourage her to take her own weight. Shoes must be well fitting and supportive. Specially adapted shoes may be advised.
- The usual baby pushchairs, car seats and body slings, are suitable for initially

getting around. These can be adapted to meet her growth. Always ensure you secure her in correctly.

- Develop the child's confidence and independence in gaining mobility. Remember that fear and anxiety can increase spasms. Help her develop control over her own body by offering only essential support.

GOOD PRACTICE

- The physiotherapist will develop a programme using exercises and aids specific to the needs of the individual child.
- The physiotherapist will also teach you how to lift a child to ensure the child has the correct, safe support. This will help you to limit associated muscle tension and spasms which are different for each child.
- Your role is to understand this and know how to implement the care plan.

PROGRESS CHECK

1 What are the main points to remember when moving a child with CP?
2 How would you manage a child who was having a spasm?
3 What is the best position for a child to be placed in for rest?

Managing feeding

Initially some babies need to be fed by tube and this may lead to difficulty in the baby learning to suck. A mother will need understanding and support at this time. Tensions developing from such a situation are easily passed onto the baby.

A baby with CP may have fixed body positions or develop spasms. Consider this when supporting her at mealtimes (see page 356).

Early feeding

- A baby who is stiff will respond by further extension of her neck and arms when her mouth is open. So when feeding try to hold her so this cannot be achieved. Position her firmly in the crook of your arm, with her flexed arm tucked behind your back and the extended one flexed against her chest. When she is older she can be effectively supported in her own chair facing you.
- A baby who is floppy needs checking that she is well supported under the ribs to help her keep an upright position and extend her chest. Ensure there is good head support. Initially chewing may need to be encouraged by moving the jaw around. When she is using a chair, support her fully, possibly using an additional pillow and with her feet flat against the chair sides.

Weaning

Prompt weaning allows for the introduction of solids to help develop chewing and tongue control which are important in promoting speech and for healthy teeth and gums. It is sometimes easier, but not advised, to continue with sloppy foods longer than for the ordinary child.

- Always make sure the child is comfortable, correctly positioned and can see well, before starting a meal so:

BODY POSITIONS

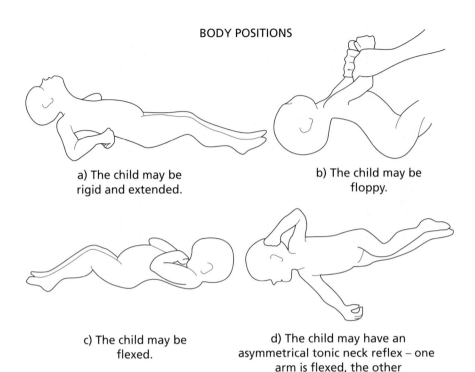

a) The child may be
rigid and extended.

b) The child may be
floppy.

c) The child may be
flexed.

d) The child may have an
asymmetrical tonic neck reflex – one
arm is flexed, the other
extended with the head turned towards it.

*A child with CP may have fixed body positions or develop spasms. Consider this
when supporting her at mealtimes*

- – sit her in her own special chair
- – sit her well forward, with her elbows rested on the tray in front and feet flat
  on the foot rest
- – try to position the chair so that she can be a part of family meals
- – keep her head upright and in midline, to reduce the risk of choking.
- ■ Use the time to talk, sing and encourage her development and make it fun.
- ■ Always tell her what you are offering her.
- ■ Check the temperature carefully.
- ■ Allow plenty of time.
- ■ Follow a usual weaning plan, with one food being introduced at a time, varying
  textures and tastes.
- ■ Always use plastic or unbreakable spoons and beakers, as a strong bite reflex
  may be present, causing potential dangers.
- ■ Place food far back on the tongue and to the side.
- ■ Swallowing can be encouraged and the bite reflex overcome, if necessary, by
  rotating the lower jaw and firmly stroking upwards and backwards under the jaw.
- ■ Crumbly foods can sometimes increase the chances of choking.

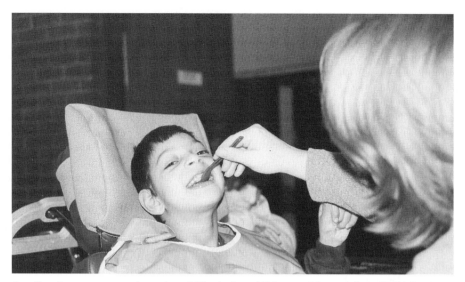

Swallowing can sometimes be difficult for children with CP. Place food far back and to the side if the child cannot manage by himself

■ As the child grows encourage her to hold the spoon. Help her grasp by checking the wrist is well back.

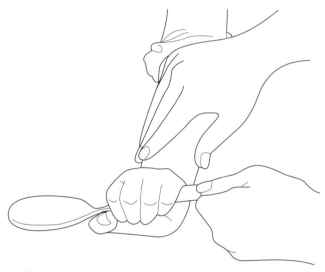

Encourage the child to keep the wrist well bent back to help maintain grasp

■ Experiment with different types of spoons to find the most suitable for her – possibly ones with wide, shallow bowls and easy-grip rubberised handles.
■ Use bowls with suction pads to prevent slipping.
■ Encourage her to push food onto her spoon using another one or a fork. This also helps her use both sides of her body even if one is weaker.

- Allow for mess and protect the child and the floor well.
- Make the time enjoyable to encourage her to try new foods and develop confidence with solids.
- Praise the child's efforts.
- If you feed her, sit at her side, always checking her position.

Drinking

Often the lower jaw is moved up and down as she drinks – this can be stopped by supporting the jaw from behind. Help her hold her mug and check her thumbs are turned *out*.

- Mugs should have two handles to promote symmetry and the use of both sides of the body. Weighted mugs may also be valuable.
- The tongue can continue to come forward (tongue thrust) in a child with CP and this can make both drinking and eating difficult. Sucking through a straw can help limit this and at the time strengthen lips and palate muscles. Blowing bubbles can teach a sucking motion.

PROGRESS CHECK

What safety precautions must you be aware of when feeding a child with CP?

GOOD PRACTICE

- You should aim to promote independence at mealtimes, even if it is initially messier and takes longer than for an ordinary child.
- Mealtimes should be sociable, friendly times with opportunity to interact and learn.

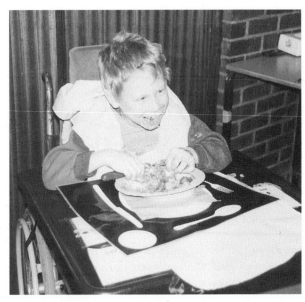

Mealtimes can provide taste, smell, language and tactile opportunities

Physical care

Dressing
- Aim to develop independence.
- Choose clothes that are easy to put on and take off.
- Put clothes on the affected limb first. Never pull her fingers as this will increase elbow flexion.
- Before putting on shoes and socks check her legs are bent. This will limit ankle and foot stiffness and toe curling.
- Encourage choice and involve her in selecting her own clothes.

Hygiene
- The usual routines will be required. Always use non-slip bath mats.
- In view of her reduced chewing capacity, pay special attention to dental care.
- As she grows and becomes heavier adaptations to help at bathtimes may be advised by the occupational therapist.

Toileting
- Muscular tension may increase her difficulties in gaining bladder and bowel control. Exercises to help this may be advised by the physiotherapist.

Sleep routines
- Develop a settling routine involving a bath and relaxing story or song.
- Occasionally the child may find it difficult to settle. If she is less mobile than her peers she may just be less tired. Check her general comfort.
- If she has spastic CP she may need to be moved during the night to prevent spasms and make her comfortable.
- A special sleeping position may be recommended – usually on her side or tummy as she grows older.
- A Portage scheme is available in some areas for children with CP (see page 152).

Play
As with any other child this is an important part of promoting her development.
- Check her position to ensure she is comfortable and well supported. Use wedges and standing frames to allow her access to toys. Remember, if she is placed on her back you may promote spasms.
- Encourage fine movements to develop hand control.
- Develop games to promote balance and control of movement.
- Stimulate and encourage her speech (see section on encouraging speech development, pages 272 to 273, chapter 8). Liaise with the speech therapist (see sections on promoting oral speech, pages 313 to 315, chapter 8 and managing hearing impairment, page 317, this chapter).
- Swimming will both help movement and be fun.
- Short bursts of play are better than long sessions.
- Use music, stories and rhymes freely.

KEY POINTS

- The child may take longer to learn a game.
- She may tire more easily.
- Always praise and encourage effort.

Activity

Make a 'feely' box for a two-year-old. Choose a variety of textures, shapes and sizes for your box.

What areas of development could this box help?

GOOD PRACTICE

- A child with CP has the same needs as other children for love, security, stimulation and protection. Always apply routine rules and discipline as with any child.
- Treat the child as a unique and individual person with her own personality, likes and dislikes. This is especially important if she has communication difficulties.

ONGOING MANAGEMENT

Management issues of handling and promoting mobility, and developing independence and the self-esteem of a child with CP will continue throughout childhood.

Added difficulties will need to be addressed if identified (for hearing and visual impairments see pages 307 and 321, this chapter; for learning difficulties see Down's syndrome, this chapter and for managing behaviour problems see page 276, chapter 8).

Conductive education

Conductive education is becoming increasingly popular for children with CP or 'motor dysfunction'. It is an intensive teaching and learning system designed to enable children with disabilities to function more independently. A child is fully assessed before undertaking the programme, to ensure that she will benefit.

Conductive education was first developed in Hungary by Dr Andras Peto in 1952. Specially trained 'conductors' provide the child with a fully integrated day, without disruptions from different professionals (speech, occupational and physiotherapists, etc). The conductor's role is to be aware of, and develop all aspects of the child, through establishing a strong relationship with her, and many feel this is the key to the programme's success.

The following are the main aims of conductive education.

- To stimulate active exploration of the world through movement during the child's whole day.

- To develop a routine to include a series of interlinked tasks undertaken with the child in different positions – lying, standing, etc.
- To encourage transferring skills learnt in these various positions to other activities, including educational ones, throughout the day. For example a child will sit at a table, lean forward to develop manipulative skills in matching or drawing and stand to paint at an easel. Thus sitting, leaning forward and standing are accompanied by manipulation, matching, memory skills and painting.
- To set achievable but increasingly demanding tasks and goals that cover both learning and motor development, so allowing the child to achieve success and raise self-esteem.
- To assume movement and language are interconnected. The child is taught to use spoken language as a means of preparing herself mentally for movement – 'I stand up tall', etc.
- To look at the whole child, not just her special need.
- To build on the child's interests and personality.
- To provide the programme within a group of children with similar needs, so developing strong peer relationships and helping motivation.
- To use a specially designed room to make progress from one activity to another streamlined. There are strategically placed bars and ladders for the child to hold on to.
- Children are encouraged to challenge their disability – to walk and not use a wheelchair, to speak and not use other forms of communication, etc.
- Parents and carers play an important part in the programme; skills that are learnt by the child should be applied and reinforced in daily life.

KEY POINT

Conductive education is not suitable for all children. It is not a cure for the condition, but aims to promote independence. It is currently only available on a very limited basis in the UK and funding is not universally available, but at the discretion of the local education authority.

Children with CP for whom conductive education is considered to be unsuitable include:
- children who are blind or deaf
- children with learning difficulties
- children with uncontrolled epilepsy.

Adaptations for children with these additional needs may incorporate a variety of therapies and methods including patterning (see page 159, chapter 5).

GENERAL IMPLICATIONS

A child with a severe disability can be a challenging and stimulating addition to a family, but exhausting – it is important to be sensitive to this. Respite care and holiday play-schemes in which a parent has confidence may be needed to allow time for families to refresh themselves.

Adaptations and changes to the home together with information regarding benefits may also be required as the child grows.

KEY POINT

The range of disability is enormous in CP. Many children will lead full and active lives with little effects from the condition, whereas other children will need some degree of lifelong support and protection.

ADDITIONAL DEVELOPMENTS

Sometimes drug therapy is needed to control epilepsy, and spasticity in limbs may be reduced with the use of muscle relaxants if a child is particularly distressed, but on the whole medicines are not routinely used for a child with CP.

Increasingly sophisticated technical developments are valuable for a child with CP. Microtechnology means computers can be worked with fingers, toes, tongues, voice and eye and breath movements, allowing access to the wider world. Communication aids now allow synthetic speech. Electric wheelchairs can even be worked with switches operated from the chin.

CASE STUDY

Mary was born prematurely with cerebral palsy and difficulties over feeding were immediately present. She was late in all aspects of her physical development, not sitting until she was eighteen months old and then only for a few seconds at a time. At four years old she was not yet walking unaided. She was alert and interested, but her speech was not distinct and although her parents understood exactly what she said, others did not. She could count, sing nursery rhymes and was always wanting more stories. She became frustrated and easily bored as she could not reach her surroundings easily.

Recently she has started attending a special playgroup where conductive educational methods are used. The individual attention and contact with other children have had a dramatic effect upon Mary. She sleeps much better, is keen to do things for herself and appears more tranquil. Her mother finds the respite from her loved, but demanding and increasingly heavy, daughter valuable, allowing her to give much needed attention to Mary's older brother of seven. The support from other parents attending the playgroup is helpful – 'knowing how she feels' is the way Mary's mother describes it.

1 What support could have been identified and organised earlier, both for Mary and her mother?
2 Which peripatetic therapists could have helped Mary in her home?

RESOURCES

SCOPE
12 Park Crescent
London W1N 4EQ

SCOPE Education & Assessment Centre
16 Fitzroy Square
London W1P 6LP

The Peto Andras Centre for Conductive Education (UK)
17 Fitzroy Square
London W1P 5HP

National Institute of Conductive Education
Cannon Hill House
Russell Road
Moseley
Birmingham B13

Child abuse

Until comparatively recently society in general found it difficult to accept that children with special needs could be abused. However, children with differing disabilities are in fact at an increased risk of abuse, the rate being 1.7 times higher than for children generally.

Many groups now consider that definitions of 'abuse' should be extended for children with a disability to include the following.
- Lack of stimulation/supervision.
- Over-protection.
- Confinement to cot, bed or room/physical restraints such as strapping into chairs.
- Intrusive or insensitive medical photography or procedures.
- Incorrect drug use.
- Forced feeding, insensitive personal hygiene management, lack of privacy.
- The withholding of aids such as wheelchairs, crutches, etc. in order to promote mobility.

Vulnerability of children with special needs
Children with special needs are particularly vulnerable because of the following.
- Intimate care is needed in bathing, toileting and dressing which often has to be undertaken by someone else for the child longer than expected for the ordinary child.
- Intimate contact in residential care may be undertaken by someone of the opposite sex.

- Communication difficulties such as with speech difficulties, the deaf child, or the withdrawn child may mean a child is unable to speak out – allowing an abuser to continue unhindered.
- Low self-esteem in some children with disability may make it less likely they complain.

Vulnerability of parents/carers
The following are factors that place parents/carers under particular pressure.
- Children with behavioural difficulties may be particularly demanding for some carers.
- Children who need constant attention, especially at night, may increase pressure on families.
- Some physical and behavioural signs may be mistaken for complications of the condition itself.
- Parents and carers may be unaware of the impact of the condition itself.

GOOD PRACTICE

- Children with special needs must be cared for in an environment of dignity, respect and empowerment.
- Policies must be developed and adhered to in order to monitor children at particular risk of abuse.
- Nursery workers must consider their own feelings and attitudes to children with disability.
- Families and carers working with children with multiple and demanding needs must have support systems and networks available to them. Their needs, too, must be understood.
- The development of an ongoing programme of information regarding care of children with additional needs, should be undertaken.

RESOURCES

KIDSCAPE
152 Buckingham Palace Rd
London SW1W 9TR

NSPCC
42 Curtain Road
London EC2A 3NH
(NSPCC Child Protection Helpline 0800 800 500)

KEY TERMS

You need to know what these words and phrases mean. Go back through the chapter and make sure that you understand:

astigmatism
asymmetry
bilingualism
Braille
British Sign Language
cerebral palsy, ataxic CP, athetoid CP,
    spastic CP
child abuse (the wider definitions to
    be considered for children with
    special needs)
conductive education
conductive impairment
contractures
deaf culture
Down's syndrome
fragile X

hearing impairment
heart and auditory lesions
myelomeningocele
oral approach
otitis media with effusion
paralysis
pressure sores
ritualistic behaviour
sensory rooms
shunting mechanisms
spina bifida and hydrocephalus
squint
total communication
vision impairment and WHO
    definition

APPENDIX: Developmental norms

0 to 1 year

	Physical development – gross motor	Physical development – fine motor	Social and emotional development	Cognitive and language development
At birth	Reflexes: ■ Rooting, sucking and swallowing reflex ■ Grasp reflex ■ Walking reflex ■ Moro reflex If pulled to sit, head falls backwards If held in sitting position, head falls forward, and back is curved In supine (laying on back), limbs are bent In prone (laying on front), lies in fetal position with knees tucked up. Unable to raise head or stretch limbs	Reflexes: ■ Pupils reacting to light ■ Opens eyes when held upright ■ Blinks or opens eyes wide to sudden sound ■ Startle reaction to sudden sound ■ Closing eyes to sudden bright light	Bonding/attachment	Cries vigorously, with some variation in pitch and duration
1 month	In prone, lifts chin In supine, head moves to one side Arm and leg extended on face side Begins to flex upper and lower limbs	Hands fisted Eyes move to dangling objects	Watches mother's face with increasingly alert facial expression Fleeting smile – may be wind Stops crying whenpicked up	Cries become more differentiated to indicate needs Stops and attends to voice, rattle and bell
3 months	Held sitting, head straight back and neck firm. Lower back still weak When lying, pelvis is flat	Grasps an object when placed in hand Turns head right round to look at objects Eye contact firmly established	Reacts with pleasure to familiar situations/routines	Regards hands with interest Beginning to vocalise

continued

0 to 1 year continued

	Physical development – gross motor	Physical development – fine motor	Social and emotional development	Cognitive and language development
6 months	In supine, can lift head and shoulders In prone, can raise up on hands Sits with support Kicks strongly May roll over When held, enjoys standing and jumping	Has learned to grasp objects and passes toys from hand to hand Visual sense well established	Takes everything to mouth Responds to different emotional tones of chief caregiver	Finds feet interesting Vocalises tunefully Laughs in play Screams with annoyance Understands purpose of rattle
9 months	Sits unsupported Begins to crawl Pulls to stand, falls back with bump	Visually attentive Grasps with thumb and index finger Releases toy by dropping Looks for fallen objects Beginning to finger-feed Holds bottle or cup	Plays peek-a-boo – can start earlier Imitates hand-clapping Clings to familiar adults, reluctant to go to strangers – from about 7 months	Watches activities of others with interest Vocalises to attract attention Beginning to babble Finds partially hidden toy Shows an interest in picture books Knows own name
1 year	Walks holding one hand, may walk alone Bends down and picks up objects Pulls to stand and sits deliberately	Picks up small objects Fine pincer grip Points at objects Holds spoon	Cooperates in dressing Demonstrates affection Participates in nursery rhymes Waves bye bye	Uses jargon Responds to simple instructions and understands several words Puts wooden cubes in and out of cup or box

1 to 4 years

	Physical development – gross motor	Physical development – fine motor	Social and emotional development	Cognitive and language development
1 year	Walks holding one hand, may walk alone Bends down and picks up objects Pulls to stand and sits deliberately	Picks up small objects Fine pincer grip Points at objects Holds spoon	Cooperates in dressing Demonstrates affection Participates in nursery rhymes Waves bye bye	Uses jargon Responds to simple instructions and understands several words Puts wooden cubes in and out of cup or box
15 months	Walking usually well established Can crawl up stairs frontwards and down stairs backwards Kneels unaided Balance poor, falls heavily	Holds crayon with palmar grasp Precise pincer grasp, both hands Builds tower of 2 cubes Can place objects precisely Uses spoon which sometimes rotates Turns pages of picture book	Indicates wet or soiled pants Helps with dressing Emotionally dependent on familiar adult	Jabbers loudly and freely, with 2–6 recognisable words, and can communicate needs Intensely curious Reproduces lines drawn by adult
18 months	Climbs up and down stairs with hand held Runs carefully Pushes, pulls and carries large toys Backs into small chair Can squat to pick up toys	Builds tower of 3 cubes Scribbles to and fro spontaneously Begins to show preference for one hand Drinks without spilling	Tries to sing Imitates domestic activities Bowel control sometimes attained Alternates between clinging and resistance Plays contentedly alone near familiar adult	Enjoys simple picture books, recognising some characters Jabbering established 6–20 recognisable words May use echolalia (repeating adult's last word, or last word of rhyme) Is able to show several parts of the body, when asked Explores environment energetically
2 years	Runs with confidence, avoiding obstacles Walks up and down stairs both feet to each step, holding wall Squats with ease. Rises without using hands Can climb up on furniture and get down again Steers tricycle pushing along with feet Throws small ball overarm, and kicks large ball	Turns picture book pages one at a time Builds tower of 6 cubes Holds pencil with first 2 fingers and thumb near to point	Competently spoon feeds and drinks from cup Is aware of physical needs Can put on shoes and hat Keenly interested in outside environment – unaware of dangers Demands chief caregiver's attention and often clings Parallel play Throws tantrums if frustrated	Identifies photographs of familiar adults Identifies small-world toys Recognises tiny details in pictures Uses own name to refer to self Speaks in 2- and 3-word sentences, and can sustain short conversations Asks for names and labels Talks to self continuously

continued

1 to 4 years continued

	Physical development – gross motor	Physical development – fine motor	Social and emotional development	Cognitive and language development
3 years	Competent locomotive skills Can jump off lower steps Still uses 2 feet to a step coming down stairs Pedals and steers tricycle	Cuts paper with scissors Builds a tower of 9 cubes and a bridge with 3 cubes Good pencil control Can thread 3 large beads on a string	Uses spoon and fork Increased independence in self-care Dry day and night Affectionate and cooperative Plays cooperatively, particularly domestic play Tries to please	Can copy a circle and some letters Can draw a person with a head and 2 other parts of the body May name colours and match 3 primary colours Speech and comprehension well established Some immature pronunciations and unconventional grammatical forms Asks questions constantly Can give full name, gender and age Relates present activities and past experiences Increasing interest in words and numbers
4 years	All motor muscles well controlled Can turn sharp corners when running Hops on favoured foot Balances for 3–5 seconds Increasing skill at ball games Sits with knees crossed	Builds a tower of 10 cubes Uses 6 cubes to build 3 steps, when shown	Boasts and is bossy Sense of humour developing Cheeky, answers back Wants to be independent Plans games cooperatively Argues with other children but learning to share	Draws person with head, legs and trunk Draws recognisable house Uses correct grammar most of the time Most pronunciations mature Asks meanings of words Enjoys verses and jokes, and may use swear words Counts up to 20 Imaginative play well developed

4 to 7 years

	Physical development – gross motor	Physical development – fine motor	Social and emotional development	Cognitive and language development
4 years	All motor muscles well controlled Can turn sharp corners when running Hops on favoured foot Balances for 3–5 seconds Increasing skill at ball games Sits with knees crossed	Builds a tower of 10 cubes uses 6 cubes to build 3 steps, when shown	Boasts and is bossy Sense of humour developing Cheeky, answers back Wants to be independent Plans games cooperatively Argues with other children but learning to share	Draws person with head, legs and trunk Draws recognisable house Uses correct grammar most of the time Most pronunciations mature Asks meanings of words Enloys verses and jokes, and may use swear words Counts up to 20 Imaginative play well developed
5 years	Can touch toes keeping legs straight Hops on either foot Skips Runs on toes Ball skills developing well Can walk along a thin line	Threads needle and sews Builds steps with 3–4 cubes Colours pictures carefully Can copy adult writing	Copes well with daily personal needs Chooses own friends Well-balanced and sociable Sense of fair play and understanding of rules developing Shows caring attitudes towards others	Matches most colours Copies square, triangle and several letters, writing some unprompted Writes name Draws a detailed person Speaks correctly and fluently Knows home address Able and willing to complete projects Understands numbers using concrete objects Imaginary play now involves make-believe games

continued

4 to 7 years continued

	Physical development – gross motor	Physical development – fine motor	Social and emotional development	Cognitive and language development
6 years	Jumps over rope 25 cm high Learning to skip with rope	Ties own shoe laces	Eager for fresh experiences More demanding and stubborn, less sociable Joining a 'gang' may be important May be quarrelsome with friends Needs to succeed as failing too often leads to poor self-esteem	Reading skills developing well Drawings more precise and detailed Figure may be drawn in profile Can describe how one object differs from another Mathematical skills developing, may use symbols instead of concrete objects May write independently
7 years	Rides a 2-wheel bicycle Improved balance	Skills constantly improving More dexterity and precision in all areas	Special friend at school Peer approval becoming important Likes to spend some time alone Enjoys TV and books May be moody May attempt tasks too complex to complete	Moving towards abstract thought Able to read Can give opposite meanings Able to write a paragraph independently

GLOSSARY OF TERMS

Access
A way into; freedom to obtain or use something, for example, the environment, education, leisure facilities.

Advocacy
Speaking on behalf of, pleading for.

Advocate
Someone who pleads on behalf of another, for example a parent or professional carer for a child.

Chromosome
A thread-like structure composed of deoxyribonucleic acid (DNA), carrying genetic material.

Congenital
Born with.

Contractures
Shortening of muscles causing limbs to remain in a fixed position.

Differentiation
Adapting and presenting the curriculum (Early Years or National) in a manner appropriate to a child's needs and abilities.

Discrimination
Unfair or unequal treatment of an individual or group of people on the grounds of disability, race, religion, gender or age.

Code of Practice
A document giving guidance to local education authorities (LEAs) and all maintained schools on their responsibilities towards children with special educational needs.

Eclectic
A combination of a variety of approaches to management.

Empower
To enable, to authorise.

Elective mutism
Inability or refusal to speak due to psychological trauma.

Encopresis
Incontinence of faeces, faecal soiling.

Enuresis
Incontinence of urine, bedwetting.

Genes
Units of genetic material (DNA) carried at certain places on a chromosome and responsible for characteristics such as hair, eye and skin colour, blood group, body shape and size.

Genetics
The scientific study of inheritance. Human and medical genetics are concerned with the study of inherited disorders.

Genetic counselling
Advice on the possibility and probability of passing on inherited conditions and listening sympathetically to the concerns and anxieties of those seeking advice.

Holistic
An approach to care, management and support in which a child's total needs (physical, cognitive, emotional and social) are taken into account.

Inclusive environment
An environment which welcomes all children/adults, including those with disabilities and special needs, and is committed to caring for, valuing and respecting all children/adults equally.

Incontinence
Inability to control passage of urine or bowel movements.

Inherited
Passed down from one generation to another, for example genetic disorders.

Integrate
To include, to avoid segregation.

Learning difficulties
Greater difficulty in learning than the majority of children of the same age or having a disability which prevents or hinders a child from using the educational facilities provided for children of the same age.

Paralysis
Loss of sensation or movement.

Paraplegia
Paralysis of both legs, due to disorder or injury of the spinal cord.

Peripatetic teacher
A teacher who teaches children in a variety of settings such as school, day nursery or the home. Examples include peripatetic teachers for children with visual or hearing impairment.

Premature/pre-term
Refers to a baby born less than 37 weeks from the first day of the last menstrual period.

Respite care
A particular system of childcare and support for families with a child with special needs.

Statement of special educational needs
A legal document which sets out a child's educational needs and the special help and provision the child should receive.

Statementing
The process of drawing up a statement of special educational needs.

Stereotyping
Having a fixed pre-conceived idea or image about a person or group of people; making assumptions.

Symmetry
Opposite sides and parts of the body in exact proportion and similar in appearance.

Syndrome
A combination of characteristics, signs and/or symptoms that indicate a particular disorder.

FURTHER READING

Most voluntary organisations produce extensive reading lists and publications of their own. For addresses see Resources at the end of each chapter in Part 2.

Cameron, J. and Sturge-Moore, L. *Ordinary Everyday Families*, Mencap, 1990

Council for the Disabled, *Help starts Here*, NCB, 1995

Davenport, G. C. *An Introduction to Child Development*, (second edition), Collins Educational, 1994

DFE, *Code of Practice on the identification and assessment of special educational needs*, 1994

Hall, D. *Health for All Children*, OUP, 1996

Herbert, M. *ABC of Behavioural Methods*, The British Psychological Society, 1996
    Banishing Bad Behaviour: helping parents cope with a child's conduct disorder, The British Psychological Society, 1996

Hobart, C. and Frankel, J. *A Practical Guide to Activities for Young Children*, Stanley Thornes (Publishers) Ltd, 1994

Hobart, C. and Frankel, J. *A Practical Guide to Child Observation*, Stanley Thornes (Publishers) Ltd, 1994

Hull, D. and Johnston, D. *Essential Paediatrics* (third edition), Churchill Livingstone, 1993

Marchant, R. and Page, M. *Bridging the Gap: Child Protection Work and Children with Multiple Disabilities*, Policy, Practice, Research, 1993

Marsden, A., Moffat C. and Scott, R. *First Aid Manual: Authorised Manual of the St John Ambulance, St Andrew's Ambulance Association and The British Red Cross* (sixth edition), Dorling Kindersley, 1992

NHS Executive, *Child Health in the Community: a guide to good practice*, 1996

NSPCC, *Protecting Children: A Guide for Teachers on Child Abuse*, Revised 1994

Phillips, K. *What do we tell the children?* Books to use with children affected by illness and bereavement, Paediatric Aids Resource Centre, 1996

PLA, *Play and Learning for ALL children: children with special needs in playgroups*, 1993

Pugh, G. *Contemporary Issues in the Early Years* (second edition), NCB, 1996

Rieser, R. and Mason, M. *Disability in the Classroom: Human Rights*, Disabilty Equality in Education, 1992

Scope, *Right from the start strategy: the template*, 1995

Shah, R. *The silent minority: children with disabilities in Asian families*, NCB, 1995

Woolfson, J. *Children with Special Needs*, Faber & Faber, 1991

USEFUL ADDRESSES

British Red Cross Society
9 Grosvenor Crescent
London SW1X 7EJ

Child Accident Prevention Trust
28 Portland Place
London W1N 4DE

Children's Rights Office
235 Shaftesbury Avenue
London WC2H 8EL

Contact a Family
170 Tottenham Court Road
London W1P 0HA

Council for Disabled Children
8 Wakeley Street
London EC1V 7QE

Disabled Living Foundation
380–384 Harrow Road
London W9 2HU

EPOCH (Campaigns against physical punishment)
77 Holloway Road
London N7 8JZ

The Equality Learning Centre
356 Holloway Road
London N7

HAPA
Play for disabled children
Fulham Palace
Bishop's Avenue
London SW6 6EA

Integration Alliance
Unit 2
South Lambeth Road
London SW8 1RL

In Touch
10 Norman Road
Sale
Cheshire N33 3DF
(In Touch links families whose children have rare specific disorders and syndromes. NB: with Contact a Family, In Touch supports families with children with special needs)

MENCAP
123 Golden Lane
London EC1Y 0RT

The National Association for Special Educational Needs
NASEN House
4–5 Amber Business Village
Amber Close
Amington
Tamworth B77 4RP

National Association of Toy and Leisure Libraries
68 Churchway
London NW1 1LT

National Children's Bureau
8 Wakeley Street
London EC1V 7QE

National Playbus Association
Unit G
Amos Castel Estate
Junction Road
Brislington
Bristol BS4 5AG

One in Eight (Pressure Group to Challenge Media Stereotyping)
Disability Equality in Action
78 Mildmay Grove
London N1 4PJ

Planet (Partnership between Save the Children and Mencap)
Cambridge House
Cambridge Grove
London W6 0LE

Pre-school Learning Alliance
61–63 King's Cross Road
London WC1X 9LL

Royal Society for the Prevention of Accidents
Cannon House
Priory Queensway
Brimingham B4 6BS

Sense (The National Deaf Blind and Rubella Association)
11–13 Clifton Terrace
Finsbury Park
London N4 3SR

INDEX

child development centres 76, 98–9
child guidance clinics 100
child protection 89
child psychiatrists 26, 100
child psychologists 26, 28, 98, 100
child psychotherapists 26, 100
childcare officers 30
childhood depression 277, 279, 285
childminding services 105, 109
children
    awareness of disability and special
        needs 40–1
    empowerment 88
    rights 85–8
    see also siblings
Children Act (1989) 82–4, 88, 90, 91,
    121, 133
children with high abilities 277, 279,
    285
children with special needs 7–8, 20
    and advocacy 92
    developing independence skills
        139–46
    empowerment 88–90
    in nursery school 117–20
    and nursery voucher scheme 121–2
    rights 20, 66, 83, 86–7
    self-image 44–5
    understanding their needs 90
    vunerable to child abuse 363–4
children's homes 5, 110, 113–14, 122
choices, offering 88–9
chorionic villus sampling 291
chromosomes 14, 230, 289–90, 302
Clear Vision books 55
clothes 141–3
clotting factors 230, 235
clumsy-child syndrome 253
cochlea implants 320
Code of Practice (1994) 66, 90, 91, 133
    implementing 66–75
coeliac condition 203–9
colour blindness 325
combined nursery centres 108–9, 117
communication 268
    aids 362
    with hearing impaired children
        313–18
    needs 269
    with vision impaired children 327
communication impairment 268–76
    autism 260–1, 263
community care 84

community paediatric nurses 27, 97, 98
community-based support services
    137–9
computers 362
conductive education 159, 360–1
conductive hearing impairment 308
congenital conditions 14
conjunctivitis 323
consultants 25, 97
continuum of development 7
contractures 239, 351, 353
Convention on the Rights of the Child
    85–6
cosmetic surgery 301
Court Report (1976) 58–60
CP (cerebral palsy) 348–63
cranium bifidia 338
CSF (Cerebro-spinal fluid) 344, 345
CSIE (Centre for Studies in Inclusive
    Education) 125
cued speech 316
cystic fibrosis 218–29

Dannett, Henry 124
day nurseries 107–8, 117
daycare services 107–9
    inclusive 46–56
    see also schools
deaf culture 317, 320
deafness *see* hearing impairment
dental care 103
Department for Education and
    Employment (DfEE) 115
Department of Health (DoH) 97, 105
Department of Social Security (DSS)
    128
depression, childhood 277, 279, 285
dermatitis 180
development centres 76, 98–9
developmental continuum 7
developmental coordination disorder
    253
developmental norms
    0 to 1 year 366–7
    1 to 4 years 368–9
    4 to 7 years 370–1
diabetes 142, 187–97
diet
    and asthma 178
    coeliac condition 205–8
    and cystic fibrosis 220–2
    and diabetes 191–3, 195
    and eczema 182

General Practitioners (GPs)   26, 97, 98
genes   211, 218
genetic conditions   14, 210, 216, 218,
   289
genetic counselling   13, 217, 291, 303
glasses   332–3
glucose   189, 193
'glue ear'   308, 312
gluten   204, 205, 208
GPs (General Practitioners)   26, 97, 98
'grand mal' *see* tonic/clonic seizures
grandparents   22
grants, cash   115
grommets   312

haemoglobin   210, 211, 216
haemophilia   229–36
HAPA (Handicapped Adventure
   Playground Association)   155
head banging   278
health promotion   101
health services   15
   professionals and their skills   25–8
   systems and support   94–104, 110,
      113, 136
health visitors   18, 26–7, 59, 97–8, 98
hearing aids   102, 313, 318, 319
hearing assessment   308–9
hearing impairment   307–21
   Down's syndrome children   300
   specific facilities   55
heart lesions   299
hemiplegia   352
high abilities, children with   277, 279,
   285
HIV (Human Immuno-deficiency Virus)
   197–203, 235
holding therapy   267
holiday schemes   110–1
holistic approach to care   84
Homestart   157
Honeylands   137–8
hospices   104, 113
hospital schools   127–8
hospitals   104, 110, 113
hydrocephalus   335, 343–8
hydrotherapy   239
hygiene, personal   142–4, 359
hyperactivity *see* ADHD
hyperglycaemia   189, 194
hypermetropia   323
hypoglycaemia   189, 193

IEP (individual educational plan)   67,
   71, 118
imaginative play   261
immunisation   15
impairment, definition   9
inclusive education   126–7
inclusive environment   45–56
incontinence   141, 145–6
independence skills development   139–46
individual educational plan (IEP)   67,
   71, 118
Industrial Revolution   5
inhalers   173, 174, 175, 176
inherited conditions   13, 14
   see also chromosomes; genetic
      conditions; sex-linked inherited
      conditions
injections, diabetes   190–1, 195
insulin   187, 189, 190
integration   6, 45–6, 62, 126–7
internalised behaviours   278
isolation of parents   18

jaundice   215

keratitis   323
key workers   108, 118, 119, 146–9

labelling   8, 42, 64
language   39, 268
   development needs   268
   inappropriate   39–40
   therapy   102
language impairment   11, 268–76
   Down's syndrome   293–4
   fragile   X 302–3
learning difficulties   11, 55, 61–2, 65
   conditions which cause   245, 260,
      277, 289
   fragile X   302–7
learning goals   122
learning support assistants   29
learning support teachers   29
legislation   63–5, 81–5
lifting and carrying children   241
light adaptation   325
listening to children   66, 87
local authorities *see* education authorities;
      social services departments
longitudinal studies   282
lungs
   asthma   171–2
   cystic fibrosis   218, 219, 222

social behaviour
  inappropriate   261, 277
  ritualistic   262
  teaching Down's syndrome children
    297
social interaction   263–4
social model of disability   32
social security benefits   115, 128–9
social services
  professionals and their skills   29–30
  systems and support   96, 105–15, 136
social workers   28, 29–30, 98, 100
sociograms   282
soiling   278
sound waves   309
soundbeams   158
spacers   174, 175
spastic cerebral palsy   350–1
Spastic Society see Scope
special educational needs (SEN)   9, 61,
    124–5
  five-stage assessment model   69–73
  legislation   64, 65
  policy   67–8, 69, 127
  provision   74, 75, 92
  statement of   72–4
  Tribunal   77–81
  under fives   75–6
special equipment see equipment
special needs   7–8
  discrimination and stereotyping   42–3
  other children's awareness of   40–1
  positive images   37–40
  possible causes   12–13, 14
  prevention and early identificaton
    13, 14
  recognition   13, 16
  types of   9, 11
special needs advisers   29
special needs assistants   29
special needs coordinator (SENCO)   67,
    71, 117
special needs support teachers   29
special schools   124–6
specialists   25, 97
spectacles   332–3
speech impairment   11, 268–76
  Down's syndrome children   293–4
  fragile X   302–3
speech therapists   27, 98, 102, 271, 304
spina bifida   334–43, 344, 347–8
spina bifida cystica   336–7, 338
spina bifida occulta   336, 338

spinal tumours   344
spine   335
sporting events   6
squint   323
staff development initiatives   47–8
stammer   270, 275
statements of special educational needs
  school age children   72–4
  under fives   75–6
statistics   9
statutory assessment   71–2
statutory services and support   94–129
stereotyping   42–3
stools, bulky   220
strabismus (squint)   323
strokes   215
stutter   270
support groups   19
surgery
  and Down's syndrome   301
  and epilepsy   170
sweep tests   312

T-helper cells   198
tantrums   278, 303
TC (total communication)   316
teachers   29, 98, 115–16, 117
  see also schools
teams see multidisciplinary teams
temper tantrums   278, 303
thalassemia   216–18
therapy services   100, 103, 159
time samples   282
toileting   145–6, 359
tongue exercises   272
tonic/clonic seizures   164
total communication (TC)   315
toy libraries   114
toys   50, 176
  for vision impaired children   328–9
traits
  sickle cell   211, 212
  thalassemia   216
translocation   290
transplants, organ   228
transport   74, 115
Tribunal, special education needs
    77–81
trigger factors
  asthma   172
  sickle cell crises   211, 213
trisomy, standard   289–90
tunnel vision   323